For Susan

We don't see things as they are. We see them as we are.

—ANAÏS NIN,

quoting what she describes as Talmudic words in
Seduction of the Minotaur

CONTENTS

FILM AS HAGGADAH

TOWARD A BETTER UNDERSTANDING
OF AMERICA'S JEWS

There is growing recognition that feature films can be considered an important primary source for the study of twentieth-century life and our time. Since the birth of cinema, filmmakers have been providing us with films that reflect the world in which they live, and their work often affords great insights into the prevailing attitudes of that universe. Like the Haggadah, the traditional "telling" of the story of the Israelites' exodus from Egypt that is read at the Passover seder, cinema offers a valuable text from which to gain an understanding of the social, political, and cultural realities of the era. Movies provide a powerful lens, a window on the past, an opportunity for historical examination.

Narrative feature films, despite almost always being fictitious, have the capability of reflecting on historical reality. Historian and sometime film critic Arthur M. Schlesinger Jr. asserted, "The fact that film has been the most potent vehicle of the American imagination suggests all the more strongly that movies have something to tell us not just about the surfaces but about the mysteries of American life."[1] His observation is assuredly true for an understanding of American Jewish life. This study uses the medium of cinema to provide an understanding of the changing situation of the American Jew over the last century.

Movies convey a great deal of information, not just through story but via images and backstory—the background history of why these movies were made, who produced them, and who went to see them. The inclusion of various oral histories and interviews with principals involved in production augments our comprehension of the films studied. Consideration of conditions surrounding film production is a key element in properly studying films. John O'Connor argued that "the cultural analysis of film demands that attention be given to the ways in which the artifact was understood by historical spectators at the time of its production and release."[2] Why was this film produced? Who made it? Under what circumstances? Was the film widely distributed? Over the last half-century, historians have advanced a methodology for mining feature films for evidence of this history by contextual analysis: a close reading of the film, the circumstances of production, and the way the movie was understood by spectators at the time of its release.

Any work of this kind requires that the films themselves be carefully scrutinized and studied. Analysis of the motion picture is an essential part of this book, and that examination often focuses on specific sequences from a film, going beyond dialogue to study the visual symbols that are present in the motion picture and that bring about a reaction from the spectator. These sensory symbols, as K. R. M. Short observed, "are extremely important in creating the appropriate emotional response or climate among the audience" and often "are so deeply part of a particular social or historical context that the 'foreign observer' may be unaware of their emotive value."[3] They may trigger an emotional response with one audience and go unnoticed by another. When Jakie Rabinowitz holds up a prayer shawl, a *tallit*, in *The Jazz Singer*, as he is being forced to make a choice between career and religion, this triggers a particular emotional response. Whether consciously or unconsciously, the reaction from the Jewish viewer may be very different from that of the "foreign observer." In *Avalon*, the image of a train pulling into a station as relatives who survived the war arrive in Baltimore conjures up a very different reaction for those used to watching Holocaust films about mass forced deportations by train in Europe than it does for the uninitiated. Shot-by-shot analysis of the film provides a remarkable text for our understanding of the world that surrounds it and with which it communicates, but reactions may vary by audience.

French historian Marc Ferro noted that cinema should be seen as both a "source" of history and as an "agent" that helps shape history.[4] In an examination of the 1947 feature films that openly broached anti-Semitism as a subject (chapter 3), we see that the films not only shed light on our understanding of the period, but as "agent" actually combated anti-Semitism and effected change. Robert Sklar noted about movies that "the nature of their content and control helps to shape the character and direction of American culture as a whole."[5] The very nature of feature-film narrative draws one in and encourages the spectator to share in the experience. That experience and its entertainment function, as historian Michael Paris observes, generally reflect the "dominant ideas, attitudes and values of the culture in which the film is made." The filmgoing event also makes movies "a powerful means of mass persuasion, as it both reflects and reinforces popular ideas and preoccupations and inculcates views and attitudes deemed desirable by the filmmaker and wider society."[6] As film historian John Belton put forward, these fictional works have a "use-value." "They can be analyzed — even psychoanalyzed — to reveal something about the cultural conditions that produced them and attracted audiences to them."[7] The thrust of this study rests on the assumption that feature film can effectively be used as *text* for the study of the American Jewish experience, Jewish identity, and Jewish culture.

In the first half of the twentieth century, Hollywood's movie moguls, most of whom were Jewish, shied away from asserting a Jewish image on the screen for fear that they might be too closely identified with that representation. As Sklar pointed out, "The movies were the first medium of entertainment and cultural information to be controlled by men who did not share the ethnic and religious backgrounds of the traditional cultural elites."[8] Over the next two decades, Jewish moviemakers became more comfortable with the concept of a Jewish hero and with an overpowered, yet heroic, Israel. Then, as there was greater comfort broaching the topic of the Holocaust, it assumed center stage as the single greatest event impacting Jewish identity in America. Over the last two decades, American Jewish screenwriters, directors, and producers have become increasingly comfortable with their heritage. As a result, we are seeing an unprecedented number of movies that spotlight Jewish protagonists, experiences, and challenges. Just what are these critical Jewish visuals that have dominated the screen, and what is the inherent coding within these images?

Jews have been involved in the production of motion pictures since the beginning of filmmaking in America and have also been the subject of many of those films. In an industry strongly influenced by Jewish moviemakers who made and continue to make the decisions as to which films are produced, the complex and changing nature of the American Jewish condition has had considerable impact on American cinema and, in particular, on how Jews are reflected on the screen. If we study the American Jewish experience over time through the cinematic lens, we are able to see an evolving portrait of the American Jew over the last century: where Jews have been and possibly where they are going. A corpus of movies has recorded the evolution of Jews within America over the last century, and the cinema provides a meaningful and real accounting—a way of telling the story, a Haggadah of what has transpired for Jews in America and what continues to take place. Through movies, we can better understand America's Jews and the changes in America that had an impact on United States Jewry. Film historian Peter Rollins wrote that "films can serve the student of American culture in a far more interesting way than simply as a record of visual reality, for films register the feelings and attitudes of the periods in which they are made."⁹ A close study of the film text, the visual images, and the coding within the film offers a great deal of information. This book is an effort to explore the American Jewish story of the last century through a review and study of some of the outstanding examples of this film genre.

The book approaches the American Jewish experience by analyzing select mainstream films from the beginning of the sound era to today. Though many motion pictures lend themselves to study and interpretation, and the omission of some was often difficult, I have chosen select films that I consider representative of specific historical periods. By studying these *Jewish subject* films and their production history, we gain entrée into the changing and evolving sensibilities of the American Jew.

Woven through the study are insights from some of the creative participants in the making of these films, many of whom were interviewed by the author. Each chapter takes the critical memories and seminal events and looks at how these artists interpreted their subjects to provide an understanding of their time. With the evolution of independent cinema, the growth of film festivals, and changes in technology, cinema should, more than ever before, become an important text for better understanding the journey of Jews in America.

The idea for this book grew out of a number of experiences. While still a graduate student in cinema studies at New York University, I was introduced to Oscar Cohen, who was National Program Director at the Anti-Defamation League of B'nai B'rith. Cohen asked for my help in doing some research for a project, a possible book, that he was undertaking on "Jews and Movies." It was my first introduction to the subject of how Jews were involved in the American film industry, and I found it unquestionably eye-opening. That was over thirty-five years ago, and the question of how Jews are reflected in film has since been ably documented in several fine works by authors like Patricia Erens, Lester Friedman, and Neal Gabler. I know that Oscar would be pleased.

In 1988, while curating a film series of American Jewish-subject films at the 92nd Street Y in New York, a few acquaintances got together and talked about how best to use such films in an educational setting in order to stimulate a discussion about the American Jewish experience. The most enthusiastic of the group was Paul Cowan, who had recently authored *An Orphan in History*. I remember having several conversations with Paul about how film should be used as "*text*" for understanding the American Jewish experience. In fact, it was Paul's strong commitment to this idea that led this same group to create a video mini-course, *The Golden Land on the Silver Screen*, using cinema to explore American Jewish life, which is referenced in the filmography. We came up with the idea to film six short introductions and post-screening wrap-ups on American films that we considered important. Paula Hyman, Egon Mayer, Deborah Dash Moore, and Mordecai Newman joined Paul and me in tackling one film each. Michael Strassfeld supervised the effort. The segments were meant to precede and follow the screening of each particular film. It was a unique approach to using the then-new technology of video for education, and the experience left me wanting to do more.

As a cinema studies student in the late 1970s at New York University, I was deeply affected by the new approaches to cinema history brought to bear by some of my teachers. The influence of Jay Leyda, who revolutionized film history by focusing on production history and how various production events impact cinema, was incredibly strong. He encouraged me to take production histories from such filmmakers as Dore Schary and Elia Kazan (which are incorporated into this book), even though their personal politics and experience within the film industry were so totally opposite Jay's. He taught me how to "*read*" film text and what is required of a good film historian. Robert Sklar came to NYU just as I was completing my studies, but our paths crossed long enough for me to appreciate and adopt his approach in using Hollywood film as a lens for analyzing American society. Other teachers like William Everson, William Rothman, William Simon, and Donald Staples also influenced how I began to use cinema as a text that required deciphering. I am so deeply grateful for that incredible learning experience.

In order to study the changing situation of Jews in American society, one requires a thorough understanding and appreciation of American Jewish history. As a camper, counselor, and unit head at Camp Tel Yehudah,

I became intoxicated with Mel Reisfield's love for Jewish history, and this enthusiasm remains with me to this day. Bernard Reisman at Brandeis University helped clarify and define American Jewish life and the structure of the Jewish community in a manner that gives clarity to much of what I do. Others with whom I studied at Brandeis were Marshall Sklare, the penultimate American Jewish sociologist; Ben Halpern, an outstanding historian; Leon Jick, a remarkable teacher whose enthusiasm for American Jewish history was contagious; and Leonard Fein, who appreciated the power of cinema and who encouraged me to delve even deeper. My time spent studying with each provided me with a wonderful grounding in American Jewish history and culture.

The true pursuit of this book began when I was accepted as a fellow at the Center for Advanced Judaic Studies at the University of Pennsylvania just over ten years ago. It was there that I was able to turn my attention to the research that was required. With the assistance of an unbelievably supportive library staff, I finally was able to dedicate extended periods of time to working on this book. I also turned to other fellows in the program for feedback and insights, which was most helpful. Center head and historian David Ruderman was always there to encourage me, and I thank him for providing this period of incubation.

Over these last ten years, I have screened and rescreened films on video and DVD, a luxury that was not possible only a short while ago. Just a few years earlier, we would mount 16mm films on a flatbed editing table or screen works in special screening facilities, even on occasion setting out for the Museum of Modern Art to study a rare film. Today, with DVD, one can more easily and clearly see the genius of the filmmaker at work and try to better understand why a film is constructed the way it is. I am thankful to my students at Queens College of the City University of New York, Stern College for Women at Yeshiva University, and The Jewish Theological Seminary for insights that they offered in the course of together studying films that deal with Jewish life in America. Any teacher who does not learn from his or her students is not worthy of being called an educator.

There have been many people, foundations, and organizations who were most helpful and whom I wish to thank. Daniel Huberman was my first research assistant; he spent hours poring over the files of local research libraries. Benny Kraut invited me to teach at Queens College and joined me in planning and implementing a 2004 national symposium on "The American Jewish Experience as Reflected in Film." Always ready to assist were the librarians at New York Public Library for the Performing Arts at Lincoln Center, the Dorot Jewish Division of the New York Public Library, Yeshiva University Library, and the library of The Jewish Theological Seminary. The archive and library of the American Jewish Historical Society and YIVO Institute for Jewish Research at the Center for Jewish History in New York was also an invaluable resource. Special thanks to the archivists at American Jewish Committee and Anti-Defamation League of B'nai B'rith for allowing me access to their collections, some of which is now housed at the Center for Jewish History. The Dore Schary collection at the Wisconsin Historical Society in Madison is a treasure trove of information, and the staff was not only courteous, but also extremely helpful. Lester Friedman graciously allowed me access to his interview with Edward Dmytryk, and Nancy Kaufmann at George Eastman House in Rochester, New York, made it happen. I am thankful to the film artists who agreed to share their valuable time and respond to a variety of questions, either in person, over the phone, or by e-mail; their insights were so important to this work. Photographs included in the book are from Photofest New York, the New York Public Library, Ergo Media, the Philippe Halsman Archive, and the American Jewish Committee.

Aron Hirt-Manheimer came to me in 1975, having learned of my interest in the postwar films about anti-Semitism, and asked me to write what would be my first journal article for a special issue of *Davka Magazine*. Steven Bayme at the American Jewish Committee provided an early platform for my work by publishing my monograph on the subject, with Roselyn Bell making excellent editorial recommendations. Eli Faber encouraged me and edited an early article on Barry Levinson and *Avalon* and *Liberty Heights* that appeared some years ago in *American Jewish History*; the idea was suggested by Edna Nahshon. Richard Koffler provided support, challenged me, and meticulously reviewed my manuscript. My editors at the University of Texas Press, Lynne Chapman and Mary LaMotte Silverstein, were most constructive, a joy to work with, and incredibly helpful. My deepest gratitude to all. I am also indebted to Michael Neiditch, who first approached me to submit my manuscript to UT Press, and to Jim Burr, who shepherded the project from beginning to end. A special note of appreciation goes to the Kronhill Pletka Foundation, the Lucius N. Littauer Foundation, and the Memorial Foundation for Jewish Culture for their generous support.

Finishing this book was in part accomplished by having gone away on writing retreats. On more than one occasion, I sought solitude in the Montreal apartment of my mother-in-law, Florence Garmaise, where I was well fed and provided with quiet and total privacy. Affording oneself time to write is often harder than it might seem, but my daughters Reisha, Arielle, and Dori and son-in-law Michael were always respectful and understanding, encouraging me to complete this work. Some vacations with my wife Susan became writing weeks, where I would write in the morning and vacation in the afternoon, and I am most appreciative of her love, encouragement, and understanding. I dedicate this work to her.

THE AMERICAN JEWISH STORY
THROUGH CINEMA

CHAPTER I

INTRODUCTION

A CENTURY OF AMERICAN JEWISH LIFE

SUCCESSFUL ASSIMILATION

Throughout the early years of cinema, the first decades of the twentieth century, Jewish moviemakers focused largely on stories of successful assimilation into American society. As Neal Gabler asserted, "The grand theme of Hollywood, both in terms of films and in terms of the lives of its moguls, is idealized assimilation."[1] Such assimilation was often expressed through the intermarriage of a Jewish child with a child from another immigrant group. The resulting union celebrated the successful melding of different ethnicities and religions, a "melting pot" producing a couple that would turn out "all-American" offspring.

Silent film was often the entertainment of choice for immigrants, as language would not be a barrier; thus it was the immigrant to whom these early movies were largely directed. Suggesting the possibility of entrée into American society on-screen, such movies made the argument for assimilation seem reasonable. This view certainly reflected the sensibilities of Jewish moviemakers of that time, who desperately sought their own acceptance into America. Films like *Private Izzy Murphy* (1926), *The Cohens and the Kellys* (1926), and *Abie's Irish Rose* (1928) were representative of this genre. Each reflected belief in an America that eliminated differences and particularity and fostered acceptance. The road to success that was put forward required integration and Americanization.

The multiethnic films of the silent era continued to be made into the early

1930s. As the "talkie" replaced silent cinema, success and the possibilities that America could provide continued to be a central theme. Even *The Jazz Singer* (1927), which represents the pivotal transition into sound, has its protagonist Jakie Rabinowitz, son and descendent of generations of cantors, leave his Jewish home to seek America's opportunities. The film shows Jakie, now Jack Robin, rejecting the perceived limitations of the cantorate and synagogue for the chance to be "truly" successful as a jazz singer on Broadway. Along with his rejection of Jewish community comes Jack's easy union with the non-Jewish Mary Dale. This thematic thrust reflected the life of Jewish movie moguls, many of whom found Judaism a burden and intermarriage a way of life. This theme continued to be popular into the early 1930s. The film provides a wonderful vehicle for examining generational difference and the quest for all that America was believed to be able to offer.

Adolf Hitler's rise to power in 1933 was not lost on American moviemakers. As Judith Doneson questioned, "To what extent did Hollywood, known as a 'Jewish' industry, feel the threat to the Jews to be a major concern?"[2] There is little doubt of the effect, as clearly identified Jews abruptly disappeared from American cinema. Hollywood's Jewish producers were particularly interested in deflecting attention. Gone were the ethnic movies that had been so much a part of earlier American cinema. In addition, with the creation of the Production Code Administration, a film industry watchdog body that scrutinized films looking for, among other things, offensive references to a character's national origin, it was easy for producers to justify removing a Jewish ethnic presence from movies.

Though Jewish producers in Hollywood shied away from tackling Jewish subject matter on the screen, not every movie producer was Jewish. Darryl F. Zanuck, head of production of Twentieth Century Pictures, was a shrewd producer, acutely aware of the commercial possibilities of making contentious pictures. He was attracted to a story about the Rothschild family, a pet project of actor George Arliss. As one of the few gentile production heads in Hollywood, Zanuck was not so sensitive about Jewish visibility on the screen as were his Jewish counterparts, nor was he overtly concerned about whether to produce a film on a Jewish subject. Zanuck had been head of production at Warner Brothers when *The Jazz Singer* was made in 1927 and was heavily involved in its creation. So when Arliss gave him a book on the Rothschilds, he saw its potential and quickly turned over the project to writer Nunnally Johnson. Soon, the film *The House of Rothschild* was readied for production. Johnson was apparently awed by Zanuck's willingness to take on a film that struggled with anti-Semitism — a subject that could, particularly given the climate, be deemed divisive. Zanuck's Jewish associates, such as Joseph Schenck, the first president of United Artists and later Zanuck's partner in Twentieth Century Pictures, as well as Jewish friends within the Hollywood community, were far from enthusiastic. It seems clear that had a Jew been running Twentieth Century Pictures at the time, the film would likely never have been made. Zanuck, by his very character, was no conformist, and understood that, by virtue of not being a Jew, he could take certain liberties that Jews would not take. The stage was set and the movie was made. There is little doubt that this experience empowered Zanuck once again to take up the subject of anti-Semitism a dozen years later, when he set out to produce *Gentleman's Agreement*.

DISCOMFORT WITH JEWISH-THEMED FILMS

After the 1934 release of Zanuck's *The House of Rothschild*, Jewish subjects disappeared from American cinema until the eve of World War II. A decade earlier, the screen had been filled with Jewish characters; now there was a dearth. Even *The Life of Emile Zola* (1937) barely reveals that the accused Alfred Dreyfus, championed by Zola and a central figure in the film, is Jewish, despite the fact that his Jewishness is the key to understanding his plight. Yet, with greater awareness of the persecution of European Jewry as the decade came to an end, this attitude seemed poised to change, as several screenwriters turned their attention toward Central Europe.

Then, in the spring of 1939, before the onset of war in Europe, Anatole Litvak's *Confessions of a Nazi Spy* opened in theaters. This film, perceived by many to be anti-Nazi, was seen as propaganda for American involvement in the events unfolding abroad. Such involvement in a war in Europe was unpopular with the American public, and an isolationist Congress, carefully scrutinizing what was being produced, called the producers of the film to task. Almost immediately screenplays about anti-Semitism that were being considered were put aside, never to be made into motion pictures. As world anti-Semitism became more of a concern, Jewish producers in Hollywood once again became much more reluctant to draw attention to themselves.

Unlike Hollywood's Jews, Charlie Chaplin, a non-Jew, proceeded with his film about Jewish persecution, *The Great Dictator* (1940), which he produced, directed, scored, and starred in. The film has Chaplin playing two parts—two look-alikes, a Jewish barber and Adenoid Hynkel, dictator of Tomania. In this brilliant tragicomedy, each takes the place of the other, with not-so-surprising results. It took a non-Jew to have the courage to make such a film, as the comfort level for Jewish producers of the day simply precluded any moviemaking on the subject. With America's entry into the war, Jewish characters finally began to emerge in a variety of war dramas—films like *The Purple Heart* (1944) and *Pride of the Marines* (1945). But the approach was still a cautious one, with the Jewish characters on-screen joining others of different ethnic origins and religions to fight America's enemy abroad.

With the end of World War II, the mood of Hollywood began to turn away from war, and there evolved a growing introspection on American life. Movies were now beginning to struggle with the issues that addressed a postwar America. With the Holocaust in Europe as backdrop, anti-Semitism seemed an appropriate subject to receive attention on the American screen. However, many other considerations made it no easy task to present this highly controversial theme openly to the American movie audience. One question was whether America was mature enough to address the issue. Another was whether Hollywood's moviemakers, the majority of whom were Jewish, were sufficiently secure to deal with this controversial subject.

In late 1946, Darryl F. Zanuck, now head of production at the merged studio Twentieth Century-Fox, announced that he had purchased movie rights to Laura Z. Hobson's *Gentleman's Agreement*, a novel about social anti-Semitism. Zanuck was excited about the prospect of doing such a film. As had been the case a dozen years earlier when he produced *The House of Rothschild*, he saw anti-Semitism as an American problem, rather than just an issue for Jews. But Hollywood's Jewish community remained concerned about drawing too much attention to itself. At this moment, American Jewry was experiencing a postwar "era of good feeling," so it might seem strange that resistance to the making of *Gentleman's Agreement* would come from the organized Jewish leadership. But just how secure did Jewish leaders feel about their status in America? Influential members of the Los Angeles Jewish community held a meeting at the Warner Brothers studio in an attempt to discourage production. Their stated fear was that by calling attention to anti-Semitism in a film, anti-Semitic feelings might be enhanced. These community leaders saw no point in raising the question in the first place. "We're getting along OK! Why raise the issue?" But Zanuck refused to give in to the pressure.

Shortly thereafter, word got out that Dore Schary, head of production at RKO Studios, was preparing *Crossfire*, a second film on anti-Semitism. Schary also met with resistance, confronted by leaders of the American Jewish Committee. Elliot Cohen, editor of the AJC-sponsored periodical *Commentary*, made it clear that he would use the power of the press (which he later did in a series of printed exchanges with Schary) if production of *Crossfire* was not stopped or, at least, the main character was not changed from a Jew to an African American. If that were not enough pressure, Hollywood colleagues threatened Schary that they would shut down distribution of the film. But the Jewish forty-one-year-old RKO producer did not buckle under this great pressure. Even a specific threat by Warner Brothers, never realized, that they would not screen *Crossfire* in their theaters, did not deter Schary.

Crossfire was released in the summer of 1947, and *Gentleman's Agreement* opened in theaters a few months later. *Crossfire* won the Best Social Film award at the Cannes Film Festival, and *Gentleman's Agreement* won the Academy Award for Best Motion Picture of 1947. A variety of studies were commissioned which showed that the films had a very positive effect in combating anti-Semitism. Interestingly enough, as 1947 began, there were at least five film projects about anti-Semitism being readied for production. But with changes taking place in Hollywood and hearings being initiated by the House of Representatives' Un-American Activities Committee, only *Crossfire* and *Gentleman's Agreement* were completed; two other film projects were shelved and forgotten, and the fifth, an adaptation of Arthur Miller's *Focus*, was not produced until 2001.

A SHIFT IN SENSIBILITY IN THE PORTRAYAL OF JEWS

In the late 1940s and early 1950s, a major shift in American cinema was about to take place. Jewish movie moguls had always influenced the kinds of films being made and how Jews were portrayed. For over a quarter of a century, they largely pushed the notion that Jews should give up their particularity and assimilate into American society. Then, for close to a decade, as the Jewish studio heads became more and more successful and as world anti-Semitism grew, they tried to deflect attention from themselves by making Jewish characters disappear from the screen. Now, Zanuck and the undaunted new Jewish production head Schary had put a story about anti-Semitism in the limelight. As one might imagine, Hollywood producers and other prominent Jews were not amused, as this went to the very heart of how secure they felt in American society. Were there still barriers that made being Jewish difficult? How would this impact the films being released, and how has this perception changed since? The answers lay ahead: The House Committee on Un-American Activities began its oversight of Hollywood, changing moviemaking forever. Television would become a competitive force, and consequently, the movie-studio system, and how decisions were to be made, would dramatically change.

The social message films following *Crossfire* and *Gentleman's Agreement* dealt with issues other than Jews. Although Jewish characters appeared in many films into the late 1950s, their Jewishness, which might have been central to the original work from which the film was adapted, was made largely peripheral in the film. Two striking examples are movies drawn from bestselling novels by Herman Wouk, *The Caine Mutiny* and *Marjorie Morningstar*. In *The Caine Mutiny* novel, Lt. Barney Greenwald's Judaism flavors his every action; this motivation we do not see in the picture. Yes, Uncle Samson comes for his nephew's bar mitzvah as *Marjorie Morningstar* opens, but Marjorie's commitment to Jewish life is minimized and almost eliminated. Simply put, Hollywood movie producers — even "independent" producers who were so much a part of the "new" moviemaking — were careful not to make their characters *too* Jewish!

THE UNABASHEDLY JEWISH PROTAGONIST

Nineteen fifty-eight turned out to be a pivotal year for Jews as portrayed in movies. Somehow, in this post–*Brown v. Board of Education*[3] period, Jews in general and filmmakers in particular felt greater comfort in America, a feeling reflected in the films that followed. Jews were accepted into the suburbs, and affiliation rates in synagogues would reach 60 percent of all American Jews, "the only time in the twentieth century that more than half of America's Jews were synagogue members."[4] "Cultural assimilation" had been achieved, but as American sociologist Herbert J. Gans pointed out in his 1953 study, Jews still maintained "continued social distinctiveness."[5] This distinctiveness was true not just in Gans's Chicago, but also in most urban centers — certainly in the movie capital, Los Angeles. It also brought about a new kind of Jewish character, one whom we would begin to see in movies: the unabashedly Jewish protagonist. True, producers were far from ready to make their leading characters *too* Jewish or "religious" (as seen in the Wouk adaptations), but they also did not shy away from characters who were clearly Jewish, as had been the case in previous decades.

In Edward Dmytryk's *The Young Lions* (1958), adapted from Irwin Shaw's novel, Noah Ackerman is meek and of slender build, but he is strong willed. When his fellow soldiers in the barracks abuse him and money is stolen from him, he demands to know who the thief is so that he may defend his honor. "I demand satisfaction!" states Ackerman. Though beaten up badly in three successive weekend fistfights that follow — with the toughest guys in the barracks — he continues to fight for his right to be there. In the fourth and final fight, he defeats his last opponent, earning the admiration and acceptance of his bunkmates, and the stolen money is returned to him. Although set before and during World War II, published after the war, and filmed a decade later, *The Young Lions* has more to say about the late 1950s than it does about the past in which it is set. In the case of Noah Ackerman, he is more the Jew of the 1950s — the time when the film was made.[6] As Pierre Sorlin notes:

> Historical films are concerned with the problems of the present. . . . On the surface, they deal with historical events . . . but from the vast range of possible choices, film-makers have singled out those characters, circumstances and dates that have a direct bearing on contemporary circumstances.[7]

Ackerman is a member of his unit, lives in the barracks like everyone else, and bunks next to men from all parts of the country. But do they include him? Not really! Noah Ackerman truly symbolizes the American Jew, distinct and different, secure in his Jewishness, aware that he has "rights" as an American and ready to fight for them — and how Ackerman does fight!

But there is another side of Noah Ackerman, showing the evolving Jew, just starting to break into the mainstream of society. He is the young man who falls in love with Hope Plowman, the gentle non-Jewish woman who invites Noah to New England to meet her father. Hope has not only accepted Noah, but has fallen in love with him. Joined by her father at the bus station to meet Noah, Hope waits until the last possible moment to share an unknown fact: "He's Jewish, father." Long before Ackerman will take on the barracks bullies, he must face Hope's father. Thus begins one of the most intriguing sequences in the film and a telling insight into the changing status of the Jew in American life. Will Mr. Plowman invite Noah Ackerman to dinner? And for turkey—the all-American feast! After 1950, "America's image of the Jew changed from conspiratorial foreigners to good neighbors,"[8] observed J. J. Goldberg. In 1958, will the Jew finally be invited to the American table? *The Young Lions* provides a wonderful film text for exploration.

THE UNAMBIGUOUSLY HEROIC ISRAELI

As 1960 came, Jews found themselves far more secure and suddenly more visible in most walks of American life than ever before. Various barriers had fallen and with them, the timidity of the early postwar period seemed to disappear. A few Jewish moviemakers even turned their attention to the new State of Israel. With the groundbreaking release by Otto Preminger of Leon Uris's *Exodus*, Israel and, with it, the Holocaust became central themes in Hollywood. Not only did Preminger introduce the story of Israel's birth, but Holocaust survivors were portrayed on-screen.[9] As Leonard Fein put it, "The coincidence in time between our learning the full dimensions of the European tragedy and our rejoicing at Israel's independence has irretrievably linked the two events."[10]

With the exception of Edward Dmytryk's adaptation of Michael Blankfort's *The Juggler* in 1953, the Shoah—the Holocaust—had been mostly a taboo subject in Hollywood. *The Diary of Anne Frank*, shorn of much of its Jewish character, reached the screen in 1959. The previous year, *The Young Lions* had contained a scene in which American servicemen (including Ackerman) liberate a concentration camp. Now Preminger, in one film, coupled the birth of the State of Israel with the horrors of the war. It was a pivotal moment, reflecting how Jewish Americans felt both about their relationships with Israel and about themselves as Jews. Howard Morley Sachar pointed to 1960 as a turning point for American Jewry, with John F. Kennedy's endorsement of Israel in the 1960 elections bringing about "a decisive shift in relations, equally with American Jews and Israel."[11]

Exodus, and images of Israel in general, provided something that previous films on Jews had not—an attractive, strong, and bold Jewish presence. Paul Newman's Ari Ben Canaan is handsome, blue-eyed, and muscular. As historian Omer Bartov showed, "The familiarity that American viewers may have felt with this kind of hero, who conformed to the rules of Hollywood cinematic characterization, may have been paralleled by the reaction of Jewish audiences, especially in the United States, who were finally provided with a Jewish character who was so recognizably and unambiguously heroic."[12] The American presence in the film is Kitty, the blonde gentile nurse who will eventually become Ari's love interest. In this way, Preminger and Uris connect the Israeli Jew with all Americans, a stylistic device aimed at keeping the story from becoming too particular, making it appealing for a broader American audience.

THE JEWISH ANTIHERO: JEWISH SELF-HATRED OR HONEST INTROSPECTION?

In 1969, Philip Roth's writing ushered in the period of the Jewish antihero on-screen, with the cinematic version of *Goodbye, Columbus* creating as much a stir as the literary version had a decade earlier. Director Larry Peerce's striking portrayal of a Jewish *simcha* (celebration) left audiences across America in stitches, while many Jewish filmgoers cringed with embarrassment. The Jew in America had finally arrived socioeconomically, and we were seeing that portrayal on the large screen. This time it wasn't film studio heads who were feeling self-conscious, but rather a sizable portion of the Jewish audience, who felt ill at ease and humiliated. Was this "hidden" anti-Semitism, as some speculated? Were Roth and Peerce (son of cantor and opera star Jan Peerce) self-hating Jews?

During this time, films portrayed Jewish gluttons at weddings and bar mitzvahs, Jewish men lusting after gentile women, and even movie moguls symbolically throwing bagels at non-Jews. *Goodbye, Columbus* and films of this kind, such as Elaine May's *The Heartbreak Kid* (1972) and Howard Zieff's *Hearts of the West* (1975), struggled with American Jewry's discomfort with its newfound acceptance. As Lester Friedman pointed out in *Hollywood's Image of the Jew*, "These films attest to the Jews' growing stature in American society and to the centrality of the Jewish experience within the American experience of the sixties."[13] As Jews moved closer to the center of American society, they felt more comfortable scoping their own distinctiveness. With this new standing in America, the safe anonymity that previous generations of Jewish filmmakers had so meticulously cultivated would evaporate.

With the 1970s, Hollywood opened up American society to greater introspection. This new license for reflection broke down barriers in all aspects of filmmaking. As for the characterization of Jews, film historian Patricia Erens noted, "Many Jewish observers were fearful, as in the past, that the new openness would result in a backlash, and that, by allowing negative Jewish portrayals, disreputable characters, and anti-Jewish sentiments, films would stimulate negative attitudes."[14] This never was the case. With anonymity gone and license given for self-examination, a new group of Jewish movie-makers set out to elucidate the Jews' place in America.

Perhaps most representative of this period is Sydney Pollack's *The Way We Were*, based on a screenplay by Arthur Laurents. The film focuses on the relationship between Katie Morosky (Barbra Streisand) and Hubbell Gardner (Robert Redford). Katie is a curly-haired Jewish woman active in politics and protest. Hubbell has Hollywood looks, is quite athletic, and strives to be a writer. They are drawn to each other, and that attraction eventually leads to their involvement and marriage. Each is so different from the other, not just in religion, politics, and interests, but in matters of conscience and even food! "What's the matter? You don't like my pot roast?" asks Katie. Like a whole generation of activists in the 1960s and 70s, Katie wants to change the world, while Hubbell is simply trying to find a niche for himself as a salaried Hollywood writer. They are very much the American Jew and non-Jew of the time, now able to interact freely and come together. In 1920s movies, Jew and gentile intersected, often in an adverse environment, to blend into the American "melting pot." In 1970s motion pictures, there was an assumption that free choice was at work, and there was no reason why Katie and Hubbell could not be together. Yet Laurents and Pollack characterize Katie and Hubbell as being too different from each other for the union of Jew and non-Jew to work. Even though Morosky is ready to iron her hair and give up ethnic New York for Los Angeles, it will not be enough.

Two decades later, in *The Prince of Tides* (1991), Streisand would play Dr. Susan Lowenstein, a successful New York psychiatrist who encounters Tom Wingo (Nick Nolte), a non-Jewish football coach from the "tides" of Carolina. The two are brought together by the mental illness of Tom's sister, whose alter ego is identified as that of a Holocaust survivor. Tom is captivated by Susan, even coaching her son in the art of football; the concept of making the Jewish youth happy and more American by making him more athletic is intriguing. In the 1973 *The Way We Were*, Katie is the outsider drawn to the "all-American" man. Eighteen years later, in *The Prince of Tides*, the same "all-American" man, from the heartland of America, now becomes the outsider as he encounters New York. There he becomes enamored of a very accomplished psychiatrist, a Jewish woman who might represent what America has come to define as success. Through these two portrayals by Barbra Streisand, in her own right a success story, we see over the intervening years the transformation of Jew from outsider to insider. By the 1970s, Jews in America were establishing themselves. By 1990, they were established. Their entrée, over these two decades, would move them from outsider status to the center of American society. American cinema recorded that.

Just as this transformation was taking place, some filmmakers, most notably Woody Allen, were struggling with the Jews' new status in America. Allen wrestled deeply with his Jewish identity, his situation as a Jew in this new America, and in particular his own ambivalence at being born Jewish. That disquiet is a recurring theme in much of his early work, beginning in the 1970s and going through the end of the century. In *Sleeper* (1973), Miles, the character played by Allen, is thrust into the future, where he is the outsider, forced to assimilate. When that process is unsuccessful, two Jewish robotic tailors, Ginsberg and Cohen, are brought in to "fit him." They create a uniform, but even that mechanized creation does not "fit." Allen seems to be questioning whether the Jew, even when handled by Jews, can meld into society. *Love and Death* (1975), set during the Napoleonic wars, presents a character totally out of sync with the world he lives in. Everyone around him happily drinks, goes to war, and seeks the worldly pleasures of life. Meanwhile, Boris, played by Woody Allen, is forced by his parents to join the war effort and walks off carrying a butterfly net. When he joins his fellow soldiers, he is totally inept, unable to bear arms, and clearly out of place. *Annie Hall* (1977) showcases Alvy, who, when joining his woman-friend Annie at her parents' home for Easter ham dinner, finds himself sitting among people with whom he has nothing in common. He feels so totally uncomfortable that at one point he presents a fantasy image of himself as a Jew in Chassidic garb. Referring to Annie's grandmother, Alvy turns to the camera and points out, "Sitting at the end of the table is a classic Jew-hater." In *Zelig* (1983), Woody Allen plays Leonard Zelig, "the son of a Yiddish actor," a chameleon-like character who transforms his appearance to that of the people who surround him. He seems to lack his own persona; he is unable to be totally comfortable as he is. Bruno Bettelheim, commenting within the movie, calls him "the ultimate conformist." Irving Howe, who also acts as one of the commentators in this documentary-style motion picture, asserts in the film, "It seems to me that his story reflected a lot of the Jewish experience in America—the great urge to push in and find one's place and then to assimilate into the culture. I mean, he wanted to assimilate like crazy!"[15] Is this not Woody Allen's reading of Jews throughout history who assume the identity of those around them—the Jew who assimilates? These and subsequent Allen films, like *Hannah and Her Sisters* (1986), *Crimes and Misdemeanors* (1989), and *Deconstructing Harry* (1997), take on similar themes. In each, Woody Allen puts on film his personal struggle and the ambiguity he seems to feel as a Jew in late-twentieth-century America. A close examination of Woody Allen's film work provides an interesting slant in understanding the changing situation of the Jew in America.

FILMS FOCUSING ON THE HOLOCAUST

By 1967, possibly as a consequence of losing its underdog status in the Six-Day War that year, Israel ceased being a popular subject for American moviemakers. Within a few years, the antiheroes introduced by the likes of Larry Peerce, Elaine May, and Howard Zieff would take central stage as cinema's new Jews. Then, by the end of the 1970s, with the presentation of the 1978 NBC miniseries *Holocaust* on television, the Shoah suddenly attracted everyone's attention. The importance of that television event cannot be overstated in that it raised awareness of the subject of the Shoah to the American public and to the world. As television critic Frank Rich noted, "It is to television's credit that it tackled the subject of the Holocaust at all when so many of the other mass arts would not."[16] What would follow was the creation of a new genre in Hollywood filmmaking: the Holocaust movie.

Certainly some Holocaust-related American narratives were screened in theaters in the years that followed the end of the war. Fred Zinnemann's *The Search* (1947) tracked a group of refugee children to a United Nations Relief and Rehabilitation Administration (UNRRA) home, and in 1953, *The Juggler* focused on the plight of a survivor who comes to Israel after the war. *The Young Lions* (1958) showed not only the liberation of a concentration camp by American forces, but the sensitivity that Americans would display in dealing with survivors. Over the next two decades, many films touching on the Holocaust would be made, but it was the 1978 miniseries that firmly affixed the Shoah on the American cultural map. "The culmination of the process," as historian Peter Novick noted, "was Steven Spielberg's 1993 *Schindler's List*, which benefited not just from the director's mega-reputation but from the fact that it appeared in the same year that the Washington Holocaust Museum opened."[17]

With the Shoah, American Jewish filmmakers found a Jewish subject that they were comfortable tackling. This kind of Jewish outpouring on the part of Hollywood moviemakers was unprecedented. The Holocaust has remained a dominant theme in movies and on television, and in this regard, some have expressed concern that for too many Jews, the Holocaust and its commemoration have become the new essence of Judaism. A few observers even see this development and the obsession with fear of anti-Semitism as indicative of deep-seated concerns about the future of American Jewry. "That American Jewry in the late twentieth century elevated the Holocaust to near iconic status," posited historian Hasia Diner, "reflected the discrepancy between the reality of total acceptance and the reality that even in America, Jews had enemies."[18]

AMERICA'S JEWS THROUGH BARRY LEVINSON'S LENS

In *Avalon* (1990), writer-director Barry Levinson shows an American Jewish society in development. The family patriarch Sam relates his family's history, which can be read as representative of an entire generation in America. Whereas American Yiddish filmmakers in the 1930s would often represent Eastern Europe in their story lines as the *heym* (home), Levinson's family seemingly has no connection to or feeling for the old country. Though the family clearly comes from somewhere else, Baltimore will always represent home, with Avalon the place within Baltimore that has mythic quality. Sam's story and world begin with his arrival in the port of Baltimore on July 4, and this moment of beginning becomes central to the film. For some, what is ominous about *Avalon* is how devoid of Jewish ritual or Jewish symbols the film is. Levinson was accused of hiding the Jewishness of his characters. Responding to this, he told me, "If I wanted to hide that they were Jewish, I'd make them non-Jewish." Sam and his family are clearly Jews, but they do not celebrate their Jewishness or represent it in any way. Still, this lack of Jewish visual cues does not mask how authentically Jewish this film is. It is a motion picture about Jews assimilating into America, Jews for whom America becomes their religion, and about how a new set of rituals, history, and memory is passed down to the ensuing generations.

In 1999, Barry Levinson revisited his hometown of Baltimore in *Liberty Heights*. This time, he places the story at a point in history after the elimination of the urban immigrant ghetto. It is 1954, and the Jew is now ostensibly an integrated member of American society. *Liberty Heights*, seemingly beginning where *Avalon* left off, is about distinctions and barriers that were very real in the post–World War II era. Jews have begun to move to the suburbs, where there are fences and limits that regulate access. This film focuses on Jews who want to cross the divide and move in and out of their suburban ghettos. Where *Avalon* avoided particular Jewish moments, the Kurtzmans in *Liberty Heights* celebrate a festive Shabbat dinner, go to synagogue on the high holidays, and are clearly identified as Jews. While on one level *Liberty Heights* is about breaking down social and racial walls, it is just as much a look at a Jewish family with strong Jewish traditions, values, and history.

Toward the conclusion of *Liberty Heights*, three Jewish boys go to the local swim club and pull down the sign that reads "No Jews, Dogs, and Coloreds." Though set in the 1950s, in this 1999 cinematic moment of Jewish assertion of power and determination we then watch the boys walk defiantly into the club and onto the dock of the swimming area. Whether this is Levinson's rendering of the historical era of the 1950s or a statement of identification for today is left up to the viewer. In *Avalon*, the immigrant Jew struggles with his or her entry onto the American stage and how that arrival affects family. In *Liberty Heights*, the immigrant memory has faded. In both of his films, Levinson's search for memory, not dissimilar to the journey begun by Liev Schreiber in his 2005 *Everything Is Illuminated*, speaks to the essence of how Jewish history is mediated in American cinema today. Each of the Levinson films serves not simply as a record of visual reality, but also as a register for the feelings and attitudes of the 1990s. As Pierre Sorlin pointed out, "We know that history is a society's memory of its past, and that the functioning of this memory depends on the situation in which the society finds itself."[19] At the beginning and the end of the 1990s, Barry Levinson gave us two powerful Jewish historical film texts with which to better understand who we were and who we are. Along with a growing number of American Jewish filmmakers, he provides new cinematic canvasses from which we can draw greater clarity about the events that continue to fashion who the Jew is in America.

A NEW DIRECTION IN FILM:
SEARCHING FOR A USABLE PAST

In 2005, Liev Schreiber incorporated his own personal exploration of his family's past into Jonathan Safran Foer's novel and created *Everything Is Illuminated*. It is the story of a young American Jew who travels to Ukraine in search of identity and self-understanding. That search is representative of a new direction in American cinema over the last several years—a search for roots, one might say—that has resulted in an unprecedented number of movies spotlighting Jewish events and issues and focusing on important moments in Jewish history. This is an exciting development, for cinema, as the pioneer filmmaker D. W. Griffith once said, "is capable of conveying a given image in many ways enormously more effectively than any mode of expression the world has ever possessed."[20]

Twenty-five-year-old Jonathan Safran Foer drew a great deal of attention in 2002 with the publication of his first novel, *Everything Is Illuminated*, which was critically well received. Foer is among a group of young Jewish writers, screenwriters, and actors who are dazzling readers and moviegoers with their talent. Just as extraordinary are the efforts being undertaken by a circle of accomplished filmmakers who are making movies with Jewish subjects. Many of them see cinema as a way to engage with their Jewishness. The talented stage and screen actor Liev Schreiber, who chose Foer's work as the medium for his first film, is just one of many who have emerged over the last decade.

Schreiber's primary Jewish connection was through a grandfather who would yearly reintroduce him to the Jewish tradition at the Passover seder. With that grandfather's death and the subsequent gap left in his life, Schreiber turned to screenplay writing as a way of dealing with his grandfather's life journey and exploring how it had impacted him. As part of that, there was a realization for both Foer and Schreiber that had their grandfathers not chosen to leave for America, they themselves might have been victims of the Holocaust. With the meeting of Foer and Schreiber, a common historical thread and story was found, resulting in a trust on Foer's part to allow Schreiber to carry both of their stories and vision to film.

In his classic book *World of Our Fathers*, Irving Howe reflected on the "fractional Jew [who] may be identified by his history, by the presence of the Jewish past within him. He is a Jew in that his experience contains the possibility of linking himself with the collective and individual experience of earlier Jews."[21] Many young Jewish filmmakers have turned to cinema as their way to find those links, whether it is with the Jew of the past or the present. In the 1930s, Yiddish films provided a nostalgic connection for the immigrant masses to reflect on the old country, but none of that nostalgia exists here. Schreiber and other filmmakers of the new millennium simply want to fill in the dots in order to better understand their identity.

In *Everything Is Illuminated*, Jonathan goes to Ukraine to search, together with the Ukrainian guide Alexander, for his grandfather's hometown of Trachimbrod, which winds up being no more than the collectables preserved by its caretaker. Yet these two grandchildren of Trachimbrod, who live on opposite sides of an ocean, uncover a common memory that may be shared with the next generation. Their newfound personal histories fill in the void left by the death of the older generation, providing a new and unique Jewish sustenance in their lives. This film and many others being made today are reflective of a new genre of America moviemaking, firmly rooted and Jewishly identified, that connects with a Jewish historical starting point. That is a most exciting development.

THE JAZZ SINGER

OUT OF THE JEWISH GHETTO

In 1883, twenty-six-year-old Binyumen kissed his wife Perele Leah and said good-bye to his two children, Anna and Hershele. According to his granddaughter Cass Warner Sperling, he was preparing to leave his shtetl of Krasnashiltz in the Pale of Settlement, hoping to make his way safely to the German border and from there to the port of Hamburg. Before he left, Perele had sewn a secret pocket into the waist of Binyumen's pants. "It is for your watch," she said. "To keep it safe." The watch was a family heirloom, passed down to him by his father. With that, his meager yeshiva education, and the few zlotys that he had been able to save, Binyumen left in search of a dream in America.[1]

Binyumen, like so many of that generation, knew little of the new land, except what had been told to him by a youth named Waleski, known as the village idiot, who had left a few years before. Waleski had sent Binyumen a letter encouraging him to join him in Baltimore: "Riches . . . earn two dollars a day . . . the streets run with gold." The letter ended with a last thought: "Everyone in America wears shoes!" Not only was Binyumen a cobbler, but he figured that if Waleski could find riches in America, so could he.[2]

It was not long before the twenty-six-year-old reached America. Standing in awe in front of the immigration clerk at New York's Castle Garden, Binyumen Vernereski, tired from a grueling transatlantic journey, was asked about his name. "Is it Verner, Waner, Varner? . . . Okay. Warner it is!" That would be the first encounter with America for Binyumen Warner, who from that time forward would be Benjamin Warner.[3] He was just another Jew who had left Eastern Europe, lured by the legend of America. Yet at that moment, beginning with his change of name, his world as a Jew would be revolutionized.

Within the year, Perele, now Pearl, joined Benjamin in America with children Anna, now Annie, and Hershele, now Harry. Soon, Ben was nailing new soles on shoes on a soot-covered street in Baltimore, making three dollars a day. The story of the family's immigration to America loomed large in the collective memory of Ben's children and grandchildren. In most respects it was the story of most of the tens of thousands of Eastern European Jews who traversed the oceans at the turn of the century to seek out America. Like most children of that generation, Ben Warner's sons and daughters utilized the skills at their disposal to eke out whatever living they could. In the case of the Warners, it was a grocery store, a butcher shop, shoe repair, traveling sales, and work out of their home. Somehow, circumstance and opportunity took them to Youngstown, Ohio, where they eventually became involved in the exhibition of motion pictures. It was no mistake that it was Benjamin Warner's prized gold watch from the old country that was pawned to fetch the extra dollars needed to buy the first Warner movie projector. This was a business in which all the brothers could work together, as a family. Ben Warner was taking care of his children; he was trading in the old for the new.[4]

The Warner brothers' story is that of four brothers, Harry, Sam, Albert, and Jack—Benjamin and Pearl's sons—tied by a tight familial bond, who struggled to create a film business on par with the other great film companies of the day. They sought the American dream of success. That in 1927 they would choose, as their biggest foray into sound motion pictures, the story of a cantor's son who wants to break away from the confines of his community to seek fame is quite remarkable. This film, *The Jazz Singer*, which would be deemed the first talking picture, would revolutionize theater and cinema. But what was more remarkable is that the story not only reflected the Warner brothers' lives, it also told the story of an entire generation of immigrants who wanted better lives. In so many respects, the thrust of the film was just as much about these immigrants as it was about the story's author, Samson Raphaelson; about one of America's great Jewish composers, Irving Berlin, whose song "Blue Skies" would be performed in the film; and about its star, Al Jolson, after whom the story was fashioned. The names would be different, with new and different characters, but the thrust would be the same. Once the Jewish immigrants arrived in this New World, how would they handle their new situation? What of the next generation? Just as incredible is the fact that from that point forward the story would be told and retold, for film, radio, and television. Something in this story of a Jewish youth struggling with the competing possibilities that America offered resonated for producers and audiences. *The Jazz Singer* is the classic Jewish story of assimilation: an account of the Jew confronting America and the tension of America intersecting with the Jew.

Some forty-four years after Benjamin Warner's arrival at Castle Garden, his four sons would recast American popular culture by successfully exhibiting a motion picture that not only had sound but included some ad-libbed dialogue. That development in itself was remarkable and has become a part of history. However, the evolution of the work that became known as *The Jazz Singer* and, more importantly, how that story reflected the lives of its various authors and a changing American Jewish community is of special relevance here.

SAMSON RAPHAELSON

In the 1910s, Samson Raphaelson wrote a short story that reflected his own sensibilities growing up as a New York Jew. The oldest of eight children, Raphaelson was born in New York City and lived on the Lower East Side. He loved New York, and when his parents were about to move the family to Chicago, he prevailed on them to allow him to stay behind with his grandparents, at least until he would begin high school: "I guess all I knew were Jewish kids, when I was a child. It was Jewish everywhere." [5] On the East Side, Raphaelson was influenced by the Yiddish theater and the liturgical music that he heard in synagogue: "There was a choir at the Pike Street Synagogue where Cantor Cooper sang on the Sabbath and on holy days. I would have given my eyeteeth to be in that choir. I knew by heart all the little threnodies. . . . I had no voice, however." [6] Years later, in May of 1917, while a junior at the University of Illinois in Champaign, Raphaelson borrowed ten dollars, and to impress "a certain young lady" bought two tickets for a musical extravaganza — the one-night performance of Al Jolson in *Robinson Crusoe, Jr.* The twenty-one-year-old Raphaelson was struck by the great versatility

Samson Raphaelson's genius is evident in his writing.
Raphaelson went on to become one of Hollywood's great screenwriters. Photofest.

of the lead actor, Al Jolson, who played three completely different roles. As Raphaelson described it, he turned to his date, "dazed with memories of my childhood on the East Side — memories of the Pike Street Synagogue. . . . My God, this isn't a jazz singer. This is a cantor!"[7] Raphaelson had never seen Jolson perform before, but he was clearly moved by the experience: "The words didn't matter, the melody didn't matter. It was the emotion — the emotion of a cantor. I said to my friend, 'There's a story in this — a dramatic story.'"[8]

There remains little doubt that seeing Al Jolson perform that night impacted Raphaelson in many ways. In Jolson, he both heard and saw a Jew who had managed to find success in America, utilizing the talents that only a generation earlier would have held him captive in a finite Jewish world. For Raphaelson, who had grown up in a totally Jewish milieu, the experience of watching Jolson truly resonated for him. Now in college and interacting with students from different worlds and cultures, he no doubt identified with the "liberated" Jolson. Here was an artist who was able to translate his cantorial talents for the American stage as a jazz singer. Raphaelson's own life was that of a young man with strong Jewish roots, wishing to become a mainstream American writer. Therefore, it was not so strange that the story he would pen would be about a youth with a strong Jewish upbringing, lured by the promise of America. Though he modeled the narrative after Al Jolson, it was just as much Samson Raphaelson's life story. As historian Arthur Hertzberg pointed out: "The children of the immigrants had no role models. They resented the traps into which they were born and they were angry with the powerless fathers who could not liberate them. They had no choice but to invent themselves, as Jews and as Americans."⁹ That night, Samson Raphaelson had found his role model. He would follow Al Jolson!

Over the next several years, Samson Raphaelson, who would become a highly successful popular writer, penning over forty plays, teleplays, and screenplays, fashioned a story drawn, in large part, on Jolson's life story and meteoric rise to fame. The basic plot concerns an only son who refuses to follow in his father's footsteps as a cantor, thereby rejecting his father's wishes and the family tradition of generations of Rabinowitz cantors. The love of music is in his veins, but rather than sing in the synagogue, he pursues a career in popular music, causing a rift between father and son that pervades the story. At various points in the narrative, the youth feels guilty about the rupture and attempts to make amends, although he is still unwilling to give up his dream of success in secular America. These overtures, though well received by his mother, are rejected by his father, who is physically and emotionally weakened by the encounters. Finally, aided in his quest for success by a love interest, a non-Jewish woman, the youth is given his long-awaited chance to perform onstage in New York. In the climax of the story, a critically ill father lays bedridden, unable to take his place in the synagogue on what many consider the holiest day of the Jewish calendar. Jakie, having changed his name to Jack, is to open a Broadway show that very night. What can the youth do to restore his father's morale? Does he choose career or family? Ambition or tradition?

Jakie Rabinowitz, descended from ten generations of cantors, was expected to take his place in the synagogue like his father before him. Al Jolson, too, chose not to follow six generations of cantors and left his home in Washington, DC, for the lure of New York. As Jolson's older brother, Harry, described it, "the chief difficulty in our home life was that Al and I had been absorbed by American customs, American freedom of thought, and the American way of life. My father still dwelt in the consciousness of the strict, orthodox teachings and customs of the Old World."[10] Jakie, like Jolson, finally makes up his mind to pursue his dream and leaves home to tour the country. Just as Asa Yoelson would become Al Jolson, Jakie Rabinowitz becomes Jack Robin; just as Al Jolson would meet Henrietta Keller, Jack Robin would meet Amy Prentiss.

PRECURSOR

In 1902, Mark Arnstein, a talented twenty-three-year-old Polish playwright, wrote a four-act play called *Piesniarze*. Two years later, he translated it from Polish into Yiddish and produced it for the Yiddish theater in Lvov as *Der Vilner Balabesl* (*The Vilna Petit-Bourgeois*).[11] The plot was based on the real-life story of Yoel Dovid Strashunsky (also known as Loewenstein-Strashunsky), a child prodigy who lived in Eastern Europe in the first half of the nineteenth century. At the age of fifteen, Strashunsky succeeded his father as cantor of the Great Vilna Synagogue. The story is all the more remarkable because some ten years later the cantor left his position to go to Warsaw, where he was successful in breaking into the mainstream music world, giving operatic and choral recitals. Arnstein was attracted to this story of a cantor transitioning from the Jewish community to that of the secular world, and after producing the play in England in 1906, he brought it to the United States. Though the work was published in New York in 1908 and staged in London in 1912, there is no evidence of its having been performed on the American Yiddish stage until the late 1920s. A very young Raphaelson, who almost assuredly accompanied his parents and grandparents to the Yiddish theater, might have heard about the play, but he certainly never saw it, and it is doubtful that he would have read it. Though similarities in story line are striking, there is no evidence to suggest that Raphaelson drew upon the earlier Arnstein work.[12] What would prove interesting is that more than a decade after *The Jazz Singer* was produced, a Yiddish film with a very different message would be made, based on Arnstein's work.

THE SHORT STORY

Samson Raphaelson's short story, "The Day of Atonement," appeared in print in the January 1922 issue of *Everybody's Magazine*. Raphaelson's story encompassed the desires of a generation, his own, that hoped to break away from the perceived insularity of the Jewish world in order to achieve a place in the broader American society. Only outside the Jewish world did many Jews of the period feel that they could authenticate their station within American society. America was perceived as a land of opportunity; Raphaelson's theme in the story was that freedom offered many options, if one only took that risk. Often, one had to sever the bonds of neighborhood, family, friends, and religion and break completely with tradition in order to escape the "ghetto" in search of this opportunity. Raphaelson understood that the move out of the Jewish enclave required some accommodation. The question he would pose was just how much accommodation? He intimates that, once liberated from the bonds of community, one could freely pursue whatever one pleased. He also insinuates that, often, such freedom comes with a steep price.

Raphaelson's character, Jack Robin, alienates his parents, in particular his father, first by his affection for his new American way of life, then by leaving home. Sholem Asch described a similar predicament in his short novel *America*: "In these children . . . there awoke with elementary force, in an American setting, a yearning for unshackled liberty."[13] The conflict between Old World and New only worsens when Jack alerts his parents to the fact that he has chosen Amy Prentiss, a woman outside his faith, to be his wife. Wrote Asch, "They pay no heed to the words of father and mother, for it is customary to hold one's parents in slight esteem. . . . Their father's piety and ways of living became a matter of jest."[14] With the freedom to seek his own way came the freedom to choose his own future, and the future of the Rabinowitz family's distinctive Jewishness is all at once put in peril. Additionally, Jack's father will never be able to overcome this final blow—the news that, as Raphaelson presents it in his short story, "our Jakie should marry a *shiksa* [a non-Jewish woman]."[15]

The finality of Jack's father's statement assessing their son's choice looms large for the cantor, but does not yet sink in for the cantor's wife. Sara Rabinowitz tells her son: "I was thinking that if a *Yiddisher* [Jewish] boy marries a *Goyishe* [non-Jewish] girl, then it ain't so terrible. She could be learned to buy kosher meat and to have two kinds of dishes . . ."[16] Sara continues detailing a possible happy resolution for this precarious situation. As Jack's grasp tightens on his mother's hands, he responds that it cannot be. "I was brought up that way, ma, and I've been unhappy all my life. And Amy was brought up the other way, and she's been happy from the day she was a baby. I'll want my children to be happy like Amy is."[17] Jack's jab at his Jewish upbringing is the final blow; the old cantor is weakened, succumbs to illness, and will finally die. "The revolt of the young against the inherited religion represented the destruction of the authority of the father within the immigrant family," explained Arthur Hertzberg.[18] As Asch described it in *America*: "They [the children] held their father in disrespect, put him down for a 'crank,' a 'dope,' a 'greenhorn,' spoke irreverently of his study of Sacred Writ, his scholarship, his Judaism."[19] Raphaelson portrays Jakie as destroying his father and bringing about his eventual death. Just before his father's death, Jack is given one last opportunity to repair the wound inflicted, when his mother comes to him at the theater: "Your papa, he ain't feeling so good, Jakie. Maybe this will be his last Yom Kippur. He talks about you. He is all the time talking about you . . ."[20] Jack sends his mother home, with a faint hope that he might pay a visit later in the week. It will be too late.

There are more important things on Jack's mind. His show is to open on Monday night. Only a few hours before the show's opening curtain, Jack is informed of his father's passing. He immediately takes a taxi to his home on Hester Street:

> Greater perhaps than her grief at the loss of the man who had loved her and his God with equal fervor for sixty years was Mrs. Rabinowitz's panic at the thought that it was Yom Kippur eve and that the lyrical voice of a Rabinowitz would not be raised in supplication to wipe out the sins of the Chosen People before their Creator. When Jack crowded his way through the friends and neighbors who packed the dark, narrow corridor, she was clinging to the hand of Lawyer Feldman.
>
> "Look, Mr. Feldman," she was saying; "it's only two hours to Yom Kippur. It's got to be a good *Chazon* [cantor] to sing. The last words my Yosele he said to me: 'Rivke, get our Jakie.' So low he says it, Mr. Feldman,

I couldn't hardly hear him. His face was white like a *Yahrtzeit* [memorial] candle, and he says to me: 'Rivke, God will forgive our Jakie if he will sing *Kol Nidre* for me to-night. Maybe my dying,' he says, 'will make a *Chazon* from our Jakie. Tell him, Rivke,' he says. Look, Mr. Feldman; Jakie is maybe coming here. Maybe you could talk to him. In his heart, he's a good boy. Tell him — tell him — oh, Mr. Feldman, my heart is breaking in pieces — I — I can't talk no more — "[21]

Once back in his old neighborhood there is no leaving, and there will be no Broadway opening that evening for Jack Robin:

It was four-thirty. If he appeared in the show that evening, singing rag-time songs while his father lay dead — while the Hester Street Synagogue went cantorless for the first Day of Atonement in forty years — while his mother struggled under an unbearable double grief . . .[22]

Jack walks the block to the synagogue, takes his father's *tallit* (prayer shawl), and sings Kol Nidre, the prayer recited on Yom Kippur, The Day of Atonement, the great annual day for forgiveness and reconciliation. With Jack's recitation of the prayer, is Raphaelson asking for his own forgiveness in addition to absolution for the sins of mankind? How does one reach for the American dream while still maintaining close ties with Jewish and family tradition? Raphaelson does not tell us. His short story simply moves to conclusion with Jakie's prayers of supplication as substitute cantor in his father's *shul* on Yom Kippur Eve. While providing a clear roadmap for the needs of the new generation to strike out on their own, Raphaelson also shows us the potential consequence for the family. In the end, his protagonist Jakie is ready to give up his hopes in order to be with his family and people.

In a certain way, Raphaelson leaves us with some sense that Jack, though punished through the loss of his father, will at the same time be rewarded for his grand gesture. At the end of the story, Jack's agent, David Lee, totally disgruntled by Jack's abandonment of the theater the night before, reads something in the paper — apparently about how Jack Robin had drawn crowds to the synagogue. He calls his colleague:

"Harry," said Lee, "do you want to hear the greatest ragtime singer in America in the making? A wonder, Harry, a wonder! Got Hal Bolton mopped off the boards. Come down right away. It's a dirty little hole down on the East Side called the Hester Street Synagogue. I'll meet you on the corner of Hester and Norfolk."[23]

Maybe Jack Robin will still succeed as a jazz singer. His talent has clearly been recognized. Perhaps Jack's story is representative of the situation of an entire generation of American Jews.

THE STAGE PLAY

By early 1925, Raphaelson had reworked his short story into a play, which he tentatively titled *Prayboy*. In May of that year, he sold it to Broadway producer Al Lewis, who brought in up-and-coming vaudevillian George Jessel, providing for him a chance at a dramatic role. George Jessel, in contrast to Jolson, had maintained a strong Jewish connection throughout his life. Much of Raphaelson's original story stayed the same, though there were minor revisions, such as changing Jakie's woman friend's name from Amy Prentiss to Mary Dale, in order to make her sound more gentile. Less emphasis was placed on the relationship between Jack and Mary and more on the differences between father and son, particularly in the music that each chooses to perform.

As in the short story, Sara Rabinowitz visits the theater in an effort to cajole her son into returning home. Might not such a return, particularly to substitute for the cantor during Yom Kippur services, effect a change for the better in Cantor Rabinowitz's health? In both versions, Jack tries to show Sara that he belongs in the theater, and both times, his mother fails to comprehend the life that he has chosen for himself. The 1922 short story concludes with Jack returning to the synagogue, but only after learning by telephone of his father's death. Then and only then, mostly out of guilt, he assumes his father's place in the synagogue. In the 1925 theatrical adaptation, Jakie returns because of his father. He chooses fatefully to make peace with the father who had cut him off and hastily departs the theater for his parents' apartment. Yet there too, he will never see his father again, as Cantor Rabinowitz had already been brought to the hospital. Jakie's manager, Henry Lee, and Mary arrive and try to convince him to return to the theater, explaining the consequences of not performing that night. Jack vacillates. The evening service is about to begin, and Jack is set to leave for the synagogue with his mother when the phone call comes. In this stage version, it is Mary who receives the information that the cantor has died. When Mary shares the news with Jack, he reacts as follows, with emphatic stage directions:

Oh my God! [Emotion has returned to him. He sobs.] He told me God would punish me! I thought I could get away from Cantors! Well, God showed me . . . [His voice rises to a wail and then subsides.] The Day of Atonement! — I'll say it's the Day of Atonement. [Sara enters with lighted candles. Jack suddenly turns to her.] Mama! I'm going with you! I'm going to synagogue![24]

Both the original story and the play end with Jakie assuming his "rightful" place, following ten generations of Rabinowitz cantors, in leading the Yom Kippur service. Jack has decided — certainly assuaged by circumstance — to return home, to come back to his people, to rejoin the Jewish community. The message again seems clear: Stay Jewishly connected! Remain committed! If not, be prepared to accept the consequences! In each version, Jack Robin sees his father's passing as his own punishment for abandoning his people. With this ending, both Jessel and Raphaelson were in agreement. You can still be successful in your career while maintaining your Jewishness. Break away and there will be pain and suffering![25]

By September, the play, now titled *The Jazz Singer*, had opened on Broadway and was doing impressive business. Thirty-eight weeks later, Jessel left the show to fulfill a commitment to shoot the movie *Private Izzy Murphy* for Warner Brothers in Hollywood. At the time, Jessel pushed the idea of optioning the film rights to the play, and just as the play was about to close, Benjamin Warner's sons, the Warner brothers, bought the movie rights and put the option aside as a future film vehicle for Jessel.[26] Harry (the only one of the four Warner brothers born in Europe), with his signing of Jessel and his commitment to the film, showed something that none of his brothers seemed to share: great warmth for his Jewish heritage. Of all the brothers, Harry always held that the cinema could do more than entertain. He always saw film "as a unique tool for education."[27] He was said to have told George Jessel that *The Jazz Singer* "would be a good picture to do for the sake of religious tolerance, if nothing else."[28]

The Jazz Singer was slated to be just another silent picture on the Warner Brothers shooting schedule. In the meantime, George Jessel was back touring the country with the play. Finally, in February of 1927, the Hollywood

George Jessel, who played Jack Robin so successfully in the theater, was set to play the part in the film adaptation, but it was not to be. Photofest.

trade papers began to hum with the story that George Jessel would shortly begin production on the film. But much had changed at Warner Brothers. The qualified success earlier that year of *Don Juan*, with its synchronized music and sound effects, had pushed the Warner production company into the "sound era." It now appeared that of all things, *The Jazz Singer* would be their first large-budget sound effort, incorporating the new Vitaphone technology. Inherent in that decision came the concern that a "Jewish" story, with the "punishment by guilt" ending that Raphaelson had written, would be of little interest to the mass audiences that Vitaphone hoped to draw. When the play was on Broadway, the vast majority of its audience was Jewish. The *Jewish Daily Forward* reported that the play was "by a Jew, about Jews and designed for 100 percent Jewish consumption." [29] The studio could never chance such a demographic in its quest for broad national distribution. Alfred A. Cohn was hired to adapt and change the scenario, and he made several alterations, including the creation of a new ending.

THE MOTION PICTURE

When Samson Raphaelson, working with producer Albert Lewis, adapted his short story for the theater he controlled both the story and its message. As I see it, the story was always about Raphaelson's perceived crisis in American Jewish life—the tightrope one had to walk to maintain one's Jewish identity while seeking the American dream. Raphaelson's work showed what Arthur Hertzberg called the immigrant's "inner torment, when the Jewish past was forgotten." [30] With *The Jazz Singer*'s sale to Warner Brothers, Raphaelson lost script control, leaving him completely out of the loop. The person most responsible at Warner Brothers for purchase of the property was New York–based brother Harry, who managed the business side of the organization. But Harry, the most Jewishly committed of the brothers, would have the least to say about its evolution. The film and its story were now in the hands of Jack and Sam, the two brothers who would control production of the film. With twenty-four-year-old head of production Darryl F. Zanuck chosen to oversee the actual making of the film, brother Sam was delegated to oversee the technical side of things, particularly the implementation of the new Vitaphone sound technology. Jack, the youngest of the brothers, was in command and now controlled the story. He would make sure that it echoed his and Sam's sensibilities, as well as reflected their lives. Jack, "the frustrated performer," [31] was the only brother to play vaudeville and saw himself as the ultimate entertainer. He saw "show business" as his religion, and he was proud to let everyone know it. Brother Sam had no qualms about breaking with and shocking his family when he married a Catholic, Ziegfeld dancer Lina Basquette, in 1925—the first in the family to marry out of the faith. Sam certainly could relate to Jack Robin's romance with dancer Mary Dale in *The Jazz Singer*.

The four Warner brothers worked hard to make their new vehicle for entertainment, the Vitaphone—the "talking movie"—successful. Harry, Jack, Sam, and Abe Warner, 1926. Photofest.

In May of 1927, George Jessel was replaced by Al Jolson as the lead in *The Jazz Singer*.[32] There was little written about the cast change in the press; George Jessel's name was simply no longer associated with the project. Over the years, there have been several explanations. Jack Warner, in his autobiography *My First Hundred Years in Hollywood*, claimed that Jessel was simply unreasonable, demanding more money for starring in what would now be a sound production. He also said that Jessel, in demanding a contract countersigned by brother Harry, showed a distrust that Jack was unable to accept.[33] Jessel, in his memoir *The World I Lived In*, also writes of having asked for more money, which he felt was deserved given the size of the project.[34] In addition, he was opposed to having non-Jews play the parts of his Jewish parents.[35] Most important, changes in the script made by writer Alfred Cohn appalled him.[36] Clearly, when the rankling between the Warner brothers and Jessel began, whatever the cause, the Warners took advantage of the moment to squeeze out Jessel, still relatively unknown as a performer, in order to pursue Jolson, by now a superstar and sure to be a bigger draw at the box office. No doubt, questions of economics had impact on the decision, now that the new production would incorporate several songs, and Jolson could sing them. Al Jolson was clearly the greatest entertainer of his day, and George Jessel was perceived as "too Jewish." As Neal Gabler pointed out, "Jack and Sam could never have identified with a strident professional Jew like Jessel, and it was almost inevitable, after searching vainly for a replacement, that they would ultimately cast a Jew as totally assimilated as they were."[37] The story was just as much Jolson's as it was that of the Warner brothers. Ruth Perlmutter observed that "the fact that the star could recreate his own climb from an ordinary guy to stardom not only made the struggle worthwhile but extended the audience's belief in the system's rewards for the acceptance of its values."[38]

The Jazz Singer is bookended by the Kol Nidre prayer and Day of Atonement service. Alfred Cohn added a new beginning, where we see a young Jakie Rabinowitz rejecting his father's wishes and departing for the outside world while the cantor ventures into the synagogue to recite the Kol Nidre. As in the story and play, the film's opening reflects a dismissal of the past; it was its conclusion that presented the real challenge. After all — in real life — would either Jack or Sam Warner, let alone Jolson, really give up their careers in order to return to the old Jewish neighborhood and sing in the synagogue? George Jessel claimed that his problem with the film was less over money and more about content. It was the new ending, added by screenwriter Cohn, that most angered him:

> Instead of the boy leaving the theater and following the tradition of his father in the synagogue, as in the play, the scenario had him return to the Winter Garden as a blackfaced comedian with his mother applauding wildly from a box seat. I raised hell. Money or no money, I would not do this version.[39]

Harry Warner's granddaughter disagreed: "The end of *The Jazz Singer* was innovative in that it resolved a conflict familiar to children of immigrants at that time. Everyone gets what they want: the traditional father reconciles with his son and hears him sing in the synagogue, but the son goes back to be a success onstage."[40]

The Jazz Singer opens with young Jakie Rabinowitz (Robert Gordon) performing at a local saloon. It is just hours before the commencement of Yom Kippur and preparations are underway for the meal that will precede the day-long fast. Jakie's father, the cantor (Warner Oland), waits impatiently for him, as the youth is to stand next to him for the recitation of the Kol Nidre prayer that opens the evening service. Upon learning that Jakie is singing at a saloon, the cantor makes his way across town to the bar to forcibly bring the boy home. It was Yudelson (Otto Lederer), official of the synagogue and keeper of the faith, so to speak, who spotted Jakie at the saloon and reported his activity to the cantor. Exactly what wrong has the boy done? Is it that he sings outside the confines of the synagogue? Is it that he is not at home preparing himself for the advent of the fast day? Both reasons seem to be in play as the cantor leaves his home for the crosstown "journey" to find his son.

The cantor's fast-paced walk through the teeming streets of the Lower East Side of New York is a visual parable of American Jewry at that time. This trek, along with the walk that Yudelson takes to summon the cantor, are the only exterior sequences of the film. That director Alan Crosland chose to insert these extended outdoor sequences is telling. On the way to and from the saloon, the cantor leaves home and walks past a variety of pushcarts manned by vendors who are struggling to carve out a living for their families. The cantor is walking through the streets of New York's Lower East Side, and all around him are merchants trying to find equilibrium between their Jewish world and the possibilities of America. The "journey" for the cantor is clear and simple: he will bring his son back to the synagogue, saving him from the lure of cabaret life. Yet for Jakie, this same walk is a tightrope that he frequently has had to tiptoe across. On one side is "home"; on the other is the "workplace." At home, we witness Old World values; in the saloon, we experience New World ambition. Can Jakie truly straddle these two worlds on the tightrope that has become his life? There are those like Yudelson, a traditional Jew who by the very act of visiting the bar is making a statement that he has no desire to isolate himself from this "outside" world. Yet, for the cantor, this New World foray has no place in his world or in the life of his son.

Sunset and the advent of the Day of Atonement are approaching, and we note the lights of the synagogue going on in the background. In spite of the boy's mother's protest, Jakie, upon returning to his home, is taken into the next room and strapped for his contrary actions by his father. At that point, the lad chooses to leave behind this way of life and seek his place in the outside world. His mother, Sara Rabinowitz (Eugenie Besserer), observes: "Our boy is gone and never coming back." The camera focuses on the Jewish star in the synagogue window, somehow representative of Judaism itself, which not only becomes equated with the punishment meted out on the boy, but also becomes the reason for the child's exodus. Shortly thereafter, the cantor, with tears in his eyes, is in synagogue about to recite Kol Nidre, declaring to Yudelson that "my son was to stand at my side and sing tonight, but now I have no son." Midway through his recitation, after the film cuts to a sobbing Sara in the women's section, we watch young Jakie briefly sneak back into the family's apartment, just long enough to take with him a picture of his mother. For the next several years, it will be the only thing that will connect him with his family.

In his novel *America*, essentially an assessment of early-twentieth-century American Jewish life, Sholem Asch observed that the father was "looked upon as a 'greenhorn,' a stranger to English speech and to American ways."[41] In many immigrant families, as the father was summarily rejected the mother often became the emotional center and protector of the family. We certainly see this in Raphaelson's story. Still, Joyce Antler felt that Sara seemed "frozen in time, trapped in a nostalgic Old World habitat where [she] will forever be weeping and sentimentalized."[42] Irving Howe conjectured that "Jewish folklore had elevated the mother to a figure of sanctioned tenderness . . . she became an object of sentimental veneration."[43] Though Jakie has left home, he carries his mother's picture with him and he will continue to correspond with her. His connection to his mother is a key element of the film, as seen through the songs that he chooses to sing. As Irv Saposnik shows us:

> The "American" songs are about love between parent and child (*Dirty Hands, Dirty Face*), a temporary parting with a vow of constant communication (*Toot, Toot, Tootsie*), a promised future with blue skies to look forward to (*Blue Skies*), the constancy of mother love even after widespread rejection (*Mother of Mine, I Still Have You*), and the everlasting bond between mother and child (*My Mammy*).[44]

When Jack learns that he is to return to the East Coast to debut on Broadway, the title cards displayed show his excitement: "New York," "Broadway," "Home." The last card — in big, bold letters — reads "MOTHER." The mother-son relationship that Raphaelson develops is strong, almost oedipal. Howe saw this special connection "as particularly Jewish, perhaps even a Jewish invention."[45] Yet there is no doubt that the mother-son relationship between Sara and Jack gives the film a certain dynamic and universality.

As the film had moved forward, we observed Jakie Rabinowitz perform-

*Jack's believed-to-be-triumphant return home brings rejection from his father,
Cantor Rabinowitz, who cannot accept his son's choices. Jack's mother looks on.
Eugenie Besserer, Al Jolson, Warner Oland. Photofest.*

ing at nightclubs across the continent, waiting for his chance to be discovered. He had long before left his home in "the Jewish neighborhood," with its perceived limitations, in search of the American dream. The Jew of Eastern Europe was limited in his ability to leave the confines of his externally imposed Jewish locale. But America offered no such physical boundary or restriction that encumbered the Jew, as (at least theoretically) the "outside" world was open to America's Jews.

Much has been written about Jack's return to New York and his visit home.[46] His entertaining of his mother with song, embrace, and talking monologue are important moments in film history. His father's entrance into the room and utterance of the word "STOP" constitute a powerful juncture between sound and silence, a contrast between the silent film of the past and the "talkie" of the present. The scene underwrites the role that father and mother play in the life of this first-generation American, with mother loyal to her husband yet loving and understanding, and father intolerant and of "the Old World." "STOP" will be the only dialogue heard from the cantor,

Mary with Jack in blackface, before a dress rehearsal. Jack is conflicted about his place in the theater and his responsibility to his family. Blackface was common at the time, but today it's highly controversial. Much has been written not only about what this "mask" might represent, but also about its appropriateness. May McAvoy, Al Jolson. Photofest.

and his effort to *stop* forward thinking and progress, as the filmmakers seem to be intimating, will be unsuccessful. The sequence provides an important prelude for what will occur next.

"Success" for Jack, his moment to appear on Broadway, finally arrives — thanks in large part to the intervention of his non-Jewish woman friend Mary Dale (May McAvoy), his co-star. The moment is very much Jack's chance, pivotal in his career, an opportunity for which he had toiled for years. The fact that opening night coincides with the eve of Yom Kippur, The Day of Atonement, an intense day of prayer and meditation when most Jews find themselves in synagogue, seems of little concern, but it represents Jack's final break with Jewish tradition. Jack, the cantor's son, though not rejecting Judaism, seems to have made his choice to divest himself of the *burdens* of being a Jew.

Hours before the show's opening, Jack's mother comes to see him in his dressing room, sharing the news that his father the cantor is quite ill, too sick to chant the traditional Kol Nidre prayer in synagogue. Her son is unrecognizable to her, having, for the dress rehearsal, covered his face in black-face — a performance device of the times.[47] She encourages him to take his father's place. In response, he informs her that he must perform onstage, making it clear that he is starring in a Broadway production and that he cannot squander this opportunity. He does not hesitate in his quick refusal, but after his mother leaves he stares blankly into the mirror, black makeup still covering his face. Michael Rogin points to the application of blackface as a way for Jack to mask his Semitic features and escape his Old World identity.[48] Irving Howe saw blackface as "a mask for Jewish expressiveness, with one's woe speaking through the voice of another."[49] Music historian Mark Slobin conjectured that Jolson's blackface seemed "an innocent ingredient in the stew . . . that make up the film's musical mosaic."[50] Who is Jack Robin? What of his identity? The image in the mirror slowly fades from his own to an image of his father, the cantor, dressed in white for High Holy Day services.[51] The pull of his Jewish world leaves him struggling. In a real sense, this scene represents an important moment in the lifetime of the 1920s Jew. Jakie Rabinowitz, like many American Jews of the period, has changed his name to Jack Robin. He has succeeded in masking his Semitic features by putting on blackface, the face of American vaudeville. Does he belong here in the theater, finally having achieved his goal of acceptance and recognition, with success at his fingertips? Or should he simply wash off the makeup and return to the synagogue? That moment, in front of the mirror, is a defining one in the film and for America's Jews. One could change one's name, wear the dress and face of America, but what of the pull of tradition and history, the force and power of the older generation?

It is interesting that *The Jazz Singer* includes a scene where, on tour, Jack Robin walks past a recital hall in Chicago and notices that Yossele Rosenblatt will be giving a concert of "sacred songs." He is drawn in to attend the matinee concert given by the renowned cantor and thinks of his own father and the world of Jewish music that he has left behind. Alfred Cohn's original screenplay called for the esteemed cantor Rosenblatt to sing the hymn "Eli, Eli," with Cantor Rabinowitz's choir singing the same a few scenes later. But the pious Rosenblatt refused to sing any part of the liturgy on camera, so the song that we hear the great Khazn Rosenblatt chant is "Yahrtzeit Likht" ("Memorial Light").[52] Irv Saposnik saw "Yahrtzeit Likht" as a song about unceasing memory of death, a musical piece "reserved for a select few who are literally and figuratively passing away . . . the *kaddish* [memorial prayer] for his father's dead world."[53] Yiddish film director Joseph Green, who was

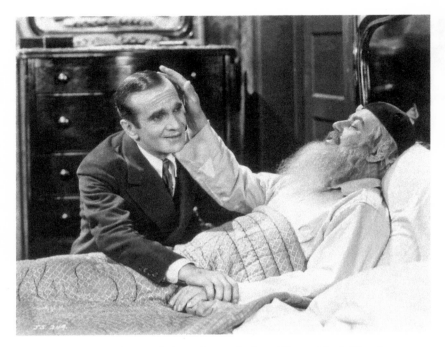

Final meeting between father and son. Al Jolson, Warner Oland. Photofest.

on the set of the movie, claimed that Rosenblatt's appearance in the film was at the personal request of the Warner brothers' father Benjamin Warner, who was a big fan.[54] According to Green, the elder Warner felt that the very incorporation of Rosenblatt singing, though it also served a purpose in plot development, showed that although the film may have rejected "Old World" in favor of "another day," the young crooner remained drawn to his Judaism and the Jewish music that was so much an important part of his childhood. It also proved that although Jack, and by inference the film and its makers, called to task Cantor Rosenblatt for his Old World ways, they did not reject his religion outright; his unwillingness to allow his son to pursue new directions was simply renounced. Jack loves his Jewish world; but he, like most of his generation, simply did not want to be constrained by it. The tradition-minded Benjamin Warner gave his sons that kind of freedom.

After seeing his mother and participating in the show's dress rehearsal, Jack goes "downtown" to see his sick father, ostensibly to pay a sick call. In the new ending created for film by Cohn, Jack does in fact see his ailing father after his mother's visit to the theater. As far as we understand, this visit

Moment of decision. Choose! Jack Robin or Jakie Rabinowitz? Does Jack take the tallit *and go with his mother and Yudelson to the synagogue? Or does he return with Mary and manager Harry Lee to the theater? Richard Tucker, May McAvoy, Al Jolson, Otto Lederer, Eugenie Besserer. Photofest.*

is to be a brief one, as Jack has every intention of returning to the theater for that night's opening performance. Upon entering his father's room, he comforts his father, but he is also seeking his own consolation. When his father wakes up, he is assured of his deep affection: "I love you!" Then, as he leaves his father's room, he is greeted by Yudelson, who thanks him for coming to take his father's place in synagogue. Jakie tries to explain that this was not the purpose of his visit, just as Mary and manager Harry Lee arrive at the apartment. A study of the sequence is quite illuminating in terms of understanding our protagonist and the American Jew of the time.

At this point in the film, all the key characters come into play. Yudelson brings Jack the *tallit*, ostensibly the same prayer shawl that Jack gave his father as a present in an earlier scene—a symbol of tradition and continuity through the generations. Mary and manager Harry Lee are in the cantor's apartment to make sure Jack understands what is at stake if he chooses not to return immediately for opening night. At the other end of the room is Jack's mother, preparing for the onset of Yom Kippur. Jack, deliberating, declares on an intertitle that "it's a choice between giving up the biggest chance of my life . . . and breaking my mother's heart!" It is interesting how the intertitle does not pivot the choice on career versus religion, but rather on career versus family. As Jack sees it, there is never a question of rejection of Judaism; rather, the question is one of choosing not to follow certain traditions. If we look closely at the images that unfold, it is the *tallit*, the Jewish mantle, which Jack is being asked to take. On one side of Jack are Harry Lee and Mary Dale; on the other side are Yudelson and Jack's mother. There is no tightrope to walk, no trek across the neighborhood — it is decision time for Jack Robin. Does he take the prayer shawl and go back to the synagogue, or does he walk away with Mary and Harry and return to the theater? As was done in each previous Raphaelson version, Jack returns to the synagogue.

What is different here in the film version is that the dying cantor has the opportunity, albeit briefly, to realize *his* dream of seeing his son replace him in the synagogue. In a real sense, this allows him to absolve his son of any guilt. Jack does finally get his father's acceptance, but only after the cantor hears Jack begin chanting the Kol Nidre prayer. The cantor tells his wife, "We have our son!" and then passes away. As the scene ends in the synagogue, with Jolson reciting the Kol Nidre, we witness the form of the old cantor, dressed in High Holiday white, coming behind Jack, placing his hand over his son's shoulder, as if he is giving his blessing.

Next is the newly added scene written by Alfred Cohn, which places Jack back at the theater as the film comes to a triumphant end. Mother and Yudelson are neatly placed in the front row as Jack sings "My Mammy" to his mother and the entire theater audience. Jack seems to have it both ways; although he chose the synagogue that night over the theater, he is still back at the Winter Palace.[55] Leonard Fein wrote: "Truth to tell, the Jews most likely to come to this land were in any case those least tied to yesterday, to the traditional ways. Whether it was freedom or fortune they sought here — or both — they came the awesome distance they did in pursuit of change, in order to invent their future."[56] Jakie Rabinowitz showed no interest in becoming the sixth-generation cantor in his family; he wanted to reinvent himself. For him and for the Warner brothers who produced the film, the synagogue represented "yesterday," while the theater represented the possibilities of the new day. John Quincy Adams postured that new immigrants to America "must cast off the European skin, never to resume it. They must look forward to their posterity rather than backward to their ancestors."[57]

Jack clutches the prayer shawl.
Al Jolson, Otto Lederer.

Jack, wrapped in the tallit, *takes his*
father's place leading the service, as his
father's spirit appears behind him, as if
to show approval. This was how Samson
Raphaelson wrote the story's conclusion,
but this ending would not be satisfactory
for the Warner brothers.

Hollywood films of the time reflected the intentions of their authors. Harry Warner liked the story's strong Jewish theme and was attracted to it, largely because of his own personal Jewish commitment and great admiration for the Jewishly identified George Jessel. Benjamin Warner, the Warner father, a traditional Jew, was so enamored of the story that he was often on the set making sure that the Jewish elements appeared realistic and was thrilled to have been able to include Yossele Rosenblatt in the film. Once the project became a Vitaphone project and took on the proportions of a major film, the less Jewishly committed brothers, Sam and Jack Warner, interceded with the changed story by Cohn, which was far more reflective of their own assimilated lifestyle. The Warner brothers transformed *The Jazz Singer* from a play about the complexities of the new American life, where family and peoplehood still had worth, into a film with a strongly assimilationist message. After all, would a true American musical talent really give up everything in order to return to synagogue to sing Kol Nidre? Certainly not, at least nobody Jack Warner knew! The choice of Al Jolson, an assimilated Jew himself, for the lead role was more in keeping with Jack Warner's thinking. This new version of *The Jazz Singer* would, at least as Jack Warner saw it, reflect the true immigrant desire to disassociate with one's ethnic enclave in an outward attempt at American socialization and assimilation. In fact, as historian David Weinberg noted, "the hero achieves success precisely because he rebels against his father's wish."[58] It must be noted, however, that the film does not reject Judaism or religion, just traditions that might inhibit fulfillment of what many believed America had to offer. In many respects, although the narrative was based on Al Jolson's life history, it was just as much the real-life story of Sam Warner and an entire generation.

Attainment of the American dream was the hope and goal of most of America's Jews at this time; it certainly was for the Jewish film producers in Hollywood. *The Jazz Singer*, as Scott Eyman so aptly put it, marked "one of the few times that the Hollywood Jews allowed themselves to contemplate their own cultural myth and the conundrums that go with it." [59] Not only did *The Jazz Singer* showcase a desire to move from the immigrant milieu to American affluence, it also reflected for the moviemakers a disconnect with the East Coast, its ghettos, its ethnicities and traditions, for the newness and fresh start that Hollywood and California were able to provide at the time. [60] Most of the films of the period, made by Hollywood's producers, generally ended "happily" with the intermarriage of Jew and non-Jew. Such endings were perceived by these producers as indicative of the American "success" chronicle, their own story, wherein a Jew could be better integrated into American life. By disassociating with tradition and ritual and by reinvention, often through intermarriage, one could become American. In *The Jazz Singer*, Jack pursues the American dream of success, seemingly ready to discard his Jewish connectedness, which might get in the way of achieving such a goal. He chooses as his woman-friend a non-Jew, who becomes influential in helping chart his path. He flirts with assimilation, an aspiration often linked with a need to reject one's tradition. Yet, as Raphaelson so powerfully portrays in *The Jazz Singer*, Jack Robin, like his generation, remains conflicted, even while gaining entrée into America.

POSTSCRIPT

Sam Warner, who was so intimately involved in preparing *The Jazz Singer* for the screen, died the day before the film was to open, apparently from an infection from abscessed teeth that he failed to treat. [61] He had been working incessantly, not paying attention to his deteriorating health, to make sure that the Vitaphone sound technology was fully operational in time for *The Jazz Singer*'s release. *The Jazz Singer* had its premier in New York City on October 6, 1927, the day before Yom Kippur. None of the Warner brothers were there; they had a funeral in California to attend.

The momentous success of *The Jazz Singer* showed that the American public was ready to see a first-generation American Jew find his way into American society. After all, that child of immigrants could have been anyone's American offspring. It also proved that the audience was not only ready, but clamoring, for sound. As film historian Robert Sklar put it, "Overnight Warner Bros. leaped from nowhere to the front rank of the industry. From one theater in 1927, they gained control over seven hundred by 1930."[62] At the very first very Academy Awards ceremony in 1929, actor Douglas Fairbanks presented a special Oscar to the Warner Brothers studio for *The Jazz Singer*, as "the pioneer outstanding talking picture, which has revolutionized the industry."[63] Accepting on behalf of the studio, production head Darryl F. Zanuck dedicated the award to Sam Warner.

REACTION IN THE YIDDISH CINEMA

While Hollywood's films were aimed at the broad American public across the nation, indeed around the world, the Yiddish movie, directed at a primarily Jewish audience, took on a different thrust. In New York, Yiddish filmmakers reacted strongly to the assimilationist tendencies of Hollywood filmmakers. Their Yiddish-language films tended to extol the virtues of Jewish life and foster Jewish continuity and community, helping instill a sense of belonging. Yiddish cinema celebrated Jewish life.

Throughout the 1930s, Yiddish producers could not find an appropriate response to what many saw as the assimilationist message of *The Jazz Singer*. Even Samson Raphaelson had found the film "dreadful and embarrassing."[64] Finally, a Yiddish version of *The Jazz Singer* came in the form of Louis Freiman's *Dem Khazns Zindl* (*The Cantor's Son*), which Mark Schweid adapted for the screen. Just as Raphaelson had based his story on the life of Al Jolson, Schweid centered his film on the life of singer/cantor Moishe Oysher, who left his home in Eastern Europe to attain success as one of America's finest voices. In *The Cantor's Son*, the action begins in Europe. Like Jack Robin, Sol Reichman (played by Oysher) leaves behind his parents to seek his dream as a member of a theatrical troupe. While Jack seemed ready to perform onstage on Yom Kippur, Sol's only sin is loving America and all its attractions. The conflict in this 1936 Yiddish film revolves around whether Sol is to remain in America, committed to the American woman who loves him or return to the old country. In America, he has found success and well-being,

In the 1937 Yiddish film classic, The Cantor's Son (Dem Khazns Zindl), *Shloimele has a love for the theater that his father does not share. He sneaks off to join a traveling theater troupe and eventually makes his way to America. Vicki Marcus, Judah Bleich, Lorraine Abarbanel, Bertha Guttenberg. Ergo Media Inc.*

but back home in Belz are his parents, the "country girl" he left behind, and his seemingly real future. Somehow, Freiman is telling us that America, with its lack of Jewishness, is no place for this Jewish lad to remain. Whereas *The Jazz Singer* is very much a celebration of breaking away, *The Cantor's Son* is a commemoration of coming home.

The 1940 Yiddish film *Overture to Glory* takes the story of *The Jazz Singer* one step further. What happens when a talented Jewish singer abandons his community? The film, also starring Moishe Oysher, drew on Mark Arnstein's 1908 play *Der Vilner Balabesl* (*The Vilna Petit-Bourgeois*), cited earlier, about the life of Yoel Dovid Strashunsky. At fifteen, upon the death of his father, Strashunsky assumed his position as Vilna cantor. His reputation as a child prodigy spread across the country. But by his midtwenties, he chose to abandon his synagogue and community in Vilna, leave his wife and son behind, and join an opera company in Warsaw. As Strashunsky becomes ever more comfortable in his new environs, his child is struck down by plague. Upon hearing the tragic news, the great cantor has a breakdown

In the 1940 Yiddish film favorite Overture to Glory (Der Vilner Shtot Khazn), *the Vilna cantor has left his congregation to sing opera in Warsaw; here he is joined by Countess Wanda. Helen Beverly, Moishe Oysher. Ergo Media Inc.*

and will sing opera no more. Whereas Jakie Rabinowitz of *The Jazz Singer* is rewarded with success onstage for leaving the Jewish community, Yoel David Strashunsky is severely punished. The film ends with the cantor's return to his synagogue, his chanting of the traditional Kol Nidre prayer, and his collapse and death, the ultimate punishment, on the *bima*, the altar.

Yiddish cinema had no sympathy for characters who were thought to have deserted their religion and who were seen as fostering the erosion of Jewish peoplehood. In *The Cantor's Son*, Sol Reichman, who is able to gain fame and success in America, will ultimately reject his new way of life and return home to family and the more comfortable Jewish setting. *Overture to Glory* shows how a Jew who forgets his roots and becomes too comfortable in the secular world will certainly find unhappiness and despair, even death. Hollywood, in these early years, flaunted the lure of the good life in a secular

American society, while the Yiddish cinema warned that American assimilation might bring about an end to the Jewish people.[65]

REMAKES

In 1936, Warner Brothers released an animated Merrie Melodies short, *I Love to Singa*, in which Professor Fritz Owl, disgusted with the antics and love for jazz of his son Owl Jolson, throws him out of the house: "Out of My House, you Jazz Singer!" the elder Owl tells his son. In the 1940s, there were several reports of attempts at remakes of *The Jazz Singer*. But Jolson's career had slid to one-night club appearances; there was little interest not only in him but in the narrative that had been taken from his real-life story. Finally, in 1946, Al Jolson's biography was adapted for the screen by a few courageous producers and released as *The Jolson Story*, with Larry Parks playing Jolson. The film was a big success, catapulting Jolson back onto radio and the stage and into the limelight. Three years later, *Jolson Sings Again* was made, with Parks again playing the entertainer. When Jolson went on tour in Korea with the USO in 1950, "the troops yelled for his appearance. He went down on his knee again and sang 'Mammy', and the troops wept and cheered."[66] He was a colossal success. In October of 1950, Al Jolson had been back from his USO tour only a month when he died of a massive heart attack at age sixty-four.

Two years after Jolson's death, in a second *Jazz Singer* directed by Michael Curtiz, singer Danny Thomas plays the part of Jerry Golding, a second-generation college graduate who returns in uniform from the Korean War. When his father announces his retirement, expecting his son to assume his place as cantor in a Philadelphia synagogue, the young GI balks at the idea, instead wanting to join his woman-friend Judy Lane (Peggy Lee) as a singer. *Cue* magazine wrote, "Where the original Samson Raphaelson play dramatized the conflict between Old World traditions and New World ways, the film now is a straight-out synagogue-singer-to-Broadway-stardom success story. Nothing more."[67] The new adaptation also removed the conflict of a Jew from a traditional home wanting to be with a non-Jewish woman. This is made clear when we hear Judy say, "I haven't been to a *seder* since I left home." If there is anything that is indicative of the growing comfort level of the 1950s American Jewish community, it is the opulence of the synagogue and the station of the congregants as portrayed in this film. The president of

The 1952 version of The Jazz Singer *starred Danny Thomas as returning Korean War veteran Jerry Golding, who would rather be in a nightclub with Judy than replace his father as cantor of the synagogue. Peggy Lee, Danny Thomas. Photofest.*

the synagogue is a doctor, and both Jerry and his dad are college graduates. In addition, these Jews seem to feel quite comfortable with their non-Jewish friends; the elder cantor's best friend is an Irish-American baseball umpire.

In the intervening years, rumors persisted about other attempts to remake the Raphaelson story. In the late 1950s, there was great surprise when the entertainment industry learned that Jerry Lewis was preparing a made-for-television version that he was reworking to fit his own life story. After the lukewarm reception to Michael Curtiz's 1952 version, nobody believed that there was room for another remake. Yet Jolson held a special place in Jerry's life, and the notion that a lad from a traditional Jewish home could break into show business had special meaning for Jerry. Shawn Levy, in his biography of Lewis, points to how Lewis's father Danny chose to become a performer after having seen Jolson perform at New York's Winter Garden.[68] Jerry's father always remembered that life-changing performance, and he imparted that memory to his son — if this very charismatic Jewish performer could make it in America, so might he. *The Jazz Singer*, after all, was not just about Jolson, but about a whole generation of would-be Jolsons.

In Lewis's television version, the young man breaks with his father's traditional Jewish life to become a clown, rather than a singer. Lewis had the protagonist's name changed from Jack to Joey, the name he himself had used throughout his childhood. He also took great pains to point out that Sarah, Joey's mother, carried the name of his beloved maternal grandmother, who had helped raise him. It would be Lewis's first non-comedic acting role, and it was met with a great deal of resistance, not just from critics who felt that he should stay with comedy, but by many who felt that the story no longer had relevance. The drama, directed by Ginny Gibbons and Ralph Nelson, was broadcast as an installment of the "Ford Startime" series of specials and made-for-TV movies on October 13, 1959, the day after Yom Kippur.

In 1980, Neil Diamond became Jess Robin, aka Yussel Rabinovitch, yet another cantor-turned-vocalist, in Richard Fleischer's film interpretation of Raphaelson's play. This story, set initially on New York's Lower East Side, has a dejected assistant cantor spending what appears to be every spare minute writing rock and roll. Jess seems happily married to Rivka (Catlin Adams), but she cares more about meeting the needs of a small synagogue that Jess and his father the cantor serve than in encouraging him to pursue his secular music career. That chance comes not from a non-Jewish woman friend, as in previous versions of the film, but from an African American buddy, Bubba (Franklyn Ajaye), who, while standing outside the Hollywood Garden of Eden Motel, cajoles Jess by phone to come to Los Angeles, which he says is "paradise." In LA Jess meets, falls in love with, and moves in with Molly Bell (Lucie Arnaz), an Italian Catholic who lights Sabbath candles and shares with Jess Friday-night kiddush wine. There is no mother in this 1980 version, just Jess's father (played by Laurence Olivier), who is a survivor of the Holocaust and who will proclaim his son dead when he meets Molly. In this version, even a trip back to synagogue for Jess to chant the Kol Nidre prayer is not enough to reconcile. That resolution comes only when Jess hands his father a photograph of his new grandson, Chaim Rabinovitch, at which point we are led to believe that the family will live happily ever after.

Neil Diamond, like Raphaelson, Jolson, and Lewis, saw *The Jazz Singer* as his story. He had spent much of his childhood in the care of his first-generation Yiddish-speaking grandparents, and became a pre-med student at New York University largely for his parents. Like Jess Robin, Diamond broke away and pursued his dream of being a songwriter, divorced his first

The 1980 remake of The Jazz Singer *stars Laurence Olivier as Cantor Rabinovitch and Neil Diamond as his son Yussel / Jess, the assistant cantor who leaves home for Hollywood. Photofest.*

wife, and married a gentile. In the film, Jess tells his father, "You got to know where you come from to know where you're going." Like the character he plays, Diamond acknowledges that his Jewishness is a key element in his life: "All my songs are based on melody, which is retrieved from my Jewish heritage."[69] "My dad was an amateur performer who lip-synced a lot of Yiddish records. They're almost operatic. The sense of melody that I have is based on that," he said.[70]

The thrust of the 1980 version is very much a celebration of America and its possibilities. Here, an assistant cantor from an ethnic enclave can escape and realize greatness. Here, Neil Diamond, a Jewish boy from Brooklyn, can leave school and write music for such artists as The Monkees and Jay and the Americans, finally achieving inconceivable fame on his own as a performer. This new film release showed an America where blacks, Jews, and Catholics prodded each other in their quest for the American dream, American success. In the concluding moments of the film, Jess, onstage, sings, "We're going to America . . . Never looking back . . . Today!" In this rendition of "America," Jess wears a shimmering blue sequined shirt with a white scarf hanging around his neck like the *tallit* he wore in the previous scene at the synagogue. Behind him is an illuminated red stage backdrop. Looking on approvingly from the audience are his dad, Molly, and his manager. Whether it is the red, white, and blue of America or the Jewish blue and white of this talent, Jess Robin, whose melody is drawn from a Jewish past, very much knows what he wants. He wants "America." Today!

One last reworking of the story was made in 1991 as one of the animated *The Simpsons* television episodes. "Like Father, Like Son" was broadcast on Fox Television. Writers Jay Kogen and Wallace Wolodarsky drew from Lewis's version of *The Jazz Singer*. The story revolved around how Krusty the Clown had been disowned by his father Rabbi Hyman Krustofski (voice by Jackie Mason) because he chose to be a clown rather than a rabbi. Bart Simpson goes on a crusade to bring the two together. America had changed dramatically from the 1920s, when generational difference and the embarrassment of having immigrant parents divided so many households. The various taboos of becoming an actor, a clown, or even a jazz singer had disappeared and if anything, the accomplishment of so many Jewish entertainers made success in the world of show business a desired goal for many. Rabbi Krustofski came to terms with this, as had a new generation of American Jews.

GENTLEMAN'S AGREEMENT
AND CROSSFIRE

FILMS THAT TOOK ON ANTI-SEMITISM IN 1947

Two years after World War II, Twentieth Century-Fox released *Gentleman's Agreement*, a well-anticipated movie that focused on the question of social anti-Semitism in America. Although the film was championed by Darryl F. Zanuck, its crusader producer, most in Hollywood were fearful about its reception by American audiences. Just a few months earlier, *Crossfire*, a mystery about the puzzling murder of a Jewish veteran of the U.S. Army, had been released, and there was tension within the film community about why such films were being made. In fact, strong efforts had been exerted on a number of fronts to keep both motion pictures from being achieved and released.

Within months of the war's end, the motion picture industry began to turn away from war and victory pictures. Movies were beginning to address America's problems. Grasping that genocide had actually taken place, anti-Semitism seemed a suitable subject for the motion picture screen. However, even at this time, it was no easy task to present this highly controversial theme openly to the American movie audience. In earlier films, anti-Semitism as a subject had received limited treatment. Carl Theodor Dreyer had made such a movie in 1921 Germany called *Die Gezeichneten* (*Love One Another*), and Darryl F. Zanuck included an ominous anti-Semitic invective (powerfully rebutted by Rothschild) in his 1934 *The House of Rothschild*. In 1940, Charles Chaplin made *The Great Dictator* and MGM released *The Mortal Storm* as attempts to depict the Nazi persecution of Jews. Other films, like *Air Force* (1943), *The Purple Heart* (1944), and *Pride of the Marines*

(1945) followed, showing Jewish men fighting in the service of their country.[1] Still, the subject of anti-Semitism, though dealt with in American literature, had never been the central theme of an American motion picture.[2] A big question was whether America was mature enough to address the issue and whether Hollywood's moviemakers were sufficiently secure to examine so controversial a subject. Making a movie about this social problem could be highly explosive.

The climate after World War II ought to have been good for producing such films. In the months following the war's conclusion, several Hollywood filmmakers, seeking a more intelligent and sophisticated audience, undertook substantial, important themes that dealt with the social fabric of American life. Yet when the idea surfaced of making a film about another such important American issue, anti-Semitism, most seemed to feel that the question should not be dealt with. A Jewish community experiencing a postwar euphoria was concerned and fearful that raising the issue of anti-Semitism might actually increase the hatred of Jews.

In the immediate post–World War II period, the question of how to deal with anti-Semitism was still a very delicate one. The Jews in America had advanced socially, culturally, and economically. Judaism was more and more seen as one of America's three major religions. Yet the massive anti-Semitism of the 1930s and World War II was still very much in memory, leaving Jews with great discomfort. Most Jews seemed to feel that anti-Semitism was still rampant and even growing. This fostered great support for so-called "defense agencies," whose role was to fight bigotry and anti-Semitism. As Arnold Forster relates, "After the war there was a sense in the air that we weren't going to take it anymore. Equality was in the air. We'd won a victory for human freedom. We wanted to continue that fight."[3] Now, when bigots staged rallies that embraced anti-Semitism, Jewish and other liberal groups felt empowered to mount even larger counterdemonstrations. These efforts often proved to have an opposite effect, as the protests were generally followed by larger anti-Semitic rallies that drew attention and extensive press coverage. Jewish rally organizers soon realized that they not only brought attention to their views but they also succeeded in raising public awareness of the anti-Semites. As a result, in 1946 the Anti-Defamation League of B'nai B'rith and other Jewish groups began to abandon such protests in favor of a posture of total indifference. S. Andhil Fineberg of the community relations division of the American Jewish Committee popularized this "quarantine treatment" and discussed the approach in a September 1946 article in *Commentary*.[4] According to Howard M. Sachar, this "silent treatment," in combination with the agreement of friendly newspapers to cooperate, provided dramatic results.[5] In 1945, one dogmatist, a promoter of so-called Christian values and probably the leading American anti-Semite of the time, the Reverend Gerald L. K. Smith, had attracted thousands of listeners and thousands of pickets. Within two years, with press coverage absent and lacking publicity, he saw his crowds and contributions dry up. The strategy, at least as it pertained to public rallies, was very effective. Still, this *Sha, shtil!* (Shhh! Quiet!) approach had its detractors.

In Hollywood, there were also commercial and political concerns. The movie business was changing, and financial officers at the studios and the bankers who funded the films were exerting greater influence on production. Could social message films be financially successful, particularly on a subject like anti-Semitism? With the beginning of the Cold War against the Soviet Union and the most conservative legislative majority in Washington the nation had seen since 1920, the studios were becoming increasingly sensitive about congressional oversight of the movie industry. Were there "outside," possibly Communist, influences on the kinds of films being made in America, and just who were the producers of these propaganda films? Congress and, in particular, influential members of the House of Representatives' Un-American Activities Committee, refocused their attention on Hollywood. It became clear that social message films were going to be scrutinized like never before.

By 1946, American movies had reached the highest level of popular appeal in their history — more people were going to the movie theater than ever before. Film-industry studies showed that the more educated the consumer, the more he or she watched films; individuals at higher income levels went to the movies more frequently; young people saw more films than older people.[6] During this first year of postwar introspection, some Hollywood filmmakers used the opportunity to undertake substantial and important themes that dealt with the social fabric of American life, with films like William Wyler's *The Best Years of Our Lives*. Yet when the idea surfaced of making a film about anti-Semitism, another important American issue, most in Hollywood felt that the question was one that needed *not* to be dealt with. Jews in Hollywood were very self-conscious about being seen as Jews, and most were petrified of drawing attention to themselves. They agreed with the "quarantine treatment" view of the Jewish defense agencies, that bringing attention to the subject might cause more injury than good.

Today, it is hard to comprehend just how controversial the subject of anti-Semitism really was for movie producers. In a 1970s interview with Michel Ciment, director Elia Kazan described the climate: "Try to put yourself back in American films in 1946, where the word 'Jew' was never mentioned before. For the first time, someone said that America was full of anti-Semitism, both conscious and unconscious, and among the best and most liberal people. That was a much bolder statement than it is now." [7] In the end, it was three individuals, two non-Jews and a Jew, who fought to forge ahead against almost insurmountable roadblocks in order to treat anti-Semitism on the screen. At Twentieth Century-Fox, it was studio head Darryl F. Zanuck, and at RKO, producer Adrian Scott and head of production Dore Schary. When the pictures were finally released, each film received considerable attention and acclaim. *Crossfire* garnered an award at the Cannes Film Festival and was dubbed best social drama by the New York Film Critics, and *Gentleman's Agreement* won the Academy Award for best motion picture of 1947.

THE BRICK FOXHOLE

At the conclusion of World War II, Richard Brooks's novel *The Brick Foxhole* was optioned by RKO Pictures. The novel, written by Brooks during his stint in the Marine Corps and high on the bestseller lists as the war was coming to an end, was about the frustrations of stateside soldiers. Adrian Scott, writer John Paxton, and director Edward Dmytryk immediately changed the murdered victim from a homosexual to a heterosexual Jew. [8] As a creative team, Paxton and Scott had worked before with director Edward Dmytryk, turning out two straight hits for RKO. According to RKO Studios historian Betty Lasky, "It had been Scott's dream to make a film about anti-Semitism on the home front, which he felt was an overwhelming global problem that had to be exposed, particularly in light of recent Nazi horrors; it was his idea that the victim in Brooks's novel could be a Jew." [9] Scott reminisced that "substituting a search for an anti-Semite instead of a jade necklace, at the same time investigating anti-Semitism, seemed to us to add dimension and meaning to melodrama, at the same time lending outlet for conviction." [10] Dmytryk felt that the original plot "wouldn't have been an interesting story. Although it could have told of a certain kind of prejudice, we felt that anti-Semitism was a more important thing [to look at] at the time." [11] The idea of a Jew as victim appeared initially to be received warmly by RKO's executives, but it was actually such a controversial idea that it took two years before a decision to produce the film was made. William Dozier was the executive in charge at the time, and Scott recalled that Dozier "was worried about anti-Semitism; and though he had no sure way of knowing, he'd [Dozier] felt from his personal experiences that anti-Semitism had grown since Hitler's demise, rather than diminished."[12] Although Dozier decided to finally option the material, he went no further.[13]

With RKO considering a first foray into this area, there were compelling reasons not to make the film, not the least of which was that the subject had never before been broached in films. With the war over and the vigorous production of propaganda war films ended, many in Hollywood had grown tired of what they called "social message films." There was such scorn for those that the popular catchphrase in Hollywood at the time was, "If you need to send a message, go to Western Union (and send a telegram)."[14] There was also mounting concern that films with a message lost money, and a fear that various film distributors and exhibitors would refuse to handle such a picture.[15] While *The Brick Foxhole* script remained in limbo at RKO, Adrian Scott went off to England together with Paxton and Dmytryk to finish work on *So Well Remembered*; when time allowed, they worked on the script for *The Brick Foxhole*.

Although it appears that everyone thought that making *The Brick Foxhole* was a good idea, nobody was ready to take the next step. In fact, a few months later, with the sudden death of studio head Charles Koerner and Peter Rathvon becoming interim production head, RKO's option on the story almost lapsed; it was only renewed at the last moment at the insistence of producer Scott. More time passed, but finally, after the appointment of new production executive Dore Schary, Scott and Dmytryk were able to meet with Schary, who "green-lighted" the project. Schary, a Jew, was excited by the challenge and pushed the idea through the studio bureaucracy, finally getting approval. Still, despite getting the go-ahead from the top brass, Schary continued to encounter internal opposition at RKO until the very end. As Schary shared with me some thirty years later, he received final approval only when he promised the RKO executives, "We'll make it inexpensively; it can't lose money."[16]

Isidore "Dore" Schary, a forty-one-year-old, New Jersey–born, committed
Jew took over production at RKO on January 1, 1947. Schary began his career
as a reporter; acting, writing, and producing skits and plays at summer re-
sorts; and as an assistant drama coach at the Newark YMHA.[17] His move to
Hollywood as a writer eventually landed him a screenwriting Academy
Award in 1938 for *Boys Town* at Metro-Goldwyn-Mayer Studios, and in
1941 he became an executive producer there. Two years later, he moved to
David O. Selznick's Vanguard Productions as executive in charge of producing B movies, where he learned the art of turning out good pictures inexpensively. During the war, Schary lectured at army camps on anti-Semitism and
witnessed firsthand bigotry in the army ranks; he also lectured on the subject to Catholic and Protestant chaplains entering the service. Dore Schary
was articulate, a man of education and culture, socially and politically liberal, and very much a nonconformist. Floyd Odlum, principal stockholder
at RKO, had been enjoying success at the studio, but his "quick-profit, short-
term-oriented policies" had left the studio with few big name stars, producers, or directors.[18] Odlum saw Schary as someone who could develop
talent and hopefully continue the successful production of profitable movies
on a low budget. He came to Schary with an offer he could not refuse. Schary
recounted how Rathvon, on behalf of Odlum, first approached him:

> *Rathvon*: You've been elected a vice-president of RKO in hopes that you
>   will become head of the studio.
> *Schary*: Look, I'm under contract to David [Selznick], number one. Num-
>   ber two, I don't know if I want to run a studio. And number three, I
>   don't think you should have done any of this without talking to me.
> *Rathvon*: Well, nothing has really been done that can't be undone. But I
>   want you to know how confident everybody is of your taking this job,
>   and that there will be no bargaining. You name your terms.[19]

The threesome of Paxton, Scott, and Dmytryk had been involved in a string
of profitable films (*Hitler's Children*, *Behind the Rising Sun*) for the studio;
almost immediately upon Schary's arrival at RKO, they presented him with
The Brick Foxhole. A year earlier, while working with RKO as an outside
Selznick producer, Schary had advised *against* doing the film because he did
not like the script.[20] Now, as production head with the ability to influence the

Writer/producer Dore Schary fought hard at RKO Pictures to produce
Crossfire. *After leaving Hollywood, Schary continued to fight for*
Jewish causes his entire life. Photofest.

script and final product, Schary came out in favor of doing the picture. As
Schary recalled, "I read it. I didn't like what they had done particularly, and
I told them how I thought it should be done, and that I would fight for it."[21]
He became truly excited by the challenge of making a movie about anti-
Semitism. By now, the film was tentatively titled *Cradle of Fear*. As Schary
pushed to renew the option on the script a third time, Peter Rathvon, now
president of RKO, told Schary that he was against moving forward on pro-
duction. "I agree that 'Cradle of Fear' is a suspenseful melodrama. I doubt

sincerely that it has the least value as a document against racial intolerance and I think there is a chance it might backfire and have an effect opposite to that intended."[22] Schary countered, "I went in, fought for it, and because I was new on the job they didn't resist me too much."[23] Despite considerable opposition from the other executives, Schary proceeded to push the idea to make the film. "They were afraid of everything. They were afraid of subject matter. They were afraid it would be a failure."[24] Eventually, the film became *Crossfire*.[25] Schary remembered:

> Scott and Dmytryk came to me with *The Brick Foxhole*, which they said they had changed from a homosexual into a Jew. They thought that I should read it right away. I read it and felt it was a little too discursive, a little long, and it needed to be compressed into something that would hold you like that! They said fine. Then I went to Peter Rathvon and I said, "I want to do this!" He said, "I thought we already went through that." "Well, we're going to do it," I said. "We'll make it inexpensively — it can't lose money." Then we went ahead and did it.[26]

There is little doubt that Schary's interest was stirred by the knowledge that in December 1946, Darryl F. Zanuck had announced the purchase of screen rights to Laura Z. Hobson's novel *Gentleman's Agreement*. Dore Schary wanted to be the first to release a picture on anti-Semitism.

GENTLEMAN'S AGREEMENT

During the two years that executives at RKO were bandying about whether to make *Crossfire*, Laura Z. Hobson was finishing the final pages of *Gentleman's Agreement*. It is the story of a journalist who, in order to expose anti-Semitism, poses as a Jew to experience the bigotry firsthand. Laura Zametkin Hobson, daughter of one of the first editors of the *Jewish Daily Forward*, was a writer and editor who had traveled in literary elite circles. Though she was a non-practicing Jew, she grew up in a home with strong Yiddishist socialist values, and Hobson was deeply influenced and affected by what she had witnessed during the war years. In her autobiography, she relates how a variety of anti-Semitic experiences that she had encountered had impacted her and changed the thrust of the novel she was writing. One of the most profound moments was in 1944, when she read a first-page story in the National

Writer Laura Z. Hobson was drawn to
write about the subject of anti-Semitism
after reading about anti-Jewish slurs being
made in the U.S. House of Representatives.
General Research Division, New York
Public Library. Astor, Lenox and Tilden
Foundations. © Philippe Halsman.
Copyright of the Halsman Archive.

Affairs section of *Time* magazine. The article related how Mississippi congressman John Rankin, addressing the House of Representatives on a bill, had referred to syndicated columnist Walter Winchell as "the little *kike* I was telling you about."[27]

> "This was a new low in demagoguery," *Time* said, but in the entire House, no one rose to protest. Far from it. At the end of Rankin's long speech, the House rose and gave him prolonged applause. And I remember that then and there.[28]

Hobson continued, "On that long-ago February day, I knew that my theme about a nation happy during war wasn't good enough."[29] Hobson decided instead to address the issue of anti-Semitism, and even managed to take aim at Rankin on the pages of her novel.

Prior to publication, *Gentleman's Agreement* ran as a four-part serial in

Cosmopolitan. Hobson and her publisher, Simon and Schuster, used this opportunity as a way to gauge public reaction to a potentially problematic subject. The response was overwhelmingly positive. Letters poured into the magazine running "a hundred to one in favor." [30] Stephen Whitfield saw the serial's success as "symptomatic of the primary impulses of her fellow Jews, who have been far better at defending the freedom to worship than in practicing it, in asserting their rights than in actually exercising them, in expressing bemusement with the contingency of Jewish identity than in cultivating its mysteries." [31]

As good as the initial response to the magazine serial seemed to be, Hobson found that Simon and Schuster was printing fewer copies than they had for her previous novel. In addition, the book was turned down by both the Book of the Month Club and the Literary Guild. Was the subject matter too controversial for the time? In late November 1946, the manuscript was submitted to all the major movie studios to see if there was "studio interest." In contrast to the response of the publishing world, three studios showed interest. Darryl F. Zanuck, head of production at Twentieth Century-Fox, took the least amount of time to react. He apparently had the book galleys sent to him at his weekend retreat in Sun Valley. By late Sunday night, he phoned his office: "Protect me on *Gentleman's Agreement.*" [32] They did. Twentieth Century-Fox bought film rights to *Gentleman's Agreement* for the tidy sum of $75,000. In the end, certainly buoyed by the film's release, more than 1.6 million copies of the book were sold.

DARRYL F. ZANUCK

Darryl F. Zanuck, the only non-Jewish head of a major Hollywood studio at the time, was excited about doing a film on anti-Semitism. [33] He was also quite conscious that any movie made on a liberal theme would be carefully scrutinized by the increasingly powerful House Committee on Un-American Activities. [34] As the political climate changed throughout 1946 and into 1947, Hollywood executives became more and more concerned. Twentieth Century-Fox's board of directors and its New York head office were pondering what impact the growing oversight by Washington might have on the financial health of the studio. Certainly, any film with a "liberal" theme was being watched with suspicion. The board at Twentieth Century-Fox, fearing government intervention, continued to pressure Zanuck to produce a film

Darryl F. Zanuck showed courage throughout his career, making films on important social issues. He never shied away from tackling difficult film projects that involved controversial Jewish subject matter. Photofest.

that would not be radical. But Zanuck's reputation as a filmmaker ready to undertake difficult subjects had been established long before, when he produced such films as *I Am a Fugitive from a Chain Gang* (1932), *The Grapes of Wrath* (1940), and *Wilson* (1944). He wanted to continue making his own kind of controversial movies. He also was experienced in making films that involved Jewish issues, as he had produced *The Jazz Singer* (1927) at Warner Brothers and *The House of Rothschild* (1934) at Twentieth Century Pictures.

Back in 1934, the timing for producing a film about the rise of an international Jewish banking family was also questionable, but Zanuck, the formidable producer, was undeterred by conventional wisdom. As Leonard Mosley described it, "It was 1933 . . . Not only were the newspapers and newsreels full of pictures of the Brownshirts on the rampage against the Jews of Berlin and Munich, but the smell of anti-Semitism reeked strongly enough to drift across the Atlantic and be sniffed eagerly by racists in the United States. . . . Zanuck . . . was stimulated by the prevailing conditions."[35] Certainly the film's portrayal of the Rothschilds is not all glowing, but the overall feeling is one of great empathy for them and the plight of the Jewish people. Though the apparent raison d'être of the Rothschilds might leave one squirming, the film proceeds to confront anti-Semitism in a most admirable manner. By today's standards the film is a bit clichéd, but the audience of that day was drawn to it and responded by coming to theaters in droves. The depiction of the irrational hatred of Jews, seen largely through the character of the fictional Count Ledrantz of Prussia (given a sinister edge by Boris Karloff), rings clearly as a repudiation of Nazi hate and a forewarning of devas-

Boris Karloff as Count Ledrantz and George Arliss as Nathan Rothschild.
© United Artists. United Artists/Photofest.

tation that looms for the Jews of Europe. Writer Nunnully Johnson's insertion of Ledrantz into the Rothschild screenplay was made to contravene any initial anti-Semitic sense that the viewer might have felt toward the family.

Just as Zanuck was undeterred when he produced *The House of Rothschild*, he quickly moved forward on *Gentleman's Agreement*. Initially earmarking $1 million for production, Zanuck had Elia Kazan direct and Moss Hart write the screenplay. Production was readied — and then came opposition from a different, outside source.

Zanuck was a shrewd producer, acutely aware of the commercial possibilities of social issue films. One of his trademarks was producing just such controversial movies, with an intensely personal drama. He fully understood that this was both an important film and one that had great potential for box-office profit. Zanuck liked the odds, and he believed that *Gentleman's Agreement* would make money. He also was convinced that the film was good for America. "He was drawn to the film by his Nebraskan populist sense of fair play," said George Custen.[36] When asked by Hobson years later why he had decided to buy film rights to her book, even before it received its wonderful reviews, Zanuck responded:

> "I have three children — Darrylin and Richard and Susan." He was looking past me, as if he were looking at the faces of his son and two daughters, then all in their teens. "If this country ever did go fascist," he went on, "and they said to me, 'Well, pop, what did *you* do to stop it? You had the studios, the money, the power — what did *you* do to fight it off?' . . . I want to be able to say to them, 'Well, I made *Wilson*, and then I made *Gentleman's Agreement*, I made *Pinky*.'"[37]

Zanuck went on to tell her, "Anyway . . . I felt in my bones your book would be a sensation, and I wanted to be *in* on a sensation."[38] As Hobson observed, "That put a cap on everything he had said so far, and if I ever were to find myself a bit skeptical about all the higher motives, I never once doubted this one."[39] Hobson's illumination makes for a good story, but all involved clearly had a sense that they were indeed "in on a sensation." The pressure was on. Zanuck knew that *Gentleman's Agreement* would be an important film. At the same time, he must have known that if the film proved financially unsuccessful, his future at Fox would be in jeopardy.

Like his board, Zanuck was concerned about the growing intrusiveness of the House of Representatives' Un-American Activities Committee (HUAC).

Congressman John Rankin of Mississippi, who largely controlled the agenda of the committee, remained unabashed about his strong anti-Semitic beliefs. At the same time, most House members on the committee seemed unprepared to be portrayed as anti-Jewish. Most feared that were the Committee itself to be perceived as anti-Semitic, rather than anti-Communist, its entire agenda could potentially be hurt.[40] With this in mind, Zanuck, Hollywood's best-known gentile and a prominent Republican, was very clever to put forward *Gentleman's Agreement* as Twentieth Century-Fox's big production of 1947. How would it look if a film subject such as anti-Semitism, rendered artistically by a gentile, were attacked by HUAC? Zanuck chose to personally supervise the production.

A large budget of close to $2 million was then assigned to the film, and certain extravagant liberties were taken in the hopes of making this a bigger and better picture. By this time, Elia Kazan had made a name for himself as one of the finest young stage and film directors in America, and Zanuck, who had enjoyed Kazan's work on *A Tree Grows in Brooklyn* (1945) and *Boomerang* (1947), wanted him for this project. According to Leonard Mosley, "He was still a little wary of Kazan, because he had brought with him from New York a reputation as an intellectual and 'I am naturally suspicious of deep thinkers in relation to motion pictures. They sometimes think so deep they miss the point . . .' It was just a question of keeping Kazan in order."[41] It was agreed that the film would be shot outside the studio, on location, and with this stipulation, Kazan agreed to direct.[42]

Zanuck also had to find the right person to adapt Hobson's novel for the screen. Stories abound as to how Zanuck chose his screenwriter. Kazan wrote that he had suggested Paul Osborn, with whom he would later collaborate on *East of Eden*, but that Osborn was not available. Apparently, everyone under contract at the studio was interested, but Zanuck wanted to go "outside" and find someone exceptional.[43] Zanuck invited Moss Hart, already an established playwright and Pulitzer Prize winner, along with his wife Kitty Carlisle, out to the West Coast to stay at his home in Palm Springs. As Leon Gutterman described it, "Every top-ranking studio and producer came running to beg for his services. But Moss was tired; he wanted to rest and relax. The studios told him that money was no object, that he could name his own price—but Moss only laughed. He had come to Hollywood to have fun."[44] Carlisle was three months pregnant; on the first night at Zanuck's home, as they were about to dine with the Zanucks and guests Merle Oberon, Joan Crawford, and Louis Jourdan, she miscarried. After a brief stay in the hos-

Kitty Carlisle with Moss Hart, circa 1950. Photofest.

pital, she and Moss stayed on with the Zanucks in Palm Springs, where the idea was proposed to Hart to write the screenplay for *Gentleman's Agreement*. Whether it was Hart's agent, Irving Lazar, who sold Zanuck on the idea of hiring Hart, or whether Zanuck went to Lazar or directly to Hart, is unclear. What is important is that Moss Hart, with all his experience as a theater and film writer, had never before written a screenplay adapted from someone else's work.[45] However, Hart was drawn to the subject matter. He was the perfect person to bring to the project, with what Steven Bach called "the wit and polish of literary New York." [46]

Moss Hart was always aware of and sensitive about being a Jew. Yet as Kitty Carlisle told me, he was not demonstrative about his Jewishness.[47]

Still, Bach claims that Kitty Carlisle's being Jewish was a key factor in their marriage.[48] Moss Hart had volunteered in 1943 to stage *We Will Never Die*, the impressive pageant organized by Ben Hecht to draw world attention to the terrible fate of Jews in Europe. When Hart learned of the project, he and composer Kurt Weill met with Hecht, telling him, "I thought I'd tell you that if I can do anything definite in the way of Jewish propaganda, call on me."[49] There is little doubt that Hart saw *Gentleman's Agreement* as a wonderful opportunity to have a positive impact on Jewish life in America. As Leon Gutterman noted, "Zanuck handed Moss a copy of the book to read. Moss read it. 'Can you see it as a fine motion picture?' asked the producer. 'I certainly can!' replied the dramatist. Said Zanuck, 'I'm looking for a great writer and one who is familiar enough with the problem of anti-Semitism. I wonder whom I might get.' Replied Moss, 'You're looking at him right now!'"[50]

Studio head Darryl Zanuck often chose one film each year to personally produce, and *Gentleman's Agreement* was the picture chosen for 1947. These were the years of the old production system, where the producer was actively involved in every step of the filmmaking process. His first task was to school Hart in the intricacies of adapting someone else's work for film. Hart was no stranger to screenwriting, but he understood that this project would be a collaborative one, with Zanuck actively involved. Fully aware of his situation, he contracted with Zanuck that the final product could not be changed by anyone else. The interaction must have been fascinating, as here was an accomplished playwright who saw drama from the fifth row of the theater being asked to transform someone else's novel into a fluid cinematic story. During this time, Laura Hobson met with Hart three different times, and he shared with her his initial writing. Hart sought her input, which she happily provided. Each seemed to have great respect for the other, and Hart shared his frustration that he believed the novel lacked a dramatic climax that could work onscreen. The story has Phil Green fall in love and become engaged to Kathy (Dorothy McGuire). Dave Goldman (John Garfield), Phil's close Jewish friend from the army, arrives in New York with a job offer in hand but is unable to find housing, both because of a housing shortage and because of the "gentleman's agreement" that exists to keep Jews and other "undesirables" out. Phil perceives Kathy as indifferent, and this pushes the two apart. Hobson explained:

> In my book I could take all the time I needed and all the episodes, to show
> Kathy probing into her hidden feelings about the anti-Semitism she de-

plores as much as Phil does. But Moss had to find some way to telescope those hundred pages into some swift, dramatic resolution, and finally he issued a specific invitation to me to come up with any idea that might help him solve his problem.[51]

Hobson volunteered to come up with some ideas and went off and wrote thirteen pages, in effect a new chapter to her book. She sent it to Hart, who used almost all of it, and this "new chapter" became the basis for a dramatic ending and for what many believed was the best scene in the movie. Elia Kazan explained:

> I believe it was the critical find, the one that made this film work. Here it is: Dorothy McGuire, anguished about her separation from her fiancé and believing his opinion of her unfair, asks Peck's best friend (John Garfield would play this part) to come and talk to her. Anxiously, she tells him how unjust Peck's accusation against her is and offers as evidence her feelings at a big dinner party she'd attended that evening, where one of the guests, a powerful and wealthy man, had dropped anti-Semitic slurs. She tells Garfield how outraged and angry she felt. . . . Through this confrontation, the issue between the lovers is resolved, she contrite, he forgiving. Hero and heroine are reunited, more in love than ever.[52]

Kazan expanded on this: "This kind of story solution was the essence of Darryl Zanuck's theory of how social issues had to be handled for the American film audience, always through a love story in which the lovers are involved in the issue under conflict. Any less personal treatment, Zanuck believed, would not hold his audience's interest. Our film was the perfect example of that day's 'liberal' films. And it worked."[53] He went on, "I think the film fit the time, the moment and it's all right . . . I think you have to judge everything in relation to when it appears."[54] Zanuck was concerned that the film might come across as "too preachy." It seems clear that he chose a Jewish writer because he felt that someone like Moss Hart could better understand the intricacies of the issues, but at the same time, he was uninterested in sermonizing. Hart, at the time, explained his position:

> What I've tried to do in the script is reach people emotionally. I'm hitting at their hearts rather than their minds. There is no preaching, no propaganda in the film that will be recognized as such. It's strict enter-

tainment—with a love story interwoven. . . . But on the other hand, its intellectual plot—a strong adult drama that is deeply conscious of its problem—will, I hope, prove to be an incentive to action on the part of those who will come to see it.[55]

THE FILM

Gentleman's Agreement features Gregory Peck as Philip Schuyler Green, a writer who does investigative reporting on a variety of subjects for *Smith's Weekly*, a New York–based magazine. A widower, he comes to New York from California with his mother and his eleven-year-old son Tommy, with the intent of settling down. His assignment is to write a series about anti-Semitism. Green struggles to find a story angle until he realizes that the best way in might be to experience what it is to be a Jew himself, so he pretends to be Jewish. After introducing himself to the magazine staff as a Jewish writer about to do a story on anti-Semitism, he finds that his own secretary, Elaine Wales (June Havoc), had to change her Jewish-sounding family name (Wilovsky) in order to get a job at the weekly: anti-Semitism was at work even at the magazine. A variety of experiences quickly follow: his son is picked on and beaten up; the family doctor reacts negatively when Phil asks about using a Jewish cardiologist to care for his mother; and after adding a second name, Greenberg, to the directory of his apartment, the superintendent asks to have it removed. He sends duplicate applications to a number of professional schools and, not surprisingly, the ones with the name Green get a different reception than those sent with the name Greenberg. Then Philip Green goes to New Hampshire with a confirmed reservation in hand for a stay at the Flume Inn resort.

The Flume Inn sequence provides one of the more incisive sequences in the film. This powerful scene, meticulously crafted by director Kazan, is significant in that it visually represents the situation of the post–World War II American Jew. A war against prejudice and hatred had been won by the Allies. Liberty, religious freedom, and an end to bigotry were to be the by-products of that victory. The Flume Inn doors were, as the book's author Laura Z. Hobson described, "opened heavily,"[56] as were America's doors, now ostensibly wide open to its Jews. Or so it seemed.

The scene opens with a lone car pulling into the "long crescent that was the approach"[57] to the Flume Inn. The birds are chirping, the weather ap-

*The reporter is shocked to learn that even his Jewish secretary, Elaine Wales,
has not only encountered anti-Semitism at the magazine where they work
but has strong anti-Jewish attitudes of her own. June Havoc, Gregory Peck.
© Twentieth Century-Fox. Twentieth Century-Fox Film Corp./Photofest.*

pears to be glorious. People are sitting on lounge chairs; others go by in their
tennis outfits or on horseback. Philip Green from New York City, the outsider arriving in the restricted upper-class world of this New England White
Mountains resort, turns up in a lone car that makes its way around the crescent. Into the hotel, through wide-open doors, enters Mr. Green, carrying a
suitcase, ready to check in. The Inn and its doors appear to be open to all, no
matter what race or religion. Are they not?

As director Elia Kazan lays out the sequence, he visually gives us an
understanding of the Jewish world of the immediate post–World War II
period. We have just transitioned from the New York kitchen of this "pretend" Jew, Philip Green. Now he finds himself in the open spaces of New
England's gentry. Around the driveway, a single automobile brings our New
York City outsider into a world not yet ready to receive his kind. "I have
a reservation for . . ." begins Green, as he arrives at the hotel desk. "Ah
yes," responds the desk clerk, as he places a registration card out on the
desk in front of Phil Green. "Oh, one more thing—is this hotel restricted?"
asks Green. So begins a dialogue between Green, the clerk, and eventually

the hotel manager. "Well, I'd hardly say it's restricted," replies the clerk. "Then it's not restricted?" At this point, the clerk excuses himself and walks into the manager's office. After a few moments, the Inn manager comes out and asks, "May I inquire. Are you—that is, do you follow the Hebrew religion yourself, or is it that you just want to make sure?" "I've asked a simple question. I'd like to have a simple answer," asks a more vocal and militant Green. "Well you see we do have a high-class clientele, and naturally . . ." Green interrupts him, "Then you do restrict your guests to gentiles?" "Well, I wouldn't say that, Mr. Green." The manager reaches over to the Rolodex in which all reservations are kept and gives it a twirl. "But in any event, there seems to be some mistake because we don't have a free room in the entire hotel." The Rolodex turns like a revolving door and the Jew's visit to this restricted world is about to end. The image is most clear. The wide-open doors were only how things appeared, not how they really were. A revolving door would have been a more appropriate image reflecting the reality of the times. "If you'd like, I could fix you up at the Brewster Hotel, near the station." The

Phil Green learns from the Flume Inn's manager that even though he has a reservation, a mistake seems to have been made and there are no rooms available. Gregory Peck, Roy Roberts. © Twentieth Century-Fox. Twentieth Century-Fox Film Corp./Photofest.

back and forth with Green continues until finally the hotel manager has had enough. "Don't raise your voice to me, Mr. Green. You speak a little more quietly please!" In the background, we see an elderly, "more refined" couple looking on, clearly annoyed by the "loud" altercation that is taking place a few yards away. Finally, the manager hits the bell, signaling the end of the conversation. Before you know it, the manager retreats to his private room, the door slams shut behind him, and Green, looking down for his bags, sees a bellman carrying them out of the lobby to the outside. Phil Green had come through doors he thought open, but in reality they were revolving doors, his stay in the lobby only a brief one. It might appear that he is welcome, but no sooner is he in, than he is back outside.

Jews had fought in the war, served their country admirably, and expected to reap the benefit. When Phil Green walked into that hotel lobby, there were no signs decreeing that Jews were prohibited. No guard stood at the entrance and eyeballed each guest who entered. In truth, had Green simply gone to the desk and picked up his room key, he would have had a comfortable night's stay. This "don't ask, don't tell" understanding made it possible for the 1940s Jew to go through the door. Making the situation viable as well was that Phil Green's name was Green, not Greenberg or Greenfield. "You keep your voice down!" was just one retort that conveyed how contempt for Jews had very much continued to be a part of American culture through the forties. With the conclusion of the war, Philip Green was able to walk inside to share in what America had to offer: affluence, an airy and bright openness, and the best that money could buy. Yet once it became obvious who he was, it was made clear that he was not welcome, as the manager hits the bell and slams the door closed. Elia Kazan's long shot of the car driving down the crescent at the beginning of the sequence symbolized that seeming openness, the Jew's arrival in America. In contrast, Green's startled look when he sees the bellman removing his bag from the spacious lobby is all the more powerful. The message: Sorry! Although it may appear that everyone is welcome, such a reception does not hold for Jews. It's okay to look but keep it brief!

In addition to Peck, the film stars Dorothy McGuire as Kathy Lacy, and Celeste Holm in an Academy Award–winning (best supporting actress) performance as Anne Dettrey. John Garfield plays Dave Goldman, and according to Garfield's son, "No one wanted to play the part in *Gentleman's Agreement*. Nobody wanted anyone to know that they were Jewish in Hollywood . . . I think it must have taken an enormous amount of guts for my father to

Phil is stunned that his luggage has been removed by the bellman, and that there is no place for Jews in this "restricted" inn.

Out for dinner, Dave Goldman, Phil's Jewish friend (seemingly always in uniform), has had enough of anti-Semitic remarks. Gregory Peck, Celeste Holm, John Garfield, Robert Karnes, Gene Nelson. © Twentieth Century-Fox. Twentieth Century-Fox Film Corp./Photofest.

take this part." [58] The screenplay was prepared and principal photography was to begin in June of 1947. The shooting schedule was set for 65 days. Interestingly, Hobson received no credit for her participation; she was not even paid for her assistance. [59]

Elia Kazan, of Greek and Turkish descent, claimed to be interested in directing the film because he had experienced anti-Semitism firsthand. "I sure experienced a lot of it. I looked like a Jew, and I've been called a 'Yid.' I can remember on the streets as a kid — I was thought of as a Jew and I was Greek. . . . I think you experience it either directly or indirectly or imagined or exaggerated or anything — I was very sensitive to it." [60] Was this the film that Kazan had expected to make? Not quite! Kazan was directing theater in New York while Hart was completing the screenplay. Kazan does say that once Moss Hart was hired, "he [Hart] had to be turned loose to write the screenplay in a series of dialogue scenes rather than action scenes. The idea of flinging the story into the streets, offices, and apartments of New York City had to be relinquished. . . . I directed it like a play." [61] Originally, Kazan had expected to creatively interpret the screenplay, but he found himself constricted, carefully following Hart's script. As Zanuck put it, the film was "eighty percent talk and twenty percent action." [62] As for the writing, Kazan explained, "I did nothing substantial, nothing of import. I had nothing to

Presenter Donald Crisp with Academy Award winners Celeste Holm and Elia Kazan.
Holm won for best supporting actress and Kazan for best director. Darryl F. Zanuck
(on behalf of Twentieth Century-Fox) also accepted an Oscar for best motion picture.
Gentleman's Agreement was nominated in eight categories. Photofest.

do with the script at all. . . . I stuck to the script as I liked Moss a lot and I thought he did a good job."[63] "Once the screenplay had been prepared, Darryl and I satisfied, Moss pleased . . . any one of thirty directors available could have done it as well as I," he wrote.[64] But Zanuck wanted Kazan to direct. (And, later, the Hollywood community felt that Kazan's effort had been superior, awarding him the Academy Award for best director.) Kazan also enjoyed a free hand in reshooting scenes he did not like, a luxury not always afforded to a director, largely because Zanuck was personally supervising production and ready to do anything necessary to make this picture successful. Kazan provided insight into his working relationship with Zanuck and how production ran:

> That was the advantage of working for the guy who ran the studio. Now he would just say to me, there are a couple of scenes I didn't do very well.

And I'd say to him, "Look. I think I screwed up a bit." You know, and he would say, "Well, wanta shoot it over?" And I'd say, "Don't you think I should?" And he'd say, "Yeah, I think I [you] can do it better." Then I'd say, "I'd like to shoot it over!" And he'd say, "When do you want to shoot it over?" And I'd say, "Right now." What's very unusual is that he would let me shoot it over the next day. It was not only generous, but it was his power to do it at that time. And you know, he had his name on the God-damned thing, so he wanted it to be as good as he could make it. And I think we did improve a couple of . . . by shooting it over immediately.[65]

MOVIES THAT HOLLYWOOD DID NOT WANT TO MAKE

In the first weeks of 1947, Dore Schary tried to "unstall" *Crossfire* at RKO, as word got out that production was moving forward on *Gentleman's Agreement*. At RKO, there had been extensive opposition to *Crossfire*, particularly from the sales department.[66] At Twentieth Century-Fox, Zanuck was under pressure from his financiers and his New York–based board of directors to produce high returns. There was also mounting external pressure against both film companies. Both films were becoming the movies "that Hollywood didn't want to make or see made."[67] The changing political climate of the country became more of a concern for the film community. In Congress, the House of Representatives' Un-American Activities Committee, which had been created prior to the war, continued to function and now took aim at Hollywood's "subversive propaganda movie-making machine."[68] One of the previously mentioned and more outspoken members of the committee, Rep. John Rankin, ranted, "They want to spread their un-American propaganda, as well as their loathsome, lying, immoral, anti-Christian filth before the eyes of your children in every community in America."[69] As Thomas Doherty pointed out:

Schooled in celluloid persuasion, postwar Americans looked upon the screen with more sophisticated eyes and discerned bright-lined messages and hidden agenda in even the most escapist motion picture fare. When the Iron Curtain descended in 1946, the contest between East and West, Soviet Communism and American Democracy, found its domestic expression in fierce debates over the subversive influence of the popular media.[70]

The Cold War had begun, and following the Republican congressional victory of November 1946, which seated a substantial right-wing majority in both houses of Congress, the Un-American Activities Committee felt newly empowered. With the influential John Rankin and a new committee chairman, J. Parnell Thomas of New Jersey, the HUAC took fresh aim at Hollywood with an agenda to root out Communist "penetration" in the film industry. HUAC's oversight of Hollywood was not a new idea; hearings had taken place in 1940, but nothing had happened. Yet in early January 1947, rabble-rouser Rev. Gerald L. K. Smith announced that all "will be happy to know that the Congressional Committee has already started its investigation and has promised that the full committee will sit in Hollywood early this year. There is much to uncover. . . . The lovers of Christ and the lovers of America have been ridiculed."[71] This declaration was not lost on the executives in Hollywood — certainly not on Schary or Zanuck. It also certainly must have been of great concern for Scott, Dmytryk, and Kazan, all of whom had at one point been associated with the Communist Party.[72] Social-message films were going to be closely studied. Washington, more than ever before, was going to carefully scrutinize what Hollywood moviemakers were producing. In May of 1947, as a prelude of things to come, a few members of the HUAC came to Los Angeles to hold hearings. The next month, *Variety* announced that two films about anti-Semitism scheduled to have been made by other studios had been cancelled: M-G-M shelved plans for *East River* and Sam Goldwyn chose not to make *Earth and High Heaven*.[73] The King Brothers, who had previously announced that they would adapt Arthur Miller's novel *Focus*, also dropped production plans.[74]

Even though Schary was finally given the go-ahead by RKO to produce *Crossfire*, Ned Depinet, RKO executive vice president, remained determined to convince the new producer not to make the film. He commissioned an audience research company to do a "want to see quotient" analysis, and found that only 8 percent of the potential viewing audience seemed interested in the subject.[75] Undeterred, Schary budgeted the film at under $500,000, and with the script that John Paxton had been working on for two years he allowed director Edward Dmytryk and producer Adrian Scott to move forward.[76] Paxton, Scott, and Dmytryk had been working on the project for some time. Scott shared his hopes for the film:

> We hoped the effect would be enormous. We weren't so sanguine as to expect the picture would, in one fell swoop, eradicate anti-Semitism. But we

did know that public discussion and lively debate have a valuable place in a democratic society. The air could be cleared. The problem could be more clearly visualized. We hoped for this, for more clarity.[77]

Paxton, Scott, and Dmytryk enjoyed great popularity at RKO because of their earlier studio movies and the newfound prosperity that these pictures had brought to RKO. Both Scott and Dmytryk, who were drawn to joining the Communist movement in 1944, had committed to making movies that would bring about change in America. At a time when "identifying with the Party" was not necessarily a revolutionary act, they chose to make pictures that were meant to be anti-Fascist and that challenged America. Their vision

Crossfire *producer Adrian Scott and director Edward Dmytryk with three writers who, together with five others, were deemed "unfriendly witnesses" when asked to testify before the House of Representatives' Un-American Affairs Committee. The group became known as the "Hollywood Ten"; they were held in contempt of Congress and given prison sentences. Herbert Biberman, Samuel Ornitz, Adrian Scott, Edward Dmytryk, John Howard Lawson. Photofest.*

for *Crossfire* was similar, showing the creation of a postwar America that was free of hatred, bigotry, and fascism. Dmytryk was truly committed:

> To me this is the only reason to make films. I'm an agnostic preacher! ... I've had messages in most of my pictures. My technique is the sugar-coated pill. I take a little tiny bit of propaganda and wrap it around with sugar. A little bit of sugar makes the medicine go down. That's the way I do it! You give them entertainment and they will accept what you give them in between![78]

As was the case for other movies that preceded *Crossfire* (the most notable being the previous year's *The Best Years of Our Lives*), the moviemakers chose to focus on the problem of the returning soldier and his struggle to adapt once he was home. Not only was *Crossfire* to be a film about anti-Semitism, but as Eileen Bowser noted, "the achievement that stands out is the recording of the mood of the time, a tone that pinpoints exactly the feelings of a population returning from war, with all its weariness, the drained-out emotions, and the fears of actually facing the old civilian life again instead of dreaming about it."[79] Edward Dmytryk, together with cameraman J. Roy Hunt, used what he called "film-noir lighting" to effectively create an atmosphere of weariness and despair.[80] "The dominant lighting throughout the film remains that of night and that of harsh, artificial illumination that can never completely light up the night," noted Keith Kelly and Clay Steinman.[81] This use of light, which Dmytryk referred to as "high contrast," was "the generally accepted style of lighting mystery, suspense, and heavy mood films."[82] It allowed Dmytryk not only to set a mood, but also to shoot the film quickly, inexpensively, and with great panache.

The opening scene of *Crossfire* certainly captures our attention as we are drawn to the lamp in the lower-right-hand corner of the frame. We then see the shadows of figures fighting in the room. Using an intriguing mix of opposing light and darkness within a film-noir context, Dmytryk creates what Keith Kelly and Clay Steinman called "a fight for light in a world of darkness."[83] The shadow fight continues for a few moments longer, and we see a man fall on the lamp, causing the light to go off and bringing about total darkness. After a few moments, a man in uniform turns on the lamp, now on the floor, creating light for the bottom half of the frame. The camera then pans left and we see a body on the floor. That body is Joseph Samuels (Sam Levene).

"A fight for light in a world of darkness."   *Joseph Samuels lies dead on the ground.*

As the film unfolds, we learn that what had taken place in the opening scene was the murder of a civilian — a Jew and a war hero — by soldiers in uniform who killed him because he was Jewish. Irish-American police inspector Finlay (Robert Young) eliminates suspects and sets a trap for the killer, whose intolerance of Jews is not merely implied. Montgomery (Robert Ryan), the suspected murderer, finally falls into a trap set by a fellow soldier (Robert Mitchum). Though caught, Montgomery flees, only to be shot down in the street by the police detective.

Leonard Leff and Jerold Simmons emphatically state that *Crossfire*'s controlling theme is "the veteran's search for identity in post-war America."[84] But where does Samuels fit into this? What is *his* identity? Who is he, anyway? Said Dmytryk:

People asked me, "Why did you have to make Samuels a hero?" . . . Remember when the sergeant brings in to the captain the war record. He was wounded. He got a metal. The reason we did that was because we did quite a bit of research on hate propaganda and counter-hate propaganda. One of the things we found out is that if in a picture you have the heaviest guy in the world say, "He's a Jew. He's a dirty Jew and I hate Jews." A lot of people in the audience are going to say, "Yeah, yeah, yeah." Or they are going to say this, "All the Jews did this. They all stayed out of the war. They got rich while we were out there fighting for them." A lot of people said that during the war. Now, unless you answer that immediately, a lot of the people who are inclined to agree with it anyway are going to say, "Yeah. That's exactly what they did." . . . So, whenever we make mention of anything of that kind in the picture, we always find some way of making a counterstatement to that quite soon, so that we can stop the people — the actual anti-Semites or the incipient anti-Semites — from saying, "Yeah, what he's saying is true!" It's a tricky thing![85]

The soldiers are interrogated by the police inspector. Robert Mitchum, Robert Ryan, Robert Taylor. © RKO Radio Pictures. RKO Radio Pictures/Photofest.

All the veterans in the film, though discharged, are in uniform. Why isn't Samuels? Is screenwriter Paxton telling us that Samuels's identity is intact? Somehow, in this opening scene, we get more than a feeling that Jews don't fit in. In contrast, why is the only one who *is* in uniform in *Gentleman's Agreement* the "real" Jew Goldman? In fact, whereas Samuels is attacked and killed largely because he is Jewish and not in uniform, Goldman is told that he is hated (at the restaurant) because he is Jewish and is in uniform. What is that message? Is it that the Jew is different? Is "difference" the key factor that alienates the Jew from everyone else? Does being "different" make it easy to be hated in this period of transition from war to peacetime? "I think it's suddenly not having a lot of enemies to hate anymore," says Samuels in a flashback. Yet in each film, the writers go to pains to show that there is really no real difference between Jew and gentile. So why is there bigotry? Why anti-Semitism? Finlay provides the answer in his extensive monologue, which ends *Crossfire*, and Kathy and Dave continue to struggle with it when they meet over coffee at the conclusion of *Gentleman's Agreement*.

With Zanuck's announcement that *Gentleman's Agreement* was to be made and preproduction plans in gear, Schary charted a course of action that would allow him to quickly pull together the resources he required.

There is little doubt that Schary had sought to produce *Crossfire* because of his strong Jewish identity and commitment. Schary, involved in what he termed "so-called left-wing organizations" and a strong admirer of Franklin Delano Roosevelt's brand of New Deal politics, also had a vision for a better America.[86] Not to be underestimated, Schary was a competitor, and he wanted to be the first that year to release a film on anti-Semitism. Another element was that Moss Hart and Dore Schary had known each other since the time that Hart directed the Y Players at Newark's YMHA in the 1920s. They had also spent summers at the Flagler Hotel, a Catskill Mountain resort in New York State, doing theater productions at Camp Flagler, with Schary as Hart's assistant. A lifetime of letters detail the close friendship and admiration they shared for one another.[87] It was now a race between two friends, the Pulitzer Prize–winning playwright and the Academy Award–winning production executive, to see who would come in first. For Moss Hart, the outcome was in the hands of Zanuck. But for Schary, that master of the quick and effective shooting schedule, he himself was in control. He postponed two other productions and used their sets. As Scott recalled, "Overnight,

The perpetrator and the victim. The bigot and the Jew. Montgomery and Samuels. Robert Ryan, Sam Levene. © RKO Radio Pictures. RKO Radio Pictures/Photofest.

the lot was transformed into a unit for *Crossfire*."[88] Principal photography was to last only twenty days; it started on March 4, 1947, and was completed March 28.[89] It would be three months before Twentieth Century-Fox would even begin filming *Gentleman's Agreement*.

When it became clear that RKO would release *Crossfire* first, Darryl F. Zanuck was not amused. On May 6, he sent a copy of Hobson's novel to Dore Schary with a sarcastic note reading, "My dear Schary: I would appreciate it if you would let me know if you have read Laura Z. Hobson's novel, *Gentleman's Agreement*."[90] Schary's secretary responded the next day that he was out of town, but that she was quite sure that he had read it. On May 15, upon returning to Los Angeles, Schary wrote Zanuck, "I have read Laura Z. Hobson's novel *Gentleman's Agreement*. I think it is a very good book, and I am certain that you will make of it a very good and important film."[91] The exchange of letters continued through the end of July, when Schary wrote Zanuck:

> The big danger in the exchange of letters such as we have been writing is that we both face the temptation to become smart or sharp with each other. The other temptation is to sit by and wait for the other fellow's answer, and then dash off a reply which in effect says "Answer that one!" Some day I hope we shall see each other and be able to answer a lot of unspoken questions that each of us probably has in mind.[92]

Schary recalled that Zanuck was racing him for "bragging rights" on who would be first to make a film on anti-Semitism. After the exchange of letters, there was also at least one phone call. Schary claims to have told Zanuck that "he [Zanuck] had not discovered anti-Semitism and that it would take far more than two pictures to eradicate it."[93] "I had to remind him that in effect I discovered it before he did, because I was Jewish."[94] Then word reached the Jewish community that both pictures were being made.

THE JEWISH COMMUNITY

Strange as it may seem today, many in the organized Jewish community felt that these pictures would do more harm than good. As Arthur Hertzberg pointed out, "The Jewish agenda was dominated by one desire, to expand the place of Jews in America. They wanted to be accepted by the gentiles, not to confront them — at least not then."[95] Jewish defense agencies concurred, having concluded, largely from their experience with public rallies, that it was best to handle things quietly. *Sha, shtil* — silence — about anti-Semitism seemed to be the best approach. One of the spiritual leaders of Hollywood's Jews, Rabbi Edgar Magnin, was said to have remarked, "The goddamn fools don't realize that the more you tell gentiles that nobody likes us, the more they say there must be a reason for it."[96] As Elia Kazan told me, "These two pictures came along right after World War II, and right after the Holocaust. They [Jews] were genuinely frightened about the Jewish problem."[97] When leaders of the Los Angeles Jewish community, members of the Community Relations Committee of the LA Jewish Community Council, first learned that *Gentleman's Agreement* was to be made as a film, they were incensed that so much public attention would be placed on Jews and, by inference, on them. A meeting to discourage production was quickly set up on the back lot of the Warner Brothers studio; much of the Community Relations Committee leadership and some Twentieth Century-Fox and Warner Brothers studio executives were in attendance. Elia Kazan remembered:

> Who the hell went over there? Moss Hart went over there, I think — and talked to the rest of these guys. You know, and he said . . . He just listened politely and they just went ahead as far as I know. There was no confrontation, except in essence, they felt that there was a lot of anti-Semitism. But we're getting along okay, so why bring it out? Why raise the issue?[98]

The LA Jewish community leaders' fear was that by calling attention to anti-Semitism in a film, anti-Semitic feeling might be increased. They saw no point in raising the question in the first place. The larger issue is the more interesting one. What do these encounters tell us about Jews at this time? J. J. Goldberg, author of *Jewish Power*, reminds us that just a few years earlier, "a sizable faction on the American political scene was so set against helping Jews that it was willing to pay a price, even inhibit the war effort, in order to avoid helping Jews."[99]

In the postwar period, "it became socially unacceptable to express anti-Jewish views in public,"[100] noted American Jewish historian Jack Wertheimer, but anti-Semitism in the United States did not disappear overnight. Studies actually show that there was a sharp rise in the public's awareness of anti-Semitism in June 1944, and that this did not fall off until some time between 1946 and 1950. In addition, over the period between 1938 and 1950, the proportion of those who reported "hearing criticism of Jews" was highest in 1946, with a sharp drop thereafter through 1950.[101] "Of particular interest is the assertion," wrote Charles Herbert Stember in *Jews in the Mind of America*, that, based on a 1946 study, "anti-Semitism was growing because 'the war made us conscious' of the Jews."[102] Quite aware that strong anti-Semitic sentiment was still prevalent in America, were the Jewish leaders correct in their judgment? Or were they simply frightened, believing that a tactical decision of silence and invisibility was the best overall defense? The next few months would provide many of the answers.

Whatever took place at the meeting on the Warner Brothers studio back lot, it seems certain to have influenced the inclusion by Moss Hart of a scene in the film which otherwise did not appear in Hobson's book. As Kazan told it, Hart wrote it into the screenplay shortly after the Warner back lot get-together.[103] The scene takes place at a meeting of the magazine's management, when John Minify, *Smith Weekly*'s editor, announces that Phil Green is to write an article on anti-Semitism. Minify's "good friend" Irving Weismann, an industrialist and stockholder, protests, claiming that such an article would be "harmful."

Minify: Mr. Green is going to do a series on anti-Semitism for us.

Weismann: Really, again?

Minify: Not again, for the first time. We are going to split it wide open.

Weismann: Do you mind my saying, as an old friend, that I think it a very bad idea, John? The worst, the most harmful thing you can possibly do now.

Minify: Not at all, why is it a harmful idea?

Weismann: Because it will only stir it up more. Let it alone. We'll handle it our own way.

Minify: The hush-hush way?

Weismann: I don't care what you call it. Let it alone. You can't write it out of existence. We've been fighting it for years and we know from experience the less talk there is about it the better.

Minify: Sure, pretend it doesn't exist and add to the conspiracy of silence. I should say not. Keep silent and let Bilbo and Gerald L. K. Smith do all the talking.[104] No sir! Irving, you and your 'let's-be-quiet-about-it' committees have got just about no place. We're going to call a spade a dirty spade. And I think it's high time and a fine idea.

This was Hart and Zanuck's response to the Jewish establishment. Hart simply wrote into the screenplay his interpretation of the events that took place at Warner Brothers. In a certain way, Zanuck was Minify and Hart was Green. Moss Hart had somehow been radicalized by his experience. With *Gentleman's Agreement*, he was doing what he felt was the best thing to combat anti-Semitism, what he considered best for America's Jews. Weismann, as a symbol of the Jewish communal establishment, would just have to accept it. Interestingly enough, months later, *Commentary* editor Elliot Cohen, reacting to this scene, wrote: "The picture displays a Jewish leader who belongs to an organization that believes in 'hush-hush' on the problem of anti-Semitism. This writer knows some Jewish individuals, but no organizations that stand for such a policy."[105]

Jewish leadership in Los Angeles continued to be concerned about *Gentleman's Agreement*, and leaders' anxiety only became greater with the announcement of the upcoming release of *Crossfire*. At this point, the national "defense" organizations sprang into action, led by the American Jewish Committee. Richard Rothschild, AJC's director of public education and information, was the professional at AJC who had been working on creating a Jewish liaison group in Hollywood. The AJC was actively trying to forge relationships in Hollywood, and Rothschild was in Los Angeles the last week of February to pursue this goal. He was shocked to learn that the movie plot would be "the story of how a returning war veteran killed a Jew, not because he was a scoundrel, but just because he was a Jew."[106] Rothschild arranged to see Schary first at his home and again the next week in his office, but failed to convince the producer of what he considered "the perceived dangers." Rothschild had headed AJC's Survey Committee which, using principles of market research, had been charged just prior and during the war with counteracting Nazi and anti-Semitic propaganda. Coming out of the advertising world, Rothschild was committed to using these testing principles. He was convinced that the AJC's "quarantine treatment" was the appropriate way to go, and until there was sufficient polling and testing to prove otherwise, he believed that this motion picture should not be released. Deeply concerned that the film might do more harm than good, he was further frustrated when Schary refused to give him a copy of the script.

One should not be surprised that Schary was reluctant to share the script with Rothschild, having had enough problems dealing with in-house RKO resistance. "When it was announced, a representative of the American Jewish Committee came to see me. The man who was there—his name was Rothschild—he was there to talk me out of it. He suggested that I turn the Jewish character into a Black and I said no!"[107] Schary ostensibly told Rothschild that he did not have a script ready to share because "as each of these scenes involving anti-Semitism came up, the producer and writer huddled with me and we worked out each detail as we went along."[108]

> Dick [Rothschild] understood perfectly that the producers of the picture were animated by the best of motives, but he felt that this basic idea, of killing Jews just because they are Jews, was an extremely dangerous idea to project on the screen before 50 million or more people of all shades of emotional maturity or immaturity. As a novel, it might be an interesting psychological study for intelligent adults; as a movie it could do serious harm among extreme antisemites and even among that large percentage of the population which is mildly antisemitic.[109]

The American Jewish Committee then turned to Mendel Silberberg, prominent attorney, chairman of the LA Community Relations Council, advisor to the moguls, and one of the most respected and powerful Jews in Hollywood. After a few weeks, Silberberg was able to elicit Schary's consent to provide him with a script, which was then forwarded to Rothschild.[110] Certainly aware that this would not be the end of Rothschild's interference, Schary nevertheless could not have imagined the events that would follow. Rothschild, unaware that a script was on its way and frustrated by Schary's intransigence, went directly to Eric Johnston, president of the Motion Picture Association. He inquired as to how the motion picture code would apply to the new movies about anti-Semitism, and about *Crossfire* in particular. Johnston apparently forwarded Rothschild's letter to the Breen Production Code Office, which was the arm of the film industry that reviewed and regulated content of film. This set into motion a whole series of alarms within the industry. As it was, Joseph Breen had objected to some of the ethnic slurs and had pressured RKO into removing words like "kike" and "yid" from the film.[111] In the meantime, Rothschild also took the matter to American Jewish Committee president Judge Joseph M. Proskauer, who in a letter written in early April applied pressure on Ralstone Irvine at the RKO organization:

> One of my staff has just returned from Hollywood, where he learned about a movie called "Cradle of Fear," which is in production by your

people. I want to make clear at the outset that I think your people think there is nothing antisemitic in this film. Our people think it is shot with dynamite.

I have cursorily examined the script; I agree with our people . . . The net effect of this script, as I read it, is to spread a gospel of hatred culminating in murder.[112]

Irvine then passed the letter to RKO president Peter Rathvon, who had never been terribly enthusiastic about the project. Still, backing his new head of production, Rathvon responded:

We had the picture viewed by a comprehensive group the other night representing the points of view of various Jewish groups and I feel quite confident that the picture will have approval generally of these organizations. Mr. Richard Rothschild, whom I saw and whose description of the picture caused Proskauer's uneasiness, has apparently antagonized a number of people out here and his judgment is not considered valid.[113]

In a letter that followed, American Jewish Committee executive director John Slawson relayed to a board member how he was hopeful that RKO might still hold back release of the film:

The result was that, during the following week, Mr. Rathvon asked if Dick [Rothschild] would drop down to see him about the matter in his office. At the meeting which followed, Rathvon said that he himself had had some doubts about the picture and would take it up with the West Coast people.[114]

Now, Schary had received calls from both Breen and Rathvon, and he was fuming. So was Mendel Silberberg, who felt betrayed, having brokered the deal to allow Rothschild to see the script. As for Dore Schary, he was now at war with the American Jewish Committee. In the meantime, the film was being edited and its release had been scheduled for midsummer. Elliot Cohen, editor of *Commentary*, published by the AJC, threatened to write an article critical of the picture. Said Schary:

Then Slawson of the American Jewish Committee came [to see me] sometime later. First of all, Elliot Cohen did threaten to write a piece about it.

Nothing happened! Then the picture was made, above the objections of the [sales] group at RKO.[115]

The pressures placed on Schary did not stop there. In early July, the Chicago Censor Board rejected the film because of "violation of city ordinances under contention it shows race hatred."[116] Once this was corrected, there was the threat from other studios, particularly Warner Brothers, that the picture would not be picked up for distribution. Unlike Twentieth Century-Fox, which had its own distribution arm, RKO Pictures had to rely on outside companies to distribute their movies. Schary recalled:

> When the sales department went out to sell it, Warner Brothers informed them that under no circumstances would that picture play at any Warner Brothers [movie] house. They were afraid of the subject. They kind of took an American Jewish Committee point of view, which at that time was "sha-sha" [*sic*].[117]

Leaving the question of exhibition to others, Dore Schary moved quickly to have RKO be first to release a picture on anti-Semitism. In the end, RKO's Ned Depinet, who had from the beginning been wary about making the film, met with Warner Brothers chief Jack Warner to discuss distribution. "The thing that worried Jack Warner most of all . . . concerning *Crossfire* was his great fear that many films dealing with the Jewish question will come out of Hollywood . . . I told him so far as RKO is concerned, he need have no fear on that account. I think it will be very unfortunate if the market is surfeited with such pictures."[118]

There had been several options for the ending of the film. One was that the murderer Montgomery would be caught, but then what? The American way — brought to trial and put in prison for life? Many, like F. Hugh Herbert at Twentieth Century-Fox, pushed Schary for such an ending. Schary's response: "I believe a majority of people who look at the film will be satisfied to know that the killer is dead and destroyed by an officer of the law who gives him ample opportunity to surrender himself."[119] David Robinson, assistant national director of the Anti-Defamation League of B'nai B'rith, took some credit for this conclusion. "I was relieved, very much . . . that you had concluded to heed the suggestion I volunteered with reference to the killing of Montgomery at the end of the picture. Certainly anything which would create sympathetic audience reaction in favor of so despicable a character would be a most unfortunate thing."[120] The big question left to Paxton, Scott, Dmytryk, and Schary was how to finish off "Monty." In the end, Finlay, after warning the killer to stop, does fire at him from a distance and kills him. Such a fine degree of marksmanship certainly did not totally make sense, but the effect — the end of Montgomery — was achieved.

As *Crossfire* was readied for release in early summer of 1947, Schary turned to the Anti-Defamation League of B'nai B'rith in the hope of finally getting some support from the Jewish community: "By then the attitude of AJC had changed a great deal and Frank Trager [National Program Director of ADL] became involved in wanting to do a study on whether or not this kind of picture could change opinions."[121] The ADL had for some years been taking on previewing responsibilities of controversial films on behalf of the Jewish community. Schary hoped that ADL support would generate positive press and counteract the negative pressure he was getting from the American Jewish Committee. AJC's John Slawson, upon learning of ADL's involvement, was furious at the ADL for independently testing *Crossfire*. He penned a quick letter to Trager: "I leave the question with you, and beg you to consider the importance for all of us to abandon agency imperialism in the interest of a harmonious and effective relationship."[122] As part of a special June 17 screening, chaired by psychiatrist David M. Levy, Trager arranged for a study on whether or not this kind of picture could change opinions. Leading psychologists, psychiatrists, film scholars, and educators were in attendance, and Trager also invited professionals from both ADL and AJC.[123] They studied the film to determine if it should be considered dangerous, whether it was felt to be worth the effort, and how they believed the film might affect anti-Semitism. Their majority summary report determined that an attitude as deep as anti-Semitism could "never be affected by a single film, even a succession of films."[124] Still, Levy concluded that the group found *Crossfire* to be "dangerous entertainment . . . a risky adventure in entertainment."[125] A poll of the group found that six believed the picture would reduce prejudice; seven believed it would increase it; sixteen believed it would have no effect. Still, ADL wholeheartedly endorsed the film, agreeing to develop a follow-up study to determine audience reaction.

A second preview was arranged, this time with a smaller group of presumed experts and coordinated by Trager and Louis Raths, professor of educational psychology at New York University. The tests were to be conducted with a high-school audience in Hamilton, Ohio, and "average" adult audiences in Boston and Denver. The study proved that attitudes could indeed be changed, but for just how long, no one knew. "And then we broadened that. We sent [questionnaires] to a few army camps and we proved the same thing — that they were more receptive to the film and to what it said once they had been exposed to anti-Semitism and knew what it meant," wrote Raths in his summary of the study.[126] Schary also arranged over a hundred special screenings across the country for civic and religious leaders in an attempt to get their endorsement and good prerelease word of mouth. Publicity put out by RKO in trade publications stressed the "courage" of the film and the filmmakers — "one of the most courageous films ever made."[127] Still, fearing too much controversy, RKO's newspaper publicity in its initial weeks of release emphasized that the film was a murder mystery and made almost no reference to anti-Semitism. *Crossfire* opened at New York's Rivoli Theater on July 22 to the overwhelming applause of critics and audiences. As Schary bragged, "*Crossfire* was a big hit — even the Warner Brothers circuit played it."[128] Billy Rose, in his nationally syndicated column, wrote, "A picture which had the guts to be important . . . a movie which had something to say and wasn't afraid to say it."[129] Bosley Crowther, in the *New York Times*, hedged a bit as to the quality of the film, but still came out strongly in favor of it. He showed concern for possible abuses and "future sensationalisms of questions of intolerance," but seemed quite pleased with its very presence on the screen.[130] The film grossed an all-time record for RKO at the box office during its twelve-week run. Overall, it earned RKO over four times its actual cost.[131]

Almost immediately upon *Crossfire*'s release, several writers in the Jewish press, led by Elliot Cohen in the American Jewish Committee–sponsored *Commentary*, began attacking Schary's efforts. In a powerful indictment written in the journal, Cohen penned that some experts saw the films as "potentially harmful, especially as respects the strongly antisemitic moviegoer."[132] As Edward Shapiro shows, *Commentary* was a right-leaning publication seen as "celebrating the status quo" that "generally avoided drawing attention to America's social and economic failings."[133] Arthur Hertzberg writes how "elements that were led by the American Jewish Committee" at the time followed "an assimilationist theme" that dictated that Jews would be accepted by American society only if they "behaved."[134] Schary's approach was far more activist, and he counted on the ADL and other groups within the Jewish community to take his side.

In the meantime, following Elliot Cohen's lead, much of the Jewish community that had been expected to be supportive of RKO's efforts by assisting in promoting and marketing the picture was instead throwing daggers at

Elliot Cohen, editor of Commentary, *was concerned about the negative impact of making* Crossfire. *He used his magazine to wage battle with producer Dore Schary. American Jewish Committee Archives.*

the studio. In his attack on the picture, Cohen wrote, "Research has established that propaganda may have 'boomerang' effects. It is such considerations as the above that lead some experts to argue that there is a chance that *Crossfire* may reinforce rather than abate the emotions that make for anti-Semitism — and in a most ticklish sector of the population. . . . The easygoing journalist assumption that a mere exposé suffices to cure a social ill is naïve or worse."[135] S. Andhil Fineberg at the American Jewish Committee emphasized that such movies only comforted anti-Semites by emphasizing that they were not alone in their hate.[136] Over the next weeks, Cohen and Fineberg wrote several articles, some syndicated, in various Jewish newspapers, and Elliot Cohen never faltered in his attack. In a letter to Schary, Cohen wrote, "If I am dubious about the value of the Hollywood touch on such problems as anti-Semitism, it is only because my own thinking makes me fear 'quickie' art and 'quickie' thinking in American life, especially when directed at important basic issues."[137]

The scurrilous articles and harassment continued throughout the summer, instigated by Cohen. As Schary saw it: "They [the Jewish community] were afraid . . . I happened to be not afraid. I had a feeling that you had to keep it fresh and you had to keep your hand on the shoulder of society and say, 'Don't forget — You schmucks!'"[138] In October, Schary decided to respond to his chief critic directly in "A Letter to Elliot Cohen from a Moviemaker," and *Commentary* gave him that forum. Schary claimed that *Crossfire* was never intended to convert the violent anti-Semite. He pointed out that on the basis of audience reaction, there seemed to be proof that the film would insulate people against "violent and virulent anti-Semitism."

> It is a definitive picture aimed at readjusting the real anti-Semite. No one picture nor one book, nor one group of professionals, have succeeded or can succeed in achieving that Nirvana.
>
> We consulted more than one expert in the making of *Crossfire*. We talked to many. We do not operate in an intellectual vacuum; on the other hand, we don't favor intellectual anarchy. If we had accepted all the reservations of the experts, we would have compromised — and inhibited and vitiated a picture that right now seems to be doing the job it was aimed at doing.[139]

The rankling continued throughout the early fall of 1947. Dore Schary was so frustrated by Elliot Cohen's personal crusade against him and the film that he counterattacked by including the following in his October 1947 *Commentary* response. "The motion picture art contains people of wide and varied experience and education. Some of them even went to Yale [where Cohen studied]. We have the things you imply we lack — knowledge, imagination and art. However, sometimes we lack the gall of our critics."[140]

As *Crossfire* played to audiences across the country, there was growing realization that the film was having a positive impact. Though Elliot Cohen continued his attack, his sponsoring organization, the American Jewish Committee, began a partial retreat. The Anti-Defamation League firmly endorsed the film prior to its release. "We had the film pre-tested . . . the results went far beyond our expectations. . . . We urge you to watch for it when it comes to your community."[141] National ADL director Richard Gutstadt wrote Schary, "I took a small party to see it [*Crossfire*] at the Palace. All were unanimous in the conviction that the picture will do much good. We have heard some diverse viewpoints expressed, but overwhelmingly the impressions are favorable."[142] Schary responded that he had been flooded by "wonderful letters from all kinds of people," and that only 3 percent had been opposed to the picture.[143] In the end, long after the picture opened, AJC's official posture emphatically shifted. In a circulated memorandum, S. Andhil Fineberg provided the official AJC position:

There appears to be an impression that the American Jewish Committee is opposed to the picture *Crossfire*. The fact is that the American Jewish Committee has taken no position either for or against this film . . .

We hope that further discussion of *Crossfire* will proceed in a larger frame of reference herein indicated. We believe there should be mature deliberations before motion pictures are produced which raise serious considerations. By the same token, we believe there should be consultation with experts. There is too much at stake for the Jews of America to rely on good intentions and rule of thumb judgments in dealing with intolerance. Intolerance is much too devious, subtle and misleading a phenomenon. Dangerous seeds may be planted in the very act of tearing off branches.[144]

Within the American Jewish Committee, there were some who were upset by what was clearly an attack mounted on *Crossfire*, even though the organization claimed to take no stand. In October, as staff were deliberating on how to respond to the upcoming release of *Gentleman's Agreement*, staff member Dorothy Nathan sent the following memorandum to AJC executive John Slawson: "Our whole handling of our original objections to *Crossfire* . . . made many more enemies for us in Hollywood. . . . It set our policy in regard to *Crossfire* without any real meeting of the minds to determine what that policy should be. . . . I would just like to be sure we adopt different procedures in dealing with this picture than those noted."[145]

Following the success of *Crossfire*, the country awaited the release of *Gentleman's Agreement*. In many ways, *Crossfire* had laid the groundwork for *Gentleman's Agreement* by taking all the flack. Whereas *Crossfire* had been low-budget and speedily made, *Gentleman's Agreement*, with a budget four times greater than *Crossfire*, had been made slowly and purposefully. The picture was released on November 23 to great reviews and was the eighth-highest-grossing film of 1947. Eileen Creelman of the *New York Sun* called it "a fine piece of craftsmanship, apparently a work of love on the part of everyone concerned."[146] Bosley Crowther of the *New York Times* said, "Every good and courageous thing has been done."[147]

Thirty years later, director Elia Kazan called the film "patronizing," claiming that *Gentleman's Agreement* did not have staying power. Yet when pushed on the question of its profound impact on a generation, he responded, "It worked."[148] "I feel that with all its limitations, it worked."[149]

> Our whole task was to use a conventional form to force people to listen to ideas that were, at the time, unconventional. At the time of *Gentleman's Agreement* people weren't used to hearing these thoughts and feelings come out on the screen. . . . All I did was try and make the message come across in a form that the middle class, whom I was accusing of anti-Semitism, would accept. They accept the story and thereby the guilt. Then hopefully they'll take on the responsibility for making things change. . . . I'll make it so familiar to you that there won't be any way for you not to accept the guilt.[150]

Along these same lines, Gregory Peck said, "We were conscious of what we had to say. What we wanted the audience to carry with them when they left the theater had to be presented in an entertaining form. You had to avoid polemics, outright blunt statements of social criticism and social comment. . . . It had to be woven into the fabric of the story and come out of the character."[151]

Crossfire had received a mixed reception, but *Gentleman's Agreement*, released three months later, was welcomed with open arms. Even Elliot Cohen, possibly convinced by the positive effects of *Crossfire*, more probably pressured by AJC leadership, lauded the film in *Commentary*: "The plain fact is that *Gentleman's Agreement* is a moving, thought-provoking film, which dramatically brings home the question of anti-Semitism to precisely those people whose insight is most needed — decent, average Americans."[152] As Dore Schary wrote in his autobiography, "*Crossfire* was a big hit. . . . *Gentleman's Agreement* was a bigger hit."[153]

A study was conducted by Irwin C. Rosen, professor of psychology at the University of Pittsburgh, about *Gentleman's Agreement* and how it affected attitudes toward Jews. Rosen took 349 students in the university's Introduction to Psychology courses, screened the film for them, and then gave them questionnaires based on the Levinson-Sanford scale of measurement. His results were similar to the Rath/Trager study — there was a reduction in expression of ethnic prejudice.[154] Russell Middletown of Florida State University conducted another study of the film in 1960. He chose 329 students for an experimental group and 116 for a control group and tested them using the Berkeley anti-Semitism scale. No Jews or anyone who had already seen the film were in either group. The results showed that although the film did have an immediate effect on viewers, this tended not necessarily to be a lasting one.[155] He also found the following:

> The more anti-Semitic the subject, the greater is his vulnerability to persuasive appeals, but the greater also is the tendency for the impact of the appeal to be blunted by his failure to perceive the theme and by his negative reaction to the theme.[156]

The tests basically reaffirmed previous assessments, but noted that certain controls must be borne. Overall, one clear result stood out — *Crossfire* and *Gentleman's Agreement* were not films about which one needed to be frightened!

Both films were finally released, the result of a long and courageous battle on the part of a few individuals to bring the problem of anti-Semitism to the screen. In the following years, moviemakers went on to tackle many other societal questions for the cinema. Dore Schary, in an article written in *Saturday Review of Literature*, summed it up quite well: "The visual impact of the screen is so powerful and so vivid that in the hands of irresponsible people it can be dangerous. In the hands of those who respect it, it can accomplish wonders."[157]

A few months after the release of *Gentleman's Agreement*, a group of Los Angeles Jewish communal leaders set up a meeting with Dore Schary to discuss how they might better respond to future films that dealt with Jewish issues. With everything that had happened, Schary initially wanted no part of Jewish scripts or meetings with Jewish communal representatives:

> I will hold off on any Jewish material for a while, particularly since I have to nurse a couple of wounds placed by some Jews who so far are the only people who have given me any trouble on *Crossfire*. . . . When you go through that, you say, "Leave me alone for a while." You don't want to go over and eat the same meal again. You're perfectly willing to take another battle, but on a different ground.[158]

Finally, a meeting was arranged between Schary and many of those same Los Angeles communal leaders who had tried to lobby Darryl Zanuck.

> A group of those people, [who] went to Zanuck, came to see me. By now, both pictures had been a success. Both had achieved real recognition, and both had reflected different facets. They said they wanted to now organize a committee. It was, I suppose, based on the idea the Catholics had, a "Legion of Decency." I said, "If you try and do this, I'll fight you all the way. You're gonna wind up as censors." They said, "We've got to do something." I said, "[I'll do it] because I'm a little concerned with the ways Jews have been portrayed in many films . . ." I said, "It's all your fault, not the fault of the writers. You guys! You permitted Jews to be shown as all sorts of ridiculous characters, from way back . . ." So I said, "What I do think is possible is if you don't announce anything and if any time a problem that you feel has to be at least approached, that there be a few of us that can talk it over."[159]

In this manner and as a result of activity that surrounded the *Crossfire* and *Gentleman's Agreement* releases, the Jewish Film Advisory Committee was formed. Dore Schary was its first chairman, a position that he held for over twenty years.

The moment in time had presented a unique situation for both Hollywood and America's Jews. First, there was the Jewish community's reluctance to have a Jewish problem discussed in public. Then, there was the fact that segments of the organized Jewish community decided to take on the Hollywood establishment to try and prevent the production of these two films about anti-Semitism. One had the American Jewish Committee and some of the Jewish press fighting the Jewish Dore Schary, and the Los Angeles Jewish establishment taking on the non-Jewish Darryl F. Zanuck. It also must be pointed out that the initial fight, the very public debate over whether to produce *Crossfire*, had been a battle between two strong-willed Jews, Elliot Cohen and Dore Schary. How would the discussion have moved forward had Schary not been Jewish? Certainly, Cohen was much more respectful in his dealings with Zanuck. As for the Los Angeles Jewish leadership group that challenged Twentieth Century-Fox over *Gentleman's Agreement*, the pressure they exerted was done much more quietly. Other elements cannot be overlooked: there was also the growing influence of Congress's watchful eye on what writers were writing and what filmmakers were producing. Elia Kazan, who had been a member of the Communist Party, was only called to testify before a subcommittee of the House Committee on Un-American Activities in 1952. However, two of the persons involved in making *Crossfire*, Adrian Scott and Edward Dmytryk, were not so fortunate and were subpoenaed on October 29 by the HUAC. They refused to testify whether they had been members of the Communist party, were later cited for contempt of Congress, and eventually were fired by RKO.[160] The fact that the two were involved with the film had no adverse affect on box-office receipts in late 1947, but it may have kept the film from garnering an Oscar the following March.[161] What would have happened had they been called in to testify six months earlier? The film studio culture was also in flux, with the growing influence of stockholders and bankers. In the case of both films, the studio producers were not only fighting for what they believed could better society, they were risking their own futures. There is little doubt that both Schary and Zanuck placed their professional reputations on the line. As for the perceptions of America's Jews, the "quarantine treatment" was deemed not always effective. The flexing of muscles by some in the organized Jewish world was reflective of a greater comfort level felt by American Jews in the postwar period and possibly indicative of America's growing acceptance of Jews and other minorities.[162] Like Philip Green, the Gregory Peck character in *Gentleman's Agreement* standing at the front desk, waiting to get his room key, Jews were getting tired of idly standing by while their luggage was removed. Jews were here to stay. The releases of *Crossfire* and *Gentleman's Agreement* and the battles that surrounded them were part of a coming of age for America's Jews.

THE YOUNG LIONS

GUARANTEEING ACCEPTANCE

Irwin Shaw's *The Young Lions* is considered one of the best novels about World War II of the immediate postwar period. At the time of publication, it joined Norman Mailer's *The Naked and the Dead*, a book that also dealt with the war, on the bestseller lists. Shaw, a New York City native and Brooklyn College graduate, drew from his own experiences as a soldier with the U.S. Army Signal Corps and from his adventures in North Africa, London, and Paris. Random House published the novel in October of 1948. The film, directed by Edward Dmytryk and released by Twentieth Century-Fox a decade later, premiered on April 2, 1958. One of the three protagonists, Noah Ackerman, is highly representative of the Jew trying to make his way in America during the period that followed World War II.

Shaw, whose family name was changed from Shamforoff when he was fifteen, grew up very much aware of his Jewishness, but "with no particular feeling about being a Jew."[1] Yet there is a strong Jewish presence in much of his writing. As he told an interviewer in 1977, "I didn't want to pretend to anybody that I was an Irishman, so that's one of the reasons why I write so much about being a Jew. . . . To pretend you're not a Jew is an act of cowardice. . . . I didn't want to pretend that I wasn't one."[2]

The plot follows the lives of three men, two Americans and one Austrian, whose war experiences intersect in different ways. Each is an invention of Shaw's, though according to the author, "here and there I'd used a story I'd heard or a scene I'd been witness to, and which was useful for the character."[3] Michael Whitacre, a New York show-business personality, is one

Writer Irwin Shaw waited for more than a decade before his novel was finally made into a film. Billy Rose Theatre Division, New York Public Library for the Performing Arts. Astor, Lenox and Tilden Foundations.

American; the second is Noah Ackerman, an orphaned, unassuming Jew. The Austrian, who is proud to wear a German uniform, is named Christian Diestl. The novel begins on New Year's Eve 1938, shortly before the war in Europe, when Margaret, who will become Michael's girlfriend, is on a ski vacation in Austria; her ski instructor is Christian. The novel concludes toward the end of the war, as American troops liberate a Nazi concentration camp and the three men encounter each other in the woods just beyond the camp. During the course of the narrative, we follow each man's saga as the war progresses toward its finish. Michael and Noah become friends, and Christian moves up within the ranks of the German army with the help of an officer who takes him under his wing. The evolution from the 1948 novel to the 1958 film adaptation is intriguing in several ways: the postwar encounter of the American Jew with Christian America; anti-Semitism in America's military; the changing portrayal of the German protagonist over a decade;

The three star actors, playing Christian, Michael, and Noah, together on the set of
The Young Lions. *The three were only together on-set for one day during filming.*
Marlon Brando, Dean Martin, Montgomery Clift. © *20th Century-Fox.*
20th Century Fox Pictures/Photofest.

the inclusion of a Nazi concentration camp scene; and America's association with the Holocaust. These five items and how they were dealt with and
transformed by writer, screenwriter, and director provide an interesting insight into the situation of the American Jew at the time of production.

THE JEWISH ENCOUNTER WITH CHRISTIAN AMERICA

Noah Ackerman, the shy, unpretentious Jewish man from the Midwest,
meets Hope Plowman, a gentle non-Jewish woman and new arrival to New
York from Vermont. The moment Noah sees her, there is immediate chemistry. In the novel, Noah is introduced to her one night when his roommate has
a bunch of friends over to their apartment; in the film they meet at a party
given by Michael, whom Noah has just befriended. The evolution of their

relationship over the course of one evening has the two walking about New York City and traveling a great distance by public transportation to Brooklyn, where Hope lives with an aunt. Their different religious affiliations seem to matter little to either. The scene is beautifully recounted in both prose and on film. In the film, with Montgomery Clift and Hope Lange as the young couple, we have one of the best-played scenes in the movie. "By far the most engrossing of the romantic episodes is the courtship of Montgomery Clift and Hope Lange," wrote critic Paul Beckley in the New York Herald Tribune.[4] Clift is brilliant as the reserved and modest Noah and Lange is both alluring and tender.

Montgomery Clift was enthusiastic about the part "because of its opportunities for positive statements on anti-Semitism."[5] He felt that the film delivered a strong anti-bigotry message. Clift changed his appearance in preparation for the role, altering the look of his nose and ears with putty and wax to affect a more Semitic look. "He starved eleven pounds off a torso that was already emaciated. The slouch and other mannerisms did the rest."[6] Clift's already Semitic appearance had many believing him to be Jewish. Biographer Patricia Bosworth related how on one occasion, in his apartment, Clift announced that he was going to play "the Jew Noah Ackerman in the movie *The Young Lions*. . . . I was picked because I look so Jewish. . . . Everybody thinks I'm Jewish." He said this knowingly to infuriate his father, who was anti-Semitic.[7] According to Bosworth, "Monty always admired what he called 'the Jewish genius for survival,' a quality he saw in Noah. . . . Noah became an artistic expression of faith for Monty. It was his favorite role — the performance he wrought most painfully and carefully from his own experience, his own observations."[8]

Shaw's choice of names for the two lovebirds is worth noting. Noah, the biblical figure who, unaided, a stray without anchor on his ark, was chosen by God, is here an orphan with no grounding. Noah appears in the Bible during a period of wickedness when the world is about to be destroyed, not wholly unlike the world that had been encompassed by war and imminent decimation in Shaw's novel. The Bible's Noah confronts the moral turpitude of his time, just as Noah Ackerman confronts the bigotry and indifference of his day. Hope comes along to bring him "hope" as she settles down with him and the two create a home and a family, in a country that Shaw believes provides protections from discrimination. Hope is a Plowman, firmly entrenched, "plowed" and dug in from a strong Christian family that had been ensconced in New England for generations. If we look at the Hebrew root

עקר (AKR), as in Ackerman, we see it means plucked up or uprooted, and indeed this Jew is not firmly rooted anywhere. The allegory seems clear—the wandering, uprooted Jew has found a haven in America and is to find hope through assimilation. Together, the couple will plow and plant deep roots and have children in the new America. Hope has not only accepted Noah, she has fallen in love with him.

In Irwin Shaw's novel, Noah Ackerman has no family when he meets Hope. His father Jacob, who traveled the countryside never quite making a living, had died leaving him nothing. Noah's father did have a brother, Israel, who had migrated from Odessa to Hamburg in 1919 and whom his father had tried, unsuccessfully, to bring to America. Noah has never met his uncle and at this point has no knowledge of his fate in Germany or, for that matter, the fate of the millions of Jews living in Europe. Jacob, speaking of his brother shortly before his death, foreshadows Noah's discovery of the concentration camp at the film and book's conclusion when he says, "They are burning my brother Israel in the furnace of the heathen."⁹ Noah hears this as he sits by his father's side and contemplates the Jewish condition around the world. Two Jewish brothers, Jacob and Israel—alternate names in the Bible for the same individual, the grandson of Abraham—are here separated by circumstance and an ocean: one is in America, safe though unfulfilled, and the other is still in Europe, where his situation is dubious; we only learn that he has died in a concentration camp at the novel's conclusion. Screenwriter Edward Anhalt, when adapting the book for the screen, understood that this scene was vital to understanding Noah. His connection to European Jewry and his eventual arrival in Europe as an American liberator of a concentration camp are very much part of the Jewish Noah. Twentieth Century-Fox hired the Yiddish theater actor/director Jacob Ben-Ami for the one-day shoot to play Jacob Ackerman. But unfortunately, as the motion picture was pared down in editing from two hundred minutes to 167, this scene was cut from the film, and there is no mention of Noah's history.¹⁰ He is simply an orphan with no family.

Irwin Shaw believed that assimilation in America was critical and possible. He raises the pivotal question of whether the Jew is "welcome" when Noah journeys to Vermont to meet Hope's father, whom Shaw describes as "a devout churchgoer, a hard-bitten Presbyterian elder."¹¹ Shaw, who fought in the war, is skeptical yet optimistic about the place of the Jew in America in this scene, which is set on the eve of America's entrance into World War II. As discussed in chapter 3's analysis of the 1947 films that confronted anti-

Jewish prejudice, there remained a widespread consciousness on the part of Jews throughout the war that the anti-Semitism of the 1930s did not abate in the 1940s. With the commencement of war, historian Edward Shapiro posited, "although most Americans interpreted the struggle between the United States and Germany as a conflict between democracy and totalitarianism, this did not lead to a revulsion from anti-Semitism, the most salient element within Nazi ideology."[12] Now Shaw, writing in postwar America, chooses to place the question of acceptance or non-acceptance into the hands of Hope's father. Mr. Plowman, representative of a broad spectrum of churchgoing Americans, will have his own personal debate over Christian values, forcing him to decide whether there is room for inclusion. Is America ready to accept its Jews? As Shapiro pointed out, "Perhaps the most remarkable aspect of American Jewish life after 1945 was the rejection of this gospel of despair by the vast majority of American Jews."[13] American Jews believed that they could fit in, and Irwin Shaw was a proponent of this. "I believe in absolute assimilation," Shaw told Miriam Varon, who interviewed him for an oral history by the American Jewish Committee. When she pushed him, "Assimilation, but not denying that you are a Jew?" he responded, "That's it!"[14] This sense that a Jew could assimilate into American society without being forced to give up one's Jewishness is an integral underlying element of Shaw's work. Shaw pushes the question further when he has Hope ask Noah to Vermont in order to exact acceptance or possible non-acceptance from her father before she can commit to marriage. This visit sets up self-examination in Hope's father as the two go off on a walk through the town center.

When Edward Anhalt, working with director Edward Dmytryk (*Crossfire*), was adapting this scene for the screen, he chose to condense chapter 11 of Irwin Shaw's book into one extended sequence, one of the more remarkable ones in the film. Instead of arriving on a train, as in the novel, Noah Ackerman comes to the New England town by bus. The sequence begins with an aerial shot of the hamlet as we hear church bells. The point is clearly made that we no longer are in urban New York, but in a slice of Americana that is representative of the vast swath of Christian America, where Jews are more a curiosity than a presence. The next shot is of Hope and her father chatting over coffee at a classic New England pharmacy as Mr. Plowman tries to ascertain more about Noah, whom he is about to meet. The pharmacy's doors behind them are wide open and Hope periodically glances out in anticipation. Then the bus, entering town, appears behind them. Dmytryk

Hope Plowman and her father wait for her boyfriend, Noah Ackerman. The bus arrives, coming between father and daughter. Hope Lange, Vaughn Taylor.

As Noah gets off the bus, Hope tells her father, "He's Jewish, father!" An awkward encounter and a shake of hands. Vaughn Taylor, Hope Lange, Montgomery Clift.

skillfully has the bus visually come between father and daughter, trumpeting the arrival of this intruder, the outsider arriving from beyond. Hope leaps up and her father follows as the bus turns the corner and pulls up to the bus stop. Just as the doors of the bus are about to open, Hope—having waited until the last possible moment to share her deep secret—turns to her dad and blurts out, "He's Jewish, father!"

In the decade that separated the book's publication and the film's release, the place of the Jew in America had been dramatically altered. According to research conducted by demographer Herbert Stember, one-fifth of those polled in 1948 said they did not want Jews as neighbors, but by 1959 that number had dropped to 2 percent.[15] Though this sequence is set in the early 1940s, Shaw is looking in his 1948 book toward an America where Jews would be welcome and in 1958, the viewers of the film would find that highly plausible. Mr. Plowman is caught quite by surprise by this interloper, who is the lone passenger getting off the bus, with only an overcoat in tow—no family, no heritage, no baggage. He invites Mr. Ackerman to join him for a walk, asking Hope to stay behind and finish her coffee. Mr. Plowman begins to introduce Noah to his New England world. "That's Jack Marshall's. I went to school with his father. My father with his father. Virgil Smith's law office. One of his people did the legal work when they incorporated this town—1750." Then the two pass the church, we hear the choir chanting, and they continue on to the cemetery, where Hope's mother is buried along with generations of Plowmans. Director Dmytryk, planting his camera at the far side of the cemetery, cleverly reverses the point of view to show a fence that visually keeps the two men outside of the cemetery. Then, as we see the two in medium close-up, separated from the cemetery by the pointy tips of the fence, Mr. Plowman continues his narration, "It's the family plot. Seven generations of Plowmans there; Hope's mother too."

Just what is Mr. Plowman implying? Is it that there is a great deal of history here in this town and his family is rooted back all the way to colonial times, before the founding of the nation? Seven generations? Plowman is all but saying to Noah that he is trespassing and unwanted—he should get on his ark and land somewhere else! Ackerman, quiet, looks strikingly calm, not knowing how to respond to what he sees and hears. Then, breaking his silence, he turns to Hope's father: "Mr. Plowman, I don't have a family plot. I don't have a family." After sharing his selective service status and limited net worth, he speaks of his love for Hope. "But I love Hope, and I shall love her for all my life." Mr. Plowman hears him, and then, as the family plot slowly disappears in the background, they continue to walk. All this is happening as the choir continues singing. Not coincidentally, the hymn "Thy Strong Word" is heard. The third stanza reads:

> Thy strong word bespeaks us righteous;
> bright with thine own holiness,
> glorious now, we press toward glory,
> and our lives our hopes confess:
> Alleluia, alleluia! Praise to thee who light dost send!
> Alleluia, alleluia! Alleluia without end.[16]

Martin Franzmann's hymn is calling out for light to bring order. It is a Christian plea for Mr. Plowman to heed God's word and leave behind the darkness of exclusion and allow hope to prevail. "You're doing an awful thing. Putting a man to the test of his principles. I wish to heaven you'd turn around and get on that bus and never see Hope again. But you won't do that, will ya?" With Ackerman shaking his head, Plowman continues, "Didn't think you would. Anybody from town asked to marry Hope, I'd say 'Come on out to the house, we got turkey for dinner.'" As he's saying these words, we observe behind them the church, with an open door, and a couple about to enter. The church seems to beckon for good Christian values. Plowman shrugs, "I never knew a Jew before. You go along all your life thinkin' a certain way." We see a woman quietly sitting on a bench with a young girl by her side. As the two continue past them, they walk in front of a cannon from some war past. "Someone jolts you, you have to look inside yourself." Sit

Edward Dmytryk provides a point-of-view shot to show the gated Christian cemetery where Hope's mother and generations of Plowmans are buried. The Jewish Ackerman is fenced out, not welcome.

As they walk past the church, Mr. Plowman admits to Noah that he "never knew a Jew before" and is not sure how to handle it.

Guess who's coming for dinner? Mr. Plowman announces to Hope that he is inviting Noah Ackerman home for turkey. Hope Lange, Vaughn Taylor, Montgomery Clift.

still on a bench passively or acquiesce and make a push, like from the cannon you are walking past on the town green — Plowman's options are clearly represented there for us. "That's what you made me do and I'm not fond of you for it." The camera is now on Hope, who comes to the pharmacy door to meet the two as they return. Are they bringing the right prescription? The church bells ring, as Mr. Plowman is about to deliver his verdict. "I was just telling Mr. Ackerman we've got turkey for dinner." The Jew has been asked to come for dinner, for of all things, turkey — the food of plenty, the all-American feast. Yes, it is 1958 and the Jew has finally been invited to the American table. Director Edward Dmytryk provides us with a cinematic script for a visual analysis of the situation of America's Jews, not so much of 1940–1941, but of 1958, when the film was made. As asserted by Pierre Sorlin, films touching on the past "are concerned with the problems of the present,"[17] and Dmytryk is here providing his and screenwriter Edward Anhalt's understanding of the Jew at that time in America.

Edward Dmytryk, the Canadian-born director who began in the film industry as a film-studio messenger, had by 1958 been involved with multiple film projects that dealt with aspects of the American Jewish experience. Always interested in mathematics and physics and even spending a year at the California Institute of Technology, Dmytryk left school to work his way up through the studio system as projectionist, editor, and finally director. He was considered one of the most talented young directors in Hollywood, having proven himself early on as a director of B pictures, movies that were generally the second film of a double-feature billing and made with much smaller budgets than A pictures. Dmytryk could make films economically and within budget. By 1947, after his direction of the short-budget *Crossfire* for RKO Pictures, he was being touted as "Mr. RKO." At the time, influential Jews in the film industry had serious misgivings about dealing with Jewish themes in movies, and the fact that Dmytryk (of Ukrainian lineage) was not Jewish became a great asset, particularly as he took on further film projects that dealt with Jewish themes and aspects. His work could not be seen as self-serving.

As noted in the previous chapter, within months of completing *Crossfire*, Edward Dmytryk became embroiled in the politics of the moment; he became known as one of the "Hollywood Ten," those ten members of the film community who were accused of Communist activity and who refused to cooperate with HUAC (House of Representatives' Un-American Activities Committee). The "Ten" and many others had their careers disrupted or ruined; two of the Ten, Dmytryk and Adrian Scott, were involved in the production of *Crossfire*. Dmytryk was sent to prison for refusing to testify before the committee, and after a few months in jail, he recanted and decided to go before HUAC, the only one of the Ten to do so. Dmytryk and his agent believed that he had thus salvaged his career, but his resurgence did not happen as quickly as hoped. Years later, with the repudiation of the anti-Communist fury of the late 1940s and 50s, many viewed him with contempt for having capitulated to the Committee. Still, having returned to Congress as a "friendly witness," Dmytryk was finally able to get work as a director. After doing *Mutiny* for the King Brothers, he was hired by independent and highly successful producer Stanley Kramer to make four pictures. The third film he made for Kramer was an adaptation of Michael Blankfort's *The Juggler*, for which Blankfort wrote the screenplay. The film, tastefully directed by Dmytryk and starring Kirk Douglas, relates the story of a survivor of the Holocaust, with serious psychological problems, who tries to find his place in the new State of Israel. Dmytryk then completed his commitment to Kramer with an adaptation of Herman Wouk's *The Caine Mutiny*, a film for which screenwriter Stanley Roberts had removed much of the Jewish flavor of the novel. In the film, the Jewishness of Lieutenant Barney Greenwald, the attorney, is minimized, and issues of social anti-Semitism, which are integral aspects of the novel, are relatively absent. But by now, Dmytryk had developed a clear understanding of the Jewish condition. Almost all of his friends were Jewish, and his own daughter flirted with converting to Judaism.[18] He would bring this sensitivity to his work on *The Young Lions* four years later.

ANTI-SEMITISM IN AMERICA'S MILITARY

In *Crossfire*, Edward Dmytryk had dealt with the murder of a U.S. serviceman by a fellow soldier simply because he was Jewish. In *The Young Lions*, Dmytryk would offer a scene where Noah, already married and now in Army basic training, encounters the anti-Semitism of his bunkmates, his sergeant, and captain. Though Irwin Shaw had never personally experienced bigotry, except for a brush with prejudice once on a job interview, an anti-Semitic incident one of Shaw's family members experienced in the Army would become the basis for the scene.[19] Dmytryk, on the other hand, like Montgomery Clift, had a father who was an anti-Semite, and he brought this understanding to bear. "Of course I got involved in the problems of anti-Semitism — at first from amazement, and then from awareness. These kinds of things have interested me all my life."[20] Earlier, in the Vermont sequence, Shaw had put forward an idealized America where good Christians would now accept and welcome Jews. However, anti-Semitism was still prevalent in America, and Shaw and Dmytryk fully understood that. For many Americans, even after the United States entered the war, there was no understanding, even on the part of soldiers, of what Nazism meant. America was fighting Germany and its way of life, yet fascism of a sort could still be found in the U.S. military that was conducting the war. Shaw's scene with Ackerman experiencing anti-Semitism in the military serves as a counterpoint to the earlier scene in Vermont. For Ackerman, this ugly and ancient foe would be the first of many enemies he faced in this war.

The powerful scene when bigoted Captain Colclough, during a barracks inspection, shows his contempt for Michael Whitacre and his fellow New Yorker, Jewish bunkmate Noah Ackerman. Lee Van Cleef, Herbert Rudley, Dean Martin, Montgomery Clift. © 20th Century-Fox. 20th Century Fox Pictures/Photofest.

In a 1984 introduction to a new printing of his novel *Focus*,[21] Arthur Miller wrote that the strong anti-Jewish hostility he experienced during the war had compelled him to write that novel. He was aghast at how people with whom he had been working at the Brooklyn Navy Yard misunderstood the war effort:

> We were fighting Germany essentially because she had allied herself with the Japanese who had attacked us at Pearl Harbor. Moreover, it was by no means an uncommon remark that we had been maneuvered into this war by powerful Jews who secretly controlled the federal government. Not until Allied troops had broken into the German concentration camps and the newspaper published photos of the mounds of emaciated and sometimes partially burned bodies was Nazism really disgraced among decent people and our casualties justified.[22]

With the war's commencement, many in the U.S. military understood that the Nazis and Japanese had to be stopped, but they were not sure that it was their responsibility.[23] For American-Jewish soldier-novelists (such as Shaw), wrote Sidra Ezrahi, "the war against Hitler was regarded as a mission in which they had a sanctified role to play."[24] It was with a deep sense of purpose that this author-turned-soldier chose to take on anti-Jewish bigotry. Irwin Shaw acknowledged that Hitler's rise to power and the war had changed his own Jewish stance, admitting that he "used to be an anti-Zionist before Hitler."[25] For his Jewish character Ackerman, it is anti-Semitism in the barracks that awakens his consciousness as a Jew. In the film version he fights four different men from the barracks (in the novel he battles ten) for having mocked him for being a Jew and for having stolen money that he had put aside to buy a gift for Hope. In each fight, Ackerman, frail and far from physically adept to fight the biggest men in the barracks, is beaten senseless.[26] But, persevering, he is finally victorious over his adversary in the very last fight and gains the respect of his peers. In many ways, this scene is predicated on the more nationalistic stance assumed by Shaw in the aftermath of the war, at a time when Israel was about to become a Jewish state: "When Hitler came in, I didn't see any hope for Jews except a place where they could at least stand and die fighting and I'm afraid that may be what's going to happen. But at least you have the honor of having a place to defend and taking a lot of people with you when you go, and so that's why I'm for Israel."[27] Deborah Dash Moore observed that "American Jews learned more than the bitter lessons of impotence from World War II. They acquired new perspectives on themselves and their country through their participation in the armed services of the United States."[28] This was certainly the experience of Irwin Shaw.

ADAPTING THE NOVEL INTO A FILM

With the novel published, was the country ready for a film acknowledging anti-Semitism in the military? Though films like *Crossfire* and *Gentleman's Agreement* had been released in 1947, a year before Shaw's book, the sense in Hollywood, particularly after HUAC began its hearings that year, was to stay clear of more "social message" films that tackled anti-Semitism. Said Shaw, "The Jew suffered for being a Jew in the American Army. Nobody would touch it. It took years of sophistication before they [film producers] would finally do it." [29] This Jew created by Shaw, the Jew as American, represents a new Jew who was ready to fight. Shaw contraposes his new Jew with the victimized European Jew whom we encounter in the concentration camp at the story's conclusion. The initially meek and mild-mannered Noah is that Jew who, touched by America and its war with Germany, changes, grows, and fights, thereby taking on a new character, the new Jew. He also becomes a moral compass for the second protagonist, the American Michael Whitacre, played by Dean Martin.

Then there is Christian Diestl, the young and naive Austrian. In the novel, we quickly witness his strong pro-Nazi and anti-Jewish bias when he berates Margaret for having a Jewish boyfriend. "Your young man is a Jew and you are afraid for him. So you lose sight of the larger issues . . . The larger issue is Austria. The German people . . . Myself, I know it's ridiculous to attack any race . . . But if the only way you can get a decent and ordered Europe is by wiping out the Jews, then we must do it. A little injustice for a large justice." [30] Shaw saw Germans as evil and was unafraid to portray Christian Diestl as such:

> You start out with a man who has decent instincts, young, idealistic, and he feels the only hope for Austria is Nazism. I mean so that he says, "Well, I'm going to go along with the Nazis." And bit by bit as he goes along he becomes corrupted by the idea that he has accepted, until finally he's a beast, which is what the Germans were at the end of the war. I mean they killed twenty million people in the camps. . . . So I wanted to show how, step by step through the course of the years of war, this German became the symbol of the Nazis. This is in my book. [31]

That was how Shaw and most Americans felt in 1948. Ten years later, when the film would be made, Germany had a different place in the American psyche. In 1958, the Federal Republic of Germany held a respected role as an American ally in its Cold War with the Soviet Union. Five years earlier, West Germany had concluded an agreement whereby it arranged to pay reparations and restitution to Israel; a "claims conference" representing the Jewish people had been created two years before that to negotiate the compensation process. West Germany was a strong and growing democracy that was seen as a bulwark against Communism.

Irwin Shaw had originally sold the film rights to his book in 1954 to a New York tax attorney and a producer who planned to shoot the film that summer. Shaw was not only going to receive more than $100,000, he was to get a share of profits and, for an additional sum, write the screenplay.[32] Shaw had written several plays in the thirties and had been writing screenplays since 1936, but this was to be his first attempt at adapting his own work. Nobody seemed ready to finance production and the project fell through until three years later, when producer Al Lichtman bought the film rights for Twentieth Century-Fox (the same studio that a decade earlier had made *Gentleman's Agreement*). Dmytryk, who was hired to direct, personally enlisted Montgomery Clift and Dean Martin to play two of the leads. Shaw's screenplay was finished, but Dmytryk chose not to use it. According to Shaw biographer Michael Shnayerson, "Dmytryk found Shaw's script hopeless. It was talky and disorganized — the same problems, he felt, to be found in every Shaw script he'd seen filmed."[33] According to Dmytryk, "His mediocre attempts at adapting *The Young Lions* had been at least partly responsible for keeping the novel off the screen for nine years."[34] Dmytryk felt that Shaw's screenplay focused too much on Michael Whitacre and not enough on the other two characters, particularly Ackerman, whom he believed to be the central character. So Academy Award–winning screenwriter Edward Anhalt went to work on writing a new draft.[35]

CHRISTIAN DIESTL

Anhalt, New York–born and a Columbia University School of Journalism graduate, had worked twice before with Dmytryk and fully understood the New York world of both Ackerman and Whitacre. He and Dmytryk went to work restoring what they believed to be the balance necessary for the three protagonists. In his biography, Dmytryk wrote that he believed the character of Christian needed change and made the case that "there was little to be gained by keeping the original characterization."[36] Shortly after a new treatment was prepared, Marlon Brando's agent approached the studio to have Brando play Christian. Though many changes had been made to the character of Christian, Brando did not feel them to be sufficient, and he pushed Dmytryk into altering the character even further, making the changes a condition of his employment. According to Shnayerson, "Dmytryk and Brando felt that Shaw had written *The Young Lions* in the still heated afterglow of the war and that as a Jew he had felt an irrational hatred of all Germans."[37]

> Twelve years after the war, the dyed-in-the-wool Nazi heavy was a cliché, and everybody accepted the proposition that a brutal war furnished brutal opportunities for a brutal man. Besides, we all learned by now that many thoroughly Aryan Germans had also been hanged to lampposts for refusing to cooperate in Hitler's war. . . . Christian was established as a man who is in sympathy with many Nazi ideas and ideals but finds that these degenerate into barbaric brutality as the war progresses. He resists the trend with growing intensity.[38]

Irwin Shaw claimed that Brando pushed for a different Christian Diestl to fit his own vision of the character. "He didn't want to be unsympathetic."[39] There was even talk at the time that Montgomery Clift and Brando were in competition with each other and that Brando felt that portraying a "bad guy" would not be good for his career.[40] Robert LaGuardia refutes this in his biography of Clift: "The old days when the two of them stumbled around each other, a little irritated and awed by the threat of the other's talent and individuality, were over."[41] It is clear that Marlon Brando wanted a different Christian, and *Look* magazine reported that he "issued an ultimatum in the form of a detailed character analysis of the Nazi that took him 15 hours to read aloud" to producer Lichtman, director Dmytryk, and screenwriter Anhalt.[42] In its eagerness to get Brando aboard, the studio acquiesced to his demands and made Christian Diestl less ugly and more of an idealist. According to Patricia Bosworth, Dmytryk later confirmed to Montgomery Clift that he had indeed acceded to the changes in order to entice Brando into taking the part.[43] That decision would later bring a sharp rebuke from Irwin Shaw, and the revamped Christian Diestl remains the most controversial element of the movie. Months after the film's release, Brando told his friend Maureen Stapleton, who found his portrayal offensive, that he had indeed forced Dmytryk to make the changes, but felt that the director should have shown more resistance: "If it had been Gadg [Elia Kazan], he wouldn't have let me do it."[44] In public, however, Brando was adamant about how he saw Christian. In the midst of filming in Berlin, Brando held a press conference for nearly one hundred German journalists where he explained the differences between novel and film: "Shaw wrote his great book while war hatreds were still white-hot. . . . We hope they've cooled. The picture will try and show that Nazism is a matter of mind, not geography, that there are Nazis—and people of good will—in every country."[45] In a 1978 *Playboy* interview, Brando spoke further about his disagreement with Irwin Shaw on the nature of the German character:

> Yeah. He felt that the German people were to blame for the Holocaust. I think if you hold an entire people responsible for something, nobody can survive. Whether it's the Turks, the French in Algeria, the English in Africa and Palestine, the Americans, Spanish—there isn't any people in the world that hasn't done something that defies one's sense of horror. . . . If you pick out a whole people and say, *all* the Germans are this, *all* the Jews do this, that's exactly what Hitler did. If you start thinking and feeling in broad terms like that then it's very dangerous. That was clear in Shaw's book, in his bitterness and anger. It's fully understandable. But he wanted to make that massive statement. I don't think it's possible to do that.[46]

When principal photography in France began on the picture, Shaw, living not far from Chantilly, just outside of Paris, where the film was being shot, made several visits to the set. Only then did he discover that his story had been dramatically changed, but he was powerless to take any action. In the midst of filming, CBS Paris bureau chief David Schoenbrun got word that there was some unpleasantness and arranged to interview both Shaw and Brando. He quickly uncovered the difference of opinion regarding Christian's characterization. Schoenbrun recalled asking Brando whether there was any problem in the interpretation of his character, to which Brando responded:

> "I just read the script and knew what the guy was like and played it straight. I had absolutely no problem. It was a great role" . . .
> To which Shaw responded: "Brando played him all wrong . . . He played him in a sympathetic way because he wants to be sympathetic on screen."
> Brando said to Irwin, "What are you talking about, you don't know this character."
> And Irwin said, "It's my character, I gave birth to him. I created him!"
> "Nobody gives birth to a character but an actor," Brando snapped back. "I play the role, now he exists. He is my creation."

And Irwin said, "You're a stupid actor, I'm the writer of this story, this is my character, you stupid . . ."[47]

A *Look* magazine article that came out the week that the film opened in New York contained the following repartee between Shaw and Brando:

> Shaw: You're the only one from Twentieth Century-Fox who has taken the trouble to look me up. What are they doing to my book?
>
> Brando told him that the spirit of the book was being respected, but that he himself was interpreting the Nazi differently. He added, "If you were writing the book today, would you show him that way?"
>
> Shaw: "I wouldn't change it much. This is the breed that killed 20,000,000 people, and the people they killed are still dead."
>
> Brando: "But the world can't spend its life looking over its shoulders and nursing hatreds. There would be no progress that way. No nation is all good. There are Nazis and men of good will in every country. If we continue to say that all Germans are bad, we would add to the argument that all Jews are bad."
>
> In the end, neither man fully convinced the other.[48]

In subsequent interviews, Brando made the case that he had positive feelings about Jews. In fact, he later said, "I was, in a sense, brought up by Jews. Stella Adler was the first woman, first person of culture, that I ever met."[49] Because of his relationship with Adler and her husband Harold Clurman, Brando had in 1946 even acted, along with Paul Muni and Celia Adler, in Ben Hecht's pageant *A Flag Is Born*. Hecht was a supporter of Revisionist Zionism, which pushed for an immediate end to the British Mandate in Palestine and creation of a Jewish state. He used the nationalistic play to raise funds to buy arms for the Etzel, the Irgun Zvai Leumi, a paramilitary group in Israel. Brando played the part of David, a concentration camp survivor who is convinced by Jewish Brigade soldiers from Palestine to take up the struggle:

> He takes the *talis* from him [the dead Tevya]. He takes a blue star from his own pocket. He put the star on the *talis*, cutting away the *talis* fringes with his knife. From beyond the lighted bridge comes a chorus of soldiers singing the *Hatikva* [what would become Israel's national anthem] in the distance. . . . He tacks his *talis* to a branch. . . . Holding his flag high, he walks toward the light, the singing and the sound of guns.[50]

Ironically, in contrast to what Brando was attempting to accomplish in *The Young Lions*, actors in the 1946 Hecht pageant spoke such lines as "the murderers called the Germans."[51]

The disposition of Christian is critical to our understanding of both the novel and the film. That the Austrian's name would be Christian is no coincidence, for Shaw created a man who is "young, idealistic" and sees Nazism as bringing hope to Austria. Both Christian men, Mr. Plowman and this Austrian, are searching for "hope" but find it in different ways. Plowman struggles with his conscience and finds tolerance, whereas Diestl's journey is corrupted under the tutelage of his mentor Captain Hardenberg and he moves away from anything decent or Christian until, as Shaw put it, "finally he's a beast."[52] "I wanted to show how a man can start out decent, intelligent, well-meaning, as so many people in Germany must have been, even in the greatest days of Nazism—and wind up bestialized, almost bereft of humanity," Shaw said.[53] As the novel comes to its conclusion, the bestialized Christian, unaffected by what he witnesses in the death camps, is indefatigable in his drive to stay alive, doing what it takes—whether he needs to kill a prisoner or camp commandant—to stay alive. With the imminent end of hostilities, he still chooses to continue his war by sniping at the two American targets, Ackerman and Whitacre, who stand before him rather than compromise himself and surrender. For that decision, he pays the ultimate price.

In contrast, Edward Dmytryk's film adaptation turned Christian's character into that of a decent foot soldier who, over the course of the conflict, finally comes to understand the ugliness of war and the atrocities committed by the Nazis, about which he had known nothing. He is so overwrought from witnessing the horror firsthand, having stumbled into a concentration camp, that he wanders off from there aimlessly, a would-be suicide and easy target for a bullet from Michael Whitacre. Ilan Avisar points out that "Shaw had sought to expose the way war brutality affects the individual. . . . Christian does start out as a fairly innocent person. But he is corrupted into a monster as the typical product of the Nazi system."[54] Interestingly, Shaw was actually praised for presenting a sympathetic Nazi so soon after the war.[55] But Brando sought something else; he was looking for innocence in his character. He wanted to show a naive youth who is cajoled into acts of horror by a corrupt system, and then finally rebels. Producer Lichtman, Dmytryk, and Anhalt did give in to Brando, but they chose not to vacate German malevolence and instead used the character of Diestl's mentor Captain Hardenberg, brilliantly played by Maximilian Schell in his first American film, as the personification of Nazi evil. As Lawrence Baron points out, they "compensated for Brando's exoneration of Diestl by stressing the scope and severity of Germany's extermination of European Jewry and its ruthless repression of vanquished gentile populations."[56] This is seen through the two concentration camp scenes — the first being Christian's arrival at the concentration camp, the second when the Americans come to liberate the death camp.

REACTING TO THE HOLOCAUST

The very insertion of a concentration camp scene in a 1958 American film was unique, just as it had been for an American novel in 1948. Each of the Allied armies had units that recorded on film the horrors that they came across as death camps were liberated. But the commissioned films, intended either as evidence to be used in war tribunals, for denazification, or to "shake and humiliate the Germans,"[57] were almost never shown outside of Germany. One such film, *Memory of the Camps*, on which director Alfred Hitchcock worked, was left unfinished and was first shown in the United States only in 1985 on PBS television. Stuart Schulberg's *Nuremberg*, elements of which were lost or destroyed, was finally restored and screened in 2010 at the New York Film Festival. Orson Welles did choose to incorporate actual footage from the camps in his 1946 film *The Stranger*, but he did so with a purpose. Said Welles, "I do think that, every time you can get the public to look at any footage of a concentration camp, under any excuse at all, it's a step forward. People just don't want to know that those things ever happened."[58]

Explicit portrayals of the events in camps, put on film soon after the war, became commonplace in narrative movies made in East Germany, Poland, and Czechoslovakia, but American filmmakers stayed away. Peter Novick noted, "Between the end of the war and the 1960s, as anyone who has lived through those years can testify, the Holocaust made scarcely any appearance in American public discourse, and hardly more in Jewish public discourse — especially discourse directed to gentiles."[59] Leon Jick wrote that "American Jewry sought to forget" and "collaborated or at least acquiesced in [a] campaign to make the world forget."[60] Edward Shapiro felt that "revelations of the Holocaust did not have a significant impact on American public opinion immediately after the war. . . . Movies and books on the Holocaust would not make an impact in the United States until at least a decade after the war's end."[61] Hasia Diner, in her 2009 book *We Remember with Reverence and Love*, took to task a multitude of scholars and declared that their thesis was wrong, that the Holocaust was very much on the minds of Jews in America and that they did not shy away from commemorating it.[62] Whether one turns to Novick, Jick, Shapiro, Diner, or the myriad of other respected scholars who have written about how American Jewry reacted to the Holocaust in the postwar years, Irwin Shaw's best-selling 1948 book did not shy away from at least introducing the notion that Jews died in concentration camps. He made the connection through the Ackermans—Noah, Jacob, and Israel, the American Jew and the murdered Jews of Europe. Edward Dmytryk boldly refitted a concentration camp barracks and used it in his 1958 film to convey that horror.

RE-CREATING A CONCENTRATION CAMP

Irwin Shaw chose to include a scene in his novel where, on the eve of liberation, Christian, searching for food, wanders into a concentration camp. "A small group of soldier-writers did attempt to integrate the camps into a larger scheme of meaning which also had a personal existential referent," wrote Sidra Ezrahi.[63] Shaw describes the death camp as looking "like an ordinary Army camp, quite pleasant, in the middle of wide green fields, with the sloping forested hills behind it."[64] The ordinary quality of the description brings to mind Alain Resnais's 1955 film *Night and Fog*, made seven years later, in which with bitter irony Resnais presents and describes the "styles" and "architecture" of various concentration camps made to appear as retreat centers. Shaw describes the stench that Christian encounters; while nodding his head in the direction of the smell, Diestl questions a guard, "What have you got in there?" "The usual. Jews, Russians, some politicals, some people from Yugoslavia and Greece, places like that," is the answer provided.[65] Diestl makes no further inquiry or investigation, nor is there any discussion of what is taking place there. As James Giles noted, "Diestl's personal barbarism is tied directly to Germany's national guilt. . . . Instead of any moral pain at the sight of gas ovens and skeletal figures in prison uniforms, he is outraged by the smell of the camp and by the incompetence of its commanders."[66] A prisoner revolt ensues and Christian, consumed with finding a way to survive the onslaught, dons a prisoner's uniform and slowly works his way out of the camp, in the process executing the camp commandant in order to prove that he is part of the insurrection. For this brief moment, Christian is the survivor—struggling to live. Ezrahi wrote that Irwin Shaw's concentration camp "itself is not much more than a stage prop into which Christian Diestl wanders and from which . . . he manages to escape." [67] In many ways she is correct, but she misses Giles's point that this moment conveys the Austrian soldier's collusion, while affording Shaw, in the subsequent American liberation of the camp scene, the opportunity to provide a vivid description of death. "The smell was beyond the tolerance of human nostrils . . . could see the piled, bony forms . . . the pale twisting of lips on skulls . . . I am now at the center of the world." [68] In the novel, we meet the monstrous Christian Diestl, who for Shaw represents an entire German-speaking people complicit in this crime against humanity.

Christian Diestl, detached, unaware, and complicit in the book, plays a different role in the film, as he enters what David Rousset referred to as "*l'univers concentrationnaire*" — "the other kingdom." [69] We see barbed wire, a watchtower, a series of barracks, one guard on duty, a sign reading "Konzentrationslager Nackerholtz," but no prisoners. There, ostensibly seeking food, he begins a dialogue with the camp commandant dissimilar to that in the book. The film is much more revealing and descriptive, both visually and through its new dialogue, of the reality that was the death camp. Says the camp's commandant: "Running a concentration camp is not a picnic. Believe me, with all the gas chambers, target ranges, doctors with all the experiments. . . . I had an extermination quota of fifteen hundred people a day, Jews, Poles, Russians, French, political prisoners, and I had only 260 men to do it." In the novel, Christian's reaction is blasé; in the film it is one of disbelief, thus bringing more attention to the crime perpetrated by this camp commander and his fellow SS. In the book, the soldiers at the camp are *Volkssturm*, militia that arrived a week earlier to replace the SS; in the movie, they remain SS. "In Auschwitz they kill twenty thousand a day. They want me to kill every man, woman, and child before the Americans get here—six thousand people! . . . But the equipment is broken!" The SS commandant, speaking about the imminent arrival of the Americans, turns to Christian and says, "They may not understand that a good German officer—our kind of officer—does what he's ordered to do. . . . We at least know what's important . . . the honor to say, 'I have done my duty for the Fatherland.'" Just what is that duty, and should Christian be accountable? At this point Christian, seemingly in shock from what he has just heard, walks out the door in

American soldiers liberate the concentration camp.

Captain Green (in foreground) breaks open the barracks door to discover malnourished surviving concentration camp inmates. His only words are, "My God!" Arthur Franz plays Green. © 20th Century-Fox. 20th Century Fox Pictures/Photofest.

a daze. In the book, his actions or lack of reaction tie him to the crime; in the film, as Brando had wanted, he separates himself from the mass murderers.

AMERICAN LIBERATION AND GUARANTEES

Christian's visit to the camp in the film is followed by a new sequence in which the American platoon liberates the camp. The camera pans from Christian walking away into the field to American soldiers on the road just about to reach the camp, as drums begin to beat and military marching music is heard. When the crew was filming in Strasbourg, in Alsace province, they came across a concentration camp at Struthof, in the town of Schirmeck.[70] By 1957 the camp, which was the only Nazi extermination camp on French soil,[71] had become a tourist attraction, and Dmytryk felt that it would be perfect to use. There was double barbed-wire fencing and "20-foot-high, tarred telephone poles, double in depth and copiously strung with barbed wire."[72] It looked perfect. As they began filming, they learned that those running the site had actually added additional fencing and telephone poles to make it look even more authentic. The tourists wanted "greater realism" to make the site look more scary, more ominous, which worked well for the film.

The scene begins with a Nazi flag being lowered from a flagpole and Ackerman and Whitacre's platoon entering the camp, with gallows in the foreground. Soldiers surround one of the barracks. Captain Green, their commander, to make sure that there is no resistance from German soldiers within, shoots a round of bullets with his machine gun and opens the door. All the while, there is music of action and imminent victory. Then Green, ready to fire on any German who might be hiding inside, comes across bunks three-high in a room full of male inmates scattered across the room, on the floor, and stuffed into bunks. The music turns shrill as we see a walking skeleton coming toward Green, at which point Green's only words are "My God!" The visual is reminiscent of the classic photograph in which inmate Elie Wiesel lies among emaciated prisoners at Buchenwald. It is ghastly and powerful. To my knowledge, this was the first visual of its kind fashioned for American narrative cinema. Ironically, several of the extras in the scene who played inmates had themselves been prisoners in that same camp.[73]

The next scene pulls together all of the elements of the film and also brings the three protagonists together for the first and only time. Following the liberation scene, we again meet Captain Green, now overseeing the necessary actions needed at the camp. The Americans are carting away the dead, treating those near death, and feeding and caring for the weak and hungry. We were first introduced to Green as the lieutenant who showed sensitivity to a bruised Ackerman, who had been fighting with his fellow soldiers. In fact, Green would later replace the anti-Semitic Captain Colclough, who goes on to face charges for his anti-Semitism and failure to act and protect Ackerman. A scene where Colclough is berated by the colonel was added to the film in part to provide a positive face for the Army and to show how the military would respond to known acts of bigotry. It was clearly an effort to counteract the strongly negative portrayal of the American military in the novel. "There are many kinds of soldiers that we get in a war . . . men like Green, Emerson and a few officers like you—fortunately, only a few like you. Sometimes, we find you out. Occasionally, we don't. In your case, we've been lucky!" says the colonel in the film. Court martial papers are then proffered to Colclough. In the book, Colclough is never reprimanded, remains in command, and is only forced to leave the company when he shows cowardice in battle. Now, in this scene, Captain Green is in charge of the governance of the liberated camp. Green is a kind and compassionate person, a strong antithesis to officers Colclough in an American uniform and Hardenberg in a German one.

For Noah Ackerman, his arrival at the concentration camp is the culmination of an excursion that began in Shaw's book by his father's deathbed and in Dmytryk's film in Hope Plowman's Vermont. That journey then took him into his own personal war against anti-Semitism in the Army and through

Encountering a walking near-skeleton in the barracks. Some of the inmate roles in the film were played by actual camp survivors.

A surviving rabbi comes forward to request permission from the American liberators to hold a service for the survivors. The local mayor warns of the possibility of riots. Robert Ellenstein and John Banner, center. (Banner would later play Sergeant Schultz on television's Hogan's Heroes.)

the hell of battle. Now, he is face-to-face with hatred and toxicity on an entirely different plane. "The camp is the realization of that vision of the horror prophesied [in the book] by Noah's dying father," said James Giles.[74] Noah is the product of Irwin Shaw's imagination, and like the soldier-author, he is changed as a Jew by this war. He is the postwar American Jew who is forced by the events around him into acknowledging his Jewishness. As a result, he becomes a fuller, more complex and multidimensional person.

As officer in charge, Captain Green is meeting with the local German mayor (in the book, he is an Albanian prisoner), who has offered his services and those of local townspeople to "clean up the camp." During the introductions, a rabbi enters in inmate uniform to ask for a "luxury" — permission to gather the sick and dying for a religious service. He tells the captain that he wants to hold a service for the dead, "who have come to their end here" — a mass kaddish. Green pauses for a moment, as the mayor interjects and advises the captain that as a European, he understands things that the captain might not comprehend. He warns the officer that if services are held, there will be riots and that "the other prisoners will not stand for it." Further, he tells Green, "The generals who are coming will not like what they see!" All the while, Ackerman and Whitacre are in the room, and Ackerman, overwhelmed by what he hears, turns away aghast. Green gives the mayor a quizzical look and rhetorically repeats what the mayor has said, to which the mayor responds, "That's a fact. I guarantee it!" Green looks at him quietly and responds, "I'm gonna guarantee something myself." Looking at the rabbi, he goes on, "I'm gonna guarantee that you'll hold your services.

I'm also gonna guarantee that machine guns will be set up on the roofs of the buildings. And further, I will guarantee that anyone who interferes with those services will be fired upon by those machine guns. And further, I guarantee [looking at the mayor] that if you ever come into this place again, I will personally break your neck. That is all!" Ackerman, who has had his back turned, slowly turns around and is dismissed by his captain. As he walks outside, followed by Whitacre, a truck filled with dead bodies passes by on its way out of the camp.

This scene has a redemptive quality. The same Army that made Ackerman's life miserable in basic training because he was a Jew was now "guaranteeing" to a rabbi that he could hold religious services. Ackerman is taking it all in. "Did you ever imagine it could be like that?" he asks Whitacre. "My father's brother died in one of those" — the first time we learn in the movie of any connection to family in Europe and the final disposition of his uncle. "Did you see that? — The ovens!" This event is, for Noah, the final moment in his coming to terms with his Jewish identity. "When that guy started to talk to Green, I could've gone outside and blown my brains out. And then Green said, 'I guarantee! I guarantee!'. . . When this war is over, Green is gonna be running the world. There are millions of Greens . . . they're human beings." Now, through Green, Noah finds hope — a vision of a good and decent world.

As Noah and Michael find comfort on the road, we see Diestl on a hilltop above the two men, clearly distraught by what he witnessed in the camp. He takes his weapon and smashes it into pieces on a rock. The noise is heard from below and Whitacre, seeing the Austrian approaching, shoots him. Christian, mortally wounded, puts his sights on the two Americans and then falls down the hill into a large puddle below. A few bubbles come to the surface — Christian's last breaths. In Shaw's book, Christian takes aim at the two men below and then shoots, his gun jamming after two shots. Here Noah is the one who is mortally wounded. Giles felt that "Noah had to die to symbolize the incalculable horror of the Nazis' crimes against the Jewish people and against humanity."[75] But Michael has not been hurt, and he hunts down his friend's fleeing murderer, finally finding him in the woods and shooting him dead. Christian's last words to Michael, in a mocking way, are "Welcome to Germany!" Shaw contrasts this moment of ridicule with how Hope's father welcomed Noah to Vermont and invited him home. Only now, just as hostilities are coming to an end, this American is welcomed by a different kind of Christian. The Austrian Christian Diestl welcomes Michael Whitacre to

Captain Green, representing the American army, "guarantees" a religious service for the survivors. Arthur Franz.

Whitacre and Ackerman are amazed by what they have witnessed. "When this war is over, Green is gonna be running the world. There are millions of Greens . . . they're human beings." Dean Martin, Montgomery Clift.

the country that brought about a world war, death camps, and the senseless murder of his buddy.

In the film, Diestl dies because his faith is shattered. In a way, he dies for the sins of his people, his adoptive country. In an earlier sequence, the SS camp commandant alluded to the fact that he, who had been at the death camp for a short time, would be held accountable, while those truly responsible would most likely go free. Now, Diestl, without a weapon, is shot dead. This is the characterization that Brando had carved out, and he wanted to take it even further:

> As usual, he [Brando] came to Dmytryk with a suggested change. Instead of just falling down the hill and dying face-down in a puddle of water, why couldn't he land on a roll of barbed wire and have one of the strands encircle and cut into his forehead like Christ's crown of thorns? It wasn't to be a death scene, but a crucifixion.
>
> For some reason, Dmytryk seriously entertained the idea, until Monty came over to him and said, "If Marlon does that, I'm going home."
>
> Brando immediately conceded, without ill feeling, but for some reason the whole incident got blown out of proportion when the press got hold of it. According to the endless published accounts, the story presumably is symbolic of the rivalry between Monty and Brando for top-dog status as Christ figures.[76]

That Christian Diestl evolves from being the epitome of evil in the novel to an innocent casualty of war in the film infuriated writer Irwin Shaw, who had cast Austrian soldier Diestl's lot with that of all Nazis. Ten years after the novel's publication, Dmytryk, Anhalt, and Brando had toned down the innate evil of the character to represent an emerging individual in the Cold War period: the "good German."

Though we are made to empathize with Christian, the ugly Nazi and his mass-murder machine remains just as evil in the film, as seen through Captain Hardenberg's hideousness and by expanding the ugly fiber of the concentration camp commandant, now a member of the SS. In addition, making the individual who protests the holding of a religious service a local German mayor rather than an Albanian camp inmate (as in the novel) more forcefully accentuates the complicit nature of Germans and the local populations who lived near the camps. With *The Young Lions* and films that followed, like *The Diary of Anne Frank* (1959) and *Judgment at Nuremberg* (1960), American Jews became more fully aware of the atrocities and more closely connected to the Holocaust.

Irwin Shaw, like his creation Noah Ackerman, sought total acceptance and assimilation into American society. Affirmation on that level was more easily found in America of the late 1950s, during the years when greater acceptance of all Americans was more fully guaranteed, not just by a Captain Green, but by institutions like the U.S. Supreme Court, Congress, and the presidency. In 1957, President Eisenhower sent federal troops to Arkansas to protect black students' entry to all-white Little Rock Central High School. The next year, the Supreme Court, in *Cooper v. Aaron*, affirmed that federal courts would not tolerate efforts to evade integration. In that decade, social theorist Will Herberg introduced the notion of a tri-faith American society, in which Jews were joined by Catholics and Protestants.[77] The synagogue was cast as an American institution and the practice of any religion was deemed respectable. The idea of "Americans All" dictated to all Christians that they had to be "neighborly," including in places like Mr. Plowman's Vermont. Jews, in the aftermath of the Holocaust and with the nascent State of Israel, were more readily prepared to fight for their rightful place in America and connected in a more meaningful way to other Jews both at home and around the world. Finally, a Noah Ackerman could partner with a Michael Whitacre and the rest of the platoon, in a new universe where it would be the Greens who are "gonna be running the world."

THE WAY WE WERE AND
THE PRINCE OF TIDES

BARBRA STREISAND AND THE
EVOLVING AMERICAN JEWISH WOMAN

STREISAND

The Barbra Streisand phenomenon looms large in the annals of twentieth-century popular culture. Hers is the story, set in the late 1950s, of an unabashed sixteen-year-old Jewish woman who, after graduating high school, left Brooklyn for Manhattan in search of a dream. Barbara Joan Streisand, like many of her time, wanted to be an actor and set her sights high. Her story, or rather the story of her generation, is captured in such films as Paul Mazursky's *Next Stop, Greenwich Village* (1976) and Sidney J. Furie's *Sheila Levine Is Dead and Living in New York* (1975), adapted from Gail Parent's novel. Streisand's sheer tenacity got her past early rejections to move her forward to finally attain recognition and stardom. She was the *fabrent* (on fire) child, as biographer Christopher Anderson called her, who refused to take no for an answer.[1] Though landing a career as an actress was her ultimate goal, early on she realized that her voice, which she had been led to believe was mediocre at best, was her ticket to that end. At eighteen, now spelling her name Barbra, she was singing at a chic Greenwich Village club. A few weeks short of her nineteenth birthday, she was on national television. Not yet twenty, Streisand received the accolades she had long sought for her performance on Broadway as Miss Mermelstein in *I Can Get It for You Wholesale* and soon thereafter landed a record contract with Columbia. Almost twenty-two, Barbra Streisand was back on Broadway, this time in a leading role as Fanny Brice in *Funny Girl*. Streisand was the Jewish kid from Brooklyn who had made it across the bridge!

That Barbra would play Fanny Brice was more than coincidence. Fanny Brice (née Fania Borach) was born on New York's Lower East Side in 1891, and with her talent as a physical comedienne, her beautiful voice, and incredible grace, she quickly became one of Florenz Ziegfeld Jr.'s greatest Folly stars. Brice found that her flair for dialects, particularly Yiddish (which she did not even know), provided her with work at a time when ethnic stereotyping was popular onstage and in cinema. Brice's "Semitic looks" often relegated her to playing Jewish roles, and in her early thirties, as biographer Barbara Grossman writes, she "tired of being a sight gag" and had her nose surgically straightened. Dorothy Parker (herself half-Jewish) joked at the time that Brice had "cut off her nose to spite her race,"[2] something that Streisand two generations later refused to do. Streisand and Brice's lives would become interconnected not only because of the similarities, but because it was Brice's story that brought Barbra Streisand in contact with Brice's son-in-law, Ray Stark, and to Broadway for her first lead role.

After Fanny Brice's death in 1951, writer Norman Katkov wrote a biography that horrified Brice's daughter, Frances. Frances's husband Ray Stark, then a successful Hollywood agent, paid Katkov a considerable sum of money *not* to license out the book and then went on to try to turn Brice's life story into a movie. When that failed, he turned to Jule Styne and Stephen Sondheim to create a musical. After several years, armed with a book by Isobel Lennart, music by Styne, and lyrics by Bob Merrill, Stark together with Styne turned to producer David Merrick to ready the musical for the stage. But who would play Fanny? Various leads were considered, from Mary Martin to Anne Bancroft and Carol Burnett. In the end, Styne, after hearing Streisand perform in *I Can Get It for You Wholesale*, was sold on her and began reworking the music with her in mind. The other actors had more experience and recognizable names, but the part of the Jewish girl from the Lower East Side seemed to have been written for this new singing sensation. Streisand's physical appearance certainly helped land her the role. Though many persons during Streisand's rise to stardom had advised her to alter her "Jewish-looking" nose and change her appearance, this very self-assured talent never did those things. Barbra Streisand also never shied away from connecting with the Jewish aspects of her new role as Fanny, nor would she ever do so in any future role that came her way.

Barbra Streisand is a star performer, one of the most talented artists of our day. Vocalist, actor, producer, director, writer, political activist, and consummate entertainer are but a few of the ways that she can be described. Unlike other artists who have gone to extremes not to be seen as identifiably Jewish, Streisand has embraced her Judaism. She was an unabashed Jew, at a time in America when barriers could be broken. The Jewish women she has portrayed on film have always been intelligent, self-assured, and compelling. Her Jewish connectedness surfaces in many of her films and even in some of the songs she chooses to include in her repertoire. Jewish identity is an important part of who she is.

A PROJECT FOR BARBRA

Barbra Streisand was an immense success in *Funny Girl* and, again with Streisand in the lead role, the play was adapted in 1968 for the screen. Streisand was recognized for her amazing performance, sharing a best actress Oscar with Katherine Hepburn. Almost immediately, producer Ray Stark began searching for new film projects for her, and in 1970, he produced the comedy *The Owl and the Pussycat*, starring Streisand and George Segal. Next, he turned to Arthur Laurents to write a screenplay for her. Laurents, who wrote the books for the musicals *West Side Story* and *Gypsy*, had a decade earlier directed Barbra in *I Can Get It for You Wholesale*. Laurents immediately went to work developing a story about a woman similar to Barbra in her Jewishness, with an activist passion for reform. He drew from his own past to pull together the story of Katie Morosky, basing her character on a Jewish woman he had known in college who was a member of the Young Communist League. He had always been struck by this woman's passion and it left an indelible memory. She was special! She was on a mission, an assignment to repair the world!

Barbra understood this girl and this character seemed made for her. Streisand, like many Jews of her generation, has been politically active. She sang and campaigned in New York for John Lindsay and Bella Abzug. She volunteered for George McGovern's 1968 presidential campaign and performed with James Taylor and Carole King at a much-heralded concert for him in Los Angeles. The late 1960s and early 1970s were a time of great upheaval, and for many in Hollywood, certainly for Laurents and Streisand, a political story that might turn people's heads was of great interest. Setting the story decades earlier allowed Laurents much more freedom to tackle im-

Producer Ray Stark and director Sidney Pollack on the set.
© Columbia Pictures. Columbia Pictures/Photofest.

portant issues of the day. Streisand, when asked whether she might consider running for office so that she could bring about change, responded that she felt she could do more politically through her films than as an elected official. Democratic politics was and still remains important for Streisand and is in many respects part of her Jewishness. "Many American Jews were raised with the understanding that liberalism or political radicalism constituted the very essence of Judaism," observed sociologist Steven M. Cohen.[3] Jews have historically been connected to liberal movements in this country, particularly in immigrant communities, since the turn of the twentieth century.

A political story represented a risk for producer Stark. Many in Hollywood were concerned, for this was the time when President Richard Nixon, in his attempt to "renew" America, had chosen to attack the media and liberal-left intellectuals, whom he saw as the enemy. Would Hollywood once again become a target for the government, as it has been in the late 1940s? What of its Jews? Director Sydney Pollack tells the story of how he ran into an executive from Columbia Pictures, the company that was to distribute the film for Ray Stark's production company, Rastar Productions. "Have you lost your mind? Making a film about a Communist Jew who goes to Hollywood?" Pollack understood that the story that Laurents had written, set against the background of the 1947 investigation of Hollywood by the House Committee on Un-American Activities (HUAC), was risky.[4] Everyone was acutely aware that the president himself had been a member of that committee when he was in Congress. Moviemakers had assiduously avoided dealing with portraying HUAC and the blacklist in mainstream cinema. All the same, Stark and company would not be deterred.

The female protagonist was drawn from Laurent's fiery radical college classmate, Fanny Price. Laurents described her as "a colorful beginning for the character of my heroine." The 1937 peace strike for Spain at the beginning of the film was modeled on an actual event that took place at Cornell, where Laurents went to college. "Its objective was to stop the civil war in Spain. . . . *Fanny Price* — small wonder Barbra reminded me of her — was both the prime motivator and prime obstacle to the strike."[5] Laurents loved his character, just as he greatly admired Barbra. The character evolved:

> In the end, Fanny was indestructible, a phoenix, and her name wasn't Fanny, it was Katie. . . . Katie because like Becky or Jenny, it was Jewish but less pointedly. She had to be a Jew; Barbra herself had arrived as one. Not flaunting, not defying, just simply declaring at Hollywood Customs: Here is a Jewish movie star. And Katie could only be a Jew because of her insistence on speaking out, her outrage at injustice, her passion, her values, and because I was a Jew. Besides, it was fresher and high time that the movies, the only industry founded by Jews, has a Jewish heroine.[6]

As the story evolved, Katie would be a plain-looking, frizzy-haired, politically active Jewish coed from the late 1930s who was "too passionate about too much." For Streisand, this "felt natural."[7] Arthur gave his character not only a fervor for politics, but one for writing as well, which mirrored his own. But as Laurents would write, "Prudish and naive, she was more fighter than female. . . . 'Katie Morosky' suited Barbra Streisand and sounded like a Jewish Communist who became fiercely romantic because she had to put her excess passion somewhere."[8] That passion would be directed toward the most unlikely of people — Hubbell Gardner, a handsome, blond, white Anglo-Saxon Protestant campus *jock*.

As Paul Cowan saw it, *The Way We Were* was "the realization of a Jewish fantasy of America and a Protestant American's fantasy of a Jew."[9] What separated the two were the characters' "ethnic styles," rather than any conflicting religious commitments. Cowan claims that this ethnic style goes back to the turn of the century, as the immigrant Jew sought something special, a sort of acceptance from the "American." He points to the relationship portrayed between an Orthodox Jewish young woman and her Protestant teacher in Anzia Yezierska's 1920 short story "The Miracle" as a case in point:

> My teacher was so much above me that he wasn't a man to me at all. He was a God. His face lighted up the shop for me, and his voice sang itself in me everywhere I went. It was healing medicine to the flaming fever within me to listen to his voice. And then I'd repeat to myself his words and live in them as if they were religion . . .

The woman speaks to him in a similarly passionate vein:

> "I'm afraid of my heart," I said, trying to hold back the blood rushing to my face. "I'm burning to get calm and sensible like the born Americans. But how can I help it? My heart flies away from me like a wild bird. How can I learn to keep myself down on earth like the born Americans?"

To which he responds:

> "But I don't want you to get down on earth like the Americans. This is just the beauty and the wonder of you. We Americans are too much on earth; we need more of your power to fly. If you would only know how much you teach us Americans. You are the promise of the centuries to come. You are the heart, the creative pulse of America to be."[10]

JEWS AND GENTILES

Throughout the first part of the twentieth century, American Jews had traditionally concentrated themselves in a very few urban communities. Within these communities, they followed a restricted number of occupations and settled in strongly ethnic neighborhoods (e.g., *Avalon*). By the mid-1950s, Jews were experiencing greater prosperity, and with suburbanization and the movement of Jews to different geographic areas (consider *Liberty Heights*), there was what sociologist Marshall Sklare called "a reduction in Jewish-gentile differentials."[11] More and more, the demographic profile of Jews approximated that of the general community; this strongly contributed to a growing acceptance of Jews. As sociologist Samuel Heilman noted, "What counted was what a person achieved by dint of his or her own efforts and accomplishments."[12] A 1972 survey carried out by the U.S. Census Bureau compared eight different ethnic groups: Jews had the highest median family income; the highest percentage of white-collar workers; and the highest percentage of high-school and college graduates. The survey showed that Jews were also finding their way into an increasing number of prestigious universities.[13] Observed Marshall Sklare:

> The effect of traditional Jewish culture on the individual was what made possible the achievement of an extraordinary high level of secular learning, and the result has been that although many Jews are no more than second- or third-generation Americans, the educational profile of the Jewish group resembles that of the most favored Protestant denominations of the old immigration.[14]

The educated Jew, at least on the college campus, was now on equal footing with the educated non-Jew. This is fascinating in light of how Arthur Laurents uses the college campus as the stage for the first meeting between Katie Morosky, Jewish, and Hubbell Gardner, Protestant. Otherwise, how and where could these two people, so different from each other and from completely different backgrounds, have met?

On a different level, this entrée of the Jew to the "academy" had some detrimental implications. In 1974, Sklare saw a remarkable trend in America. He noted the educational achievement of American Jews as having "important implications for group identity and cohesion":

> Higher education may have the effect of reducing family solidarity, and reduced family solidarity may produce a weakened group identity. Higher education may also have the effect of raising the rate of intermarriage. . . . the individual may become alienated from the same Jewish community whose culture initially impelled him to pursue educational attainment.[15]

Sidney Goldstein, in his 1970 demographic profile of American Jewry, noted:

It would be ironic if the very strong value that Jews traditionally have placed on education and that now manifests itself in the very high proportion of Jewish youths attending college may be an important factor in the general weakening of the individual's ties to the Jewish community.[16]

Higher education made it easier for Jew and gentile to interact and get to know each better, with all kinds of ramifications, some of which can be seen in *The Way We Were*.

Katie Morosky represents the archetypal Jew of the period. Jewish women "drew upon the political commitments that had animated the urban, working-class environments in which they had spent their formative years, even as they moved into their new, middle-class communities."[17] Though Katie's character lives in the middle part of the century, she is very much the Jewish woman of the 1970s, a product also of the civil rights and women's movements. "The social upheavals of the late 1960s and early 1970s further eroded white Christian hegemony and validated the legitimacy of diverse ethnic traditions," wrote Sylvia Barack Fishman.[18] With Katie's Jewish upbringing came a drive toward higher education, and with that came her political activism and hope for reform, for *tikkun olam* — the chance to repair the world, to make it a better place.

The year 1973, when *The Way We Were* was filmed, saw an end to U.S. involvement in the war in Vietnam. With that came the demise of the antiwar movement and the radicalism that had been so much a part of the college life of the times. The movie audience sees Katie, in her call for support of loyalist Spain in the midst of a civil war, as reflective of a 1970s activist fighting for an end to all wars. Katie is a strong-willed Jewish woman, keenly aware of the events spiraling around her, and Laurents uses this inner strength throughout the film as her modus operandi. That Katie is a forceful woman was extremely important for Streisand. In a reversal of traditional movie stereotypes, the female protagonist here is strong, while Hubbell (Robert Redford), the male protagonist, at least in the initial film treatment, comes across as only a pretty face and sex object.[19]

"Different roles have given me the opportunity to show different qualities that I admire and respect in women," Streisand told an interviewer.[20] Women in America were actively taking on a greater role in shaping what America was all about, and Barbra Streisand could very well have been a poster child for the women's movement. When presented with Arthur Laurents's treatment, these qualities in Katie are certainly what attracted Streisand to the project.[21] Not only did the story suit her, but there were a number of potential scenes — she counted five — that were incredibly powerful and challenging for her to undertake. "I just knew her," said the actress.[22] Streisand also recognized something in this story, what biographer Tom Santopietro called "that once-in-a-lifetime opportunity which defines true movie stardom: the chance to play the idealized version of herself and thereby cement permanent fan identification."[23]

Robert Redford, on the other hand, found the part of Hubbell quite limited. After several revisions of the script and a great deal of persuasion by his friend Sydney Pollack, who was to direct the film, he finally came on board. In a November 2010 episode of *The Oprah Winfrey Show* that brought Redford and Streisand together for the first time in over thirty years, Redford related that he had agreed to do the film only after the changes were made to his character. "Otherwise, I would be a Ken doll, you know? . . . That's for somebody else."[24]

In college Katie Morosky had been a strong-willed activist with an independent streak who passed out leaflets for loyalist Spain. But we first encounter her as an assistant radio producer who is trying to insert political material into the radio scripts being produced for the Office of War Information. It is 1945, and she gets invited by her boss to a club, where she immediately shows her assertiveness, berating the maitre d' for not allowing men in uniform to enter. Within a few moments the camera pans the bar and finds a golden-haired man in Navy "whites" sitting upright on a stool at the bar, asleep. The camera zooms in, just to make sure that we know whom both we and Katie are staring at — and that is our introduction to Hubbell Gardner.

Katie makes her way over to Hubbell and brushes the hair off his forehead, an image that will punctuate the film. After a few moments of staring — by Katie, by ourselves, and the camera — there is a fade-out to Hubbell, a lone runner jogging through the woods and college campus. Hubbell Gardner is, in a unique 1970s role reversal, the male object of every woman's attention. And so begins our story, with Marvin Hamlisch's Academy Award–winning score heard in the background.

As the opening titles appear onscreen, we are introduced to our two key players in a montage of opposites. Katie is the young, somewhat homely bookworm, who is either studying or working so that her education can be paid for. Hubbell is the campus leader, whose good looks and athletic prowess are about to be placed on display. Katie is busy plastering the walls with Strike! signs, while Hubbell competes in track events and sculling

Katie, now a successful radio producer, comes across Hubbell, who has had too much to drink. She will not be able to resist brushing the hair off his forehead. Robert Redford, Barbra Streisand. © Columbia Pictures. Columbia Pictures/Photofest.

competitions. On the sidelines, we hear classmates rooting on their hero: "Gardner, Gardner!" as all the while Streisand's voice can be heard singing Hamlisch's "Memories" in the background. We see Hubbell having a bite at the local restaurant with an attractive coed, while Katie works behind the counter. Then there are the young women practicing ballroom dancing in their sorority as the camera pans out of the room, through the window, and down, to show us Katie looking up from outside, at a part of campus life that she, the outsider, either cannot or chooses not to have. Hubbell's javelin toss and discus throw are contrasted with Katie, with her passion for writing, sitting at the typewriter, a photograph of Lenin prominently on display in the background. Last, there is a touch-football match on the lawn with Hubbell and friends, as Katie stands at the linotype press readying leaflets for a peace rally. This opening sequence is beautifully filmed and provides a dazzling introduction to the characters. There are few words heard, and yet we understand: Katie and Hubbell, geographically on the same college campus, are worlds apart.

*The all-American Hubbell Gardner seems to excel
in everything he does. Robert Redford.*

*While Hubbell races, Katie gets ready for the peace rally.
James Wood, Barbra Streisand.*

KATIE

Arthur Laurents created a Jewish woman of obvious working-class roots, somewhat on the periphery—outside of college leisure activity—who must work her way through college. To her character he opposed Hubbell Gardner, a gentile man of privilege—although we never know him to be *too* privileged—who is a leader and hero on campus. He is the object of everyone's attention, while she seems of little consequence, that is, until the peace-strike scene that opens as the titles and theme song end. There, on-stage, speaking for peace, she captures everyone's attention, in particular Hubbell's—the camera makes sure that we see this by zooming in on his face. Although she speaks to her audience only for a few moments, she captivates them and impresses him. At that moment, we know that Hubbell recognizes something special, unique, and deep about Katie, and during a subsequent sequence at the restaurant between customer and server, he ac-

Katie, dressed in red, addresses students at the peace rally. Barbra Streisand.
© Columbia Pictures. Columbia Pictures/Photofest.

The students, including Hubbell, seem dazzled by Katie's powerful words,
at least initially. Lois Chiles, Robert Redford.

cords her some respect, unlike the friends he has sitting with him. Next, we follow Katie's schoolgirl stares at him in the library, and finally we see the selection of Hubbell's essay by the English professor. It is Hubbell Gardner's essay, not Katie's, that is chosen. As much as she is hurt that her work was overlooked, she has a newborn respect for this talented writer.

Though this film is set in the 1930–1950s, it is essential to understand that it is really about the 1970s, when it was made. With the reading of Hubbell's essay, we are introduced to his world. "In a way, he was like the country he lived in. Everything came too easily to him . . ." We begin to understand this man and the world of the enfranchised 1970s "WASP." Katie, in contrast, works so hard at her writing, yet in the end it is Hubbell's work that is selected. At this point, Katie seems to fall for Hubbell Gardner—the guy who always seems to have it too easy but who also has talent. Katie becomes frustrated and tears up her writing. Arthur Laurents explained:

> The passion she'd poured into writing, what was she to do with that now that she faced she had no talent? Another cause? Just more of the same. Pour into a person? Not intentionally. Not unless it was in spite of herself. A person who was everything she wasn't; a person who was unattainable; a fantasy; a beautiful blond goy.[25]

A relationship between a Jewish woman and a gentile man was, by 1973, not crazy fiction. Steven M. Cohen found that increased education adversely influenced ritual observance, one way of measuring Jewish identification.[26] Sociologist Egon Mayer noted that "while the percentage of Jews who mar-

Katie and Hubbell truly love each other, but can such a relationship last? Barbra Streisand, Robert Redford. © Columbia Pictures. Columbia Pictures/Photofest.

ried persons of non-Jewish origins had remained relatively constant from the early 1940s to the end of the 1950s, it nearly *doubled*, quite suddenly, from the end of the fifties to the midsixties, and nearly *tripled* from the midsixties to the early seventies." [27] The national intermarriage rate in the 1970s was at 28 percent. [28] What is fascinating to see in *The Way We Were*, and why this picture is so important for understanding the Jewish condition of the time, is how different and yet in love these two seemed to be. In the previous generation, Jews were "accepted" by their Christian neighbors. By the 1970s, America had begun a courtship with its Jews. But could that relationship last? Katie and Hubbell are representative of that time — a love affair between the all-American boy and the American Jewish girl. The campus environment provided a meeting ground for the Jew and non-Jew who, coming from very different socioeconomic worlds, otherwise might not have met and interacted. Arthur Laurents, coming from Katie's Brooklyn, had experienced an entirely new world when he arrived at Cornell. In the case of Katie and Hubbell, the extent of their interaction was initially cursory (as seen by the casual encounter between the two at the onset of the college sequence, as Hubbell jogs past Katie, who is handing out leaflets on the campus green), but as the film moves forward, their connection evolves — in the classroom, at campus gatherings, and at events on and off campus.

COMING TOGETHER

After the college flashback, we return to the bar, where Katie sees Hubbell after years of separation. Hubbell is inebriated and happily goes with Katie to her apartment to sleep off his drunkenness. Katie looks different than she did in college. She is well dressed, with her hair no longer curly; she now straightens it with an iron. We never are quite sure that Hubbell fully recognizes her, since his only spoken remark upon seeing her is, "What do you know!" twice repeated. After making it up several flights of stairs to her apartment, he finds the bathroom, duly vomits, and then Katie, emerging from the kitchen where she has gone to prepare tea, finds him in her bed. Awakened by a whistling teakettle, naval officer Hubbell instinctively cries out "General's Quarters. Countdown. Stand Safe!" as if he is aboard ship. For Katie, it is a sort of alarm, but she does the opposite of standing safe — she undresses and crawls into bed next to him. As she lies naked next to this man whom she has adored since college days, she at once pulls a sheet up

Katie finally has Hubbell in bed with her, but is he even aware of it? Barbra Streisand, Robert Redford. © Columbia Pictures. Columbia Pictures/Photofest.

over her body as a sort of protection while moving her hands over his forehead, desirous of again brushing his hair. Her face alternates from a smile of delight to one of fright at what is happening—somehow this Jewish woman has gotten the gentile man of her dreams into her bed. He turns, caresses her, and then goes on to make love with her, as all the while music comes up in the background. But, in his drunken stupor, is he just reacting to a warm body? Does he actually know what is taking place? Does his sexual act have greater meaning? He lies on her, seemingly asleep, as she reminds him, "Hubbell, it's Katie! You do know it's Katie!"

The next morning, as Hubbell takes leave and thanks Katie for her hospitality, it becomes clear that the events of the night before are unknown to him. Laurents and Pollack played with different possibilities for this scene, ranging from Hubbell acknowledging their having had sex to the scenario that remained in the film. It is striking that the pure, clean, golden-haired, white-clad gentile American has to be in college to interact with a Jewish woman and needs to be drunk to fall into a Jewish bed. As the script dictates, the seduction by the Jewess of the WASP seems plausible only because it happens without his knowledge.

The real coming together of the two protagonists eventually happens when Hubbell returns to New York and needs a couch on which to sleep. Their relationship evolves slowly, but they finally do fall in love and become a couple. A central question in the film is why these two individuals from very different worlds are drawn to each other and whether they can sustain that relationship. The pull of opposites becomes believable as we watch their courtship evolve. They are truly in love and, in many ways, quite good for each other. At the same time, whether it's their politics, their whole approach to life, their values, or religion, it is the differences that will eventually cause a breakup. Hubbell seems ready to adapt to any situation.[29] Katie, on the other hand, may modify her politics with time, no longer being the staunch antiwar radical she was on campus in 1937, but she still takes every opportunity to try to better America.

We have no sense of Hubbell's religious connection, but Katie's Jewishness remains unapologetic, whether she wishes Hubbell "Happy Rosh Hashonoh" when presenting him with the gift of a typewriter or jokingly provides a title for a mock "eastern" film, "Shavuos!"[30] These ad libs were just some of the Jewish elements that Streisand brought to the film.[31] When she tells Hubbell that he is about to become a father, she does so by relating a story: "Loudmouth Jewish girl from New York City comes to Malibu, California, and tells her gorgeous *Goyishe* guy that, uh [he interrupts her by proclaiming 'Great alliteration'] she's pregnant and he just . . ." Though this scene is set in the forties, Streisand represents that Jewish woman of the 1970s who seeks out America, with strong Jewish convictions to make it a better place, while believing that she can meld with the rest of America. As Patricia Erens pointed out, "Here we see the Jew's passion for social justice and change, and belief in a world where all outsiders may be accepted."[32]

But just how easily is Katie accepted into Hubbell's world? Katie, the strong-willed Jewish woman, wants in. She may temporarily conquer Hubbell, but will she ever be made to feel comfortable in Hubbell Gardner's Protestant world—what she terms "Beekman Place"?[33] "It is the oddball's impulse to be what passes for normal, the minority desire to be part of the majority, the outsider's attempt to get inside," wrote Barry Gross, describing Katie's motives.[34] Katie Morosky is truly an outsider in that world, temporarily entering it as Hubbell's wife, but never fully accepted. "Your friends make me feel like I'm invited for drinks and everyone else is staying for dinner!" Katie tells Hubbell. Whether she makes herself unwelcome or whether they simply reject her almost does not matter. Katie still remains on the outside.

From the start, it is clear that the union of these two most different personalities cannot succeed, despite their love for each other. Hubbell's "Beekman Place" world is a sphere where Katie the Jew can never really fit. She may iron her hair to be like them, but in the end she turns to him and asks, "I'm not attractive in the right way, am I?" Their differences are too strong, and Hubbell's infidelity is the last straw. "To the end, you'll always be a nice Jewish girl," he tells her. "And are you still a nice gentile boy?" she asks. In the original treatment, these differences are intermingled with strong political dissimilarity — Katie's left-wing politics will lose Hubbell his job. Not only are their politics so different, but now *her* politics are about to adversely impact upon *his* life. She comes up with the idea of divorcing him so as to remove any taint attached to him. But for a variety of reasons, mostly length and concern that the film might be deemed too political, a great deal about HUAC and blacklisting was kept out of the final cut of the film.[35] The two do have a child, and Hubbell stays with Katie until the child, whom she names Rokhl, or Rachel, is born. In the end, really more because of politics than anything else, as Streisand has posited, Katie and Hubbell go their separate ways.[36]

The final scene is set in front of New York's Plaza hotel some years later, in the fifties. Katie has returned "home" to New York, allowed her hair to return to its natural curls, and is back on the street protesting, this time against use of the atomic bomb. As she approaches the area she spots Hubbell about to get into a cab with an attractive blonde woman. They see each other and she quickly moves across the street to greet him. After an exchange of pleasantries, we will learn that Katie is married to a Jewish doctor named David X. Cohen and has retreated into the New York Jewish world where she can feel most comfortable, and that Hubbell is writing for television. She leaves him to go off to her protest work across the street, when he follows her to join her. "You never give up, do you?" he asks. "Only when I am absolutely forced to!" is her response. In a very real way, this is not just Katie responding, but Streisand herself, the consummate overachiever. She continues, "But I'm a very good loser." His response: "Better than I am." To which she adds, "But I've had more practice." We the audience somehow wanted this relationship between opposites — between Jew and gentile, between blond and brunette, between two such different actors and characters — to work, even if we find the idea of intermarriage problematic. At this concluding moment of the film, they remain very much in love, though clearly they are not able to be with each other. As director Pollack observed, "The central appeal of the film is the chemistry and yearning between these two people for an impossible romance — a romance that they want and we want for them, but they can't have.[37] We also question how a father can so totally cut himself off from his child and wonder whether there might be other opportunities for these two to meet again.[38] Katie gives one more brush of Hubbell's bangs and there is one last embrace. As Hubbell retreats back across the street to hop into the cab, the theme music is heard and Katie's passion again takes form with her calls to "Ban the bomb!" The Jewish woman has taken her place in American society, comfortable in what she does but not quite ready or able to stand side-by-side with a gentile man. She truly, as she tells him, "want[s] us to love each other," very much as the 1970s Jew wanted to be loved and accepted by America. When Katie asked Hubbell if he was "still a nice gentile boy," he responded, "I never was; you only imagined it!" There was indeed a romance, but it was an "impossible" romance.

ONWARD

With *The Way We Were*, Barbra Streisand quickly became one of the most successful actresses in Hollywood. She went on to star in *For Pete's Sake* (1974), followed the next year by *Funny Lady*, again working with Ray Stark in a film dramatization of Fanny Brice's relationship with showman Billy Rose. In 1976, she served as executive producer and starred in *A Star is Born* opposite Kris Kristofferson, and after a three-year film hiatus made *The Main Event* with Ryan O'Neal. After the 1981 critical fiasco *All Night Long*, with Gene Hackman, she set her teeth into adapting Isaac Bashevis Singer's "Yentl the Yeshiva Boy." The filmmaking process would surely be a challenge, but Streisand believed in this story (though most studio executives resisted) of a young Jewish woman who wanted equality both as a Jew and as a woman — it was very much Barbra's story. The film dealt with the relationship between a father and daughter, and Barbra saw it as a way of connecting to her father, who had passed away when she was only a year old; the film is dedicated to his memory. For over a decade, Barbra peddled the story to one studio executive after another, to no avail. Finally, David Begelman, executive at United Artists and Barbra's former agent, agreed to take on the project. Streisand would produce, direct, cowrite (with Jack Rosenthal), and star in this daring film about a girl who assumes the identity of a boy in order to find her place in Jewish society, an idea not used onscreen since Molly Picon played Yidl in the Polish-made Yiddish-language *Yidl Mitn Fidl* over thirty years before.

In order to properly prepare for the adaptation of I. B. Singer's "Yentl," Streisand spent many hours examining Judaism, visiting synagogues, observing Jewish ceremonies, and studying Jewish culture and music. She also became a benefactor of many of the Jewish institutions that helped her. Much to everyone's surprise, the film was well received and did extremely well in box office receipts; Streisand also released a soundtrack recording that was highly profitable. Who could have imagined that a film about a girl who becomes a boy in order to study Jewish texts at a yeshiva could not only be made in America, but seen by hundreds of thousands around the world? Though LA's Academy of Motion Picture Arts and Sciences failed that year even to nominate her for an Oscar in any category, *Yentl* proved that Barbra Streisand could not only act and sing, but produce, write, and direct. Four years after *Yentl*, Barbra would make *Nuts*, a film in which she costarred with Richard Dreyfuss and which she coproduced. It would be four more years before she decided to undertake another major movie project; this time she would not only produce, but direct and play the lead! It would be *The Prince of Tides*. Now the story of a Jewish woman and her relationship with a non-Jewish man would take on a different look than it had in *The Way We Were*. One thing would stay the same: Barbra Streisand would play the part of that Jewish woman.

THE PRINCE OF TIDES

Pat Conroy's semi-autobiographical novel came out in 1986, and Andrew Karsch, a business associate of Conroy's, set out to produce the film. Apparently, Robert Redford was initially interested in playing the lead, but he bowed out. Then, as the film's adaptation was moving forward, MGM/UA, the studio that was to produce the film, ran out of money and backed out of the project. Streisand spent the next year searching for another studio to underwrite production, when former boyfriend Jon Peters, now cochairman at Columbia Pictures, stepped forward and worked out a deal. Streisand, who had been working with screenwriter Becky Johnston on the adaptation of the novel, wanted to consult with author Pat Conroy. Apparently for months

Conroy, believing that the messages being left by Streisand on his answering machine were a practical joke, failed to return her calls. She and Johnston moved forward and crafted a first draft in three months.

The novel dealt with Henry Wingo, an abusive shrimper in the American South, and his wife Lila and their three children. The Wingos are a totally dysfunctional family; the novel, told largely through flashbacks, touches on the nightmarish South Carolina childhood that Luke, Tom, and Savannah, the children, had to endure and the psychological impact of those years. Streisand was attracted to the subject by issues that she saw as very much her own — being neglected as a child, and her feelings of being an outsider. The character of Dr. Susan Lowenstein, the Jewish New York psychiatrist who would treat two of the adult children, was a role that resonated for Streisand, one that she saw as a rich and challenging acting opportunity. The actual "prince of tides," the Luke character at the center of the novel, almost disappears in the film adaptation. Instead, Streisand and Johnston focused on brother Tom, his inner demons, and the journey that would make him more mentally healthy. In addition, they expanded the romance between Tom and Susan, making the love affair between them a central part of the film and giving Streisand a stronger and more dynamic role, one that could work for her. Once Conroy was convinced that it really was Barbra trying to make contact, he joined her and, working together for two weeks, they crafted a final screenplay. Conroy, together with Johnston, would receive a writing credit, though Streisand's involvement looms large and very much reflects the Streisand sensibility. As Conroy noted:

> I've never seen anyone go through a total immersion in a project like she does. . . . It completely obsesses her and takes over her life. I mean, here is how much input I had on the script: I think Barbra actually wrote it. She certainly wrote more of it than I did. She whipped that thing into shape the way she liked it, and I just helped with the polish. She should have taken screenwriting credit on it. I think she even tried for one, but the Writers Guild works in Byzantine ways, which I don't understand. She certainly deserves it.[39]

When questioned as to why she chose not to share writing credit, Streisand responded, "It is common in the process of moviemaking that directors get involved in the formation of the script and not take credit for their contributions."[40]

In *The Prince of Tides*, we have a study of two worlds that collide over tragedy. We first meet Tom Wingo, "from the Carolinas," as the camera pans over the patchwork of low-country expanses of water that make up his world. He is a shrimper's son who grew up with a brother and twin sister, all rooted to the land that they love so much. Tom must leave home and journey to New York, that Sodom of the modern world, to aid his suicidal sister's Jewish psychiatrist as she delves into the Wingo family's troubled past. In sharp contrast to the opening shots, the camera now introduces us to a grim reality, and we see the ethnic, tenement-like life of Greenwich Village, with children crowded on the street, various foreign languages heard, and Tom's welcome by the barrel of a gun brandished by a neighbor who had failed to recognize him as he entered his sister's apartment. Tom has left his "safe" gentile world for the realm of ethnics — immigrants and Jews — also home to gays, artists, and psychiatrists. *Tides* is about two people from dramatically different worlds, a gentile and a Jew, brought together by circumstance and forced to come to grips with their own pain. In the process, they make startling discoveries about themselves and each other and fall in love. One might question what each could possibly represent for the other.

Streisand envisioned Robert Redford as Tom, but as we have already observed, Redford was not interested.[41] After Warren Beatty passed on the part, Barbra met with Nick Nolte, who had made quite a name for himself on the ABC miniseries *Rich Man, Poor Man* and had followed this with several fine film performances. Though Nolte's personal life was in shambles, with three failed marriages, he seemed to Streisand the perfect man to play the part, possibly because of his seeming vulnerability. But according to biographer Christopher Andersen, Streisand had her own doubts about whether she herself was right for the part of Lowenstein, whom Conroy describes in the novel as "breathtakingly beautiful":

> She invited Conroy to her house in Holmby Hills and asked him point-blank, "Do I look like Lowenstein?" When he said she didn't, Barbra asked, "Does *this* look like Lowenstein?" and flipped a switch. Up came a huge image of Barbra in character, standing in the book-lined office of a psychiatrist. "Yeah," Conroy replied, stunned. "That's Lowenstein."[42]

Throughout American cinema, the Jew was usually portrayed as the outsider attempting to assimilate into America. This is most pervasive in Woody Allen's work and can also be seen in such films as *The Jazz Singer*, *Hester*

Fenced in and kept out. The all-American coach from the Carolinas finds himself the outsider as he jogs around New York City. Nick Nolte.

Street, *The Heartbreak Kid*, *Private Benjamin*, and *Avalon*. We saw this in *The Way We Were*, as Katie exists almost entirely in Hubbell's world. In *The Prince of Tides*, curiously, it is the Jewish protagonist, Dr. Susan Lowenstein, who appears to be the *insider*. The Barbra Streisand character makes the leap, just as the American Jew had in the intervening eighteen years, to find herself comfortable and at peace with America in a Jewish milieu. In sharp contrast, Tom the "American" is the outsider in this unique American setting—the ethnic world of New York. One powerful visual has the athletic Carolinian taking a jog only to find himself fenced in at a fish market, amid loud haggling, peering through the fence at a dirty stream polluted with garbage at water's edge; this, in contrast to the stunning Carolina coast that had segued his departure from the Tides to New York City only minutes earlier. Tom seems trapped, a temporary prisoner to noise, traffic, and disturbance.

Assimilation into America has traditionally been achieved through the professions, by intermarriage, or by money. Susan Lowenstein seems to have all three—she is professionally well respected, married to a renowned non-Jewish violinist, Herbert Woodruff (Jeroen Krabbé), and by virtue of her situation seems to have accumulated some wealth, thus assuring her place in New York society. But in reality, many in America saw New York as a world unto itself, thereby leaving someone who is a New York insider still feeling like an outsider in America. Examples abound. When President Gerald Ford said he would deny federal assistance to spare New York from bankruptcy, the front page of the next morning's *Daily News* read: "FORD TO CITY: DROP DEAD."[43] New Yorkers had a sense that the rest of the country simply did not care about them.

A great deal had changed for Jews in America in the eighteen years since the release of *The Way We Were*. For one thing, according to the National

Barbra Streisand, here as psychiatrist Susan Lowenstein, not only involved herself in crafting the screenplay, she also directed The Prince of Tides *and was its costar.* © *Columbia Pictures. Photographer: Jurgen Vollmer. Columbia Pictures/Photofest.*

Jewish Population study, conducted in 1990, only half of America's Jews had any affiliation with the Jewish community, and the rate of intermarriage had soared from 17 percent to 52 percent for third- or fourth-generation Americans,[44] a figure that created what political scientist J. J. Goldberg called "a nationwide panic over impending Jewish disappearance."[45] The character of Susan Lowenstein represented an interesting demographic — the remarkable success of American Jews in the postwar years. But along with that success story, as Arthur Hertzberg noted, "came the worries about continuity and the survival of Jews in America as a discrete entity."[46] Historian Henry Feingold noted that the remarkable success of Jews, "coupled with acceptance by the host culture presented new survival problems, as the demands of the accommodation process led to a thinning of the content of Jewishness in religious and cultural spheres."[47] Back in 1973, we thought we understood Katie Morosky, but just who was Dr. Susan Lowenstein?

Susan Lowenstein is an accomplished Jewish psychiatrist who had been treating Tom Wingo's mentally ill sister, Savannah. We learn that Savannah came to New York to escape her past and write children's books. But Tom is surprised to find a drawer in her apartment with bills addressed to a Renata Halpern and a portfolio, labeled "The Holocaust and other poems," by the same person. He then picks up a children's book, *The Southern Way*, by this author in a bookstore. When he again goes through his sister's drawer, he comes across a bill from Susan Lowenstein made out to Renata Halpern. Exactly what mystery is unfolding and what is the doctor hiding from Tom? He breaks angrily into her office demanding an explanation and questioning why she has kept this from him. In response, she asks him why he is so angry. "I don't like being lied to. I don't like secrets," he replies. Indeed, it is *his* secret and that of his sister that is at the root of the grave psychological damage that has affected his family; a terrible event had taken place during their childhood. Lowenstein begins to explain: "She said her father was a furrier and both parents were survivors of the Holocaust. She couldn't fool me about being Jewish, but what fascinated me was why she chose to be the child of survivors. What *was* she trying to survive? What *is* she trying to survive?" The very decision by this Southern American woman to identify with Jews is a fascinating and telling one, as the American Savannah equates her own victimization with that of Jews in the Holocaust and throughout history. She chooses to come to New York, to live with them, and to be, albeit only in her mind, one of them. Just as Jews had to confront and survive a horrific past, so must Savannah come to grips with her personal horror, live on, and go forward.

The question of past and memory is central to both *The Way We Were* and *The Prince of Tides*. The 1973 film begins with a flashback to 1930s campus days as we hear Marilyn and Alan Bergman's lyrics to the Marvin Hamlisch song: "Memories light the corners of my mind, misty watercolor memories of the way we were. . . . Can it be that it was all so simple then?" The lyrics set the stage for recollections of a time past. But the next lyric is most telling and is central to *The Prince of Tides*: "Memories may be beautiful and yet what's too painful to remember we simply choose to forget." What brings Tom to Dr. Susan Lowenstein is the hope that she can help his sister's mental illness, but that sickness is connected to something "too painful to remember." Lowenstein's role, as the professional responsible for helping the

Wingo twins, is to try and deal with their pain and find its cause. Savannah is devoid of memory, and the therapist turns to Tom to try and retrieve whatever it is that seems to be causing her and possibly him as well so much anguish. She explores the basis of his symptomatology, feelings, and defense mechanisms, hoping for a cathartic moment of reattaching to the trauma frozen in his body. As a psychiatrist, Dr. Susan Lowenstein is highly trained and well equipped to help people deal with their pasts, and she succeeds in tapping into his memory. In fact, it is the uncovering of Tom's past that ultimately leads not only to Savannah's healing, but to his own renewal. As survivors of the Shoah were more and more confronting their past through testimony at this time, so too do Savannah (as Renata Halpern) and her brother Tom begin to confront their personal "Holocaust." Tom becomes, as she later proclaims, "her memory!"

While Tom struggles with his repressed past along with his sister's mental illness, Dr. Lowenstein's son Bernard (played by Streisand's real-life son, Jason Gould) is struggling with his own issues. His father, a world-class violinist, wants his child to follow in his footsteps, but Bernard wants a different type of acceptance. He has entrée into the arts world through his parents, but at school he wants to play football — that sport which among all American sports seems to be the one least favored by Jewish parents for their children. Tom, a former coach of this most American of hard, grueling, physical contact sports, becomes his teacher. While Susan *tackles* mental illness, Tom literally teaches Bernard how to *tackle*. It is a rite of passage for both as Tom is slowly incorporated by Susan into the New York world of the fine arts, and Bernard moves closer to a new kind of acceptance by his peers — this to the possible detriment of his violin-playing hands. In the end, Bernard overcomes his demons and learns to be a decent player, while Tom is never made fully comfortable in New York society. However, he does get Susan, at least for a while.

Susan and Tom leave behind the noise and bustle of New York City to find their romantic time together in her country home, an hour away from the city. There the all-American football coach from the Carolinas finds some happiness in Susan's affluent Jewish world. But just as Katie could not be totally happy in Hubbell's world, Tom misses the beauty and openness of his Carolina home and the family he left behind. Confronting his past and history with the assistance of Susan, he is able to finally leave her and seek out happiness on his terms and on his turf. Susan, in the meantime, ends her troubled relationship with her non-Jewish musician husband and at least

Nick Nolte as Tom Wingo. © *Columbia Pictures.*
Photographer: Jurgen Vollmer. Columbia Pictures/Photofest.

comes to one conclusion: "I gotta find me a nice Jewish boy. You guys are killing me!" (Interestingly enough, Conroy's novel uses the word "goys," not "guys.")

In both *The Way We Were* and *The Prince of Tides*, the Jewish woman is strong, educated, multitalented, and successful in her own way as she takes on America. Though *The Way We Were* is set in the 1940s, I contend that Katie reflects a 1970s heroine who tries to find her way in Hubbell's milieu, but her values and conflicting style get in the way. Susan is a self-assured accomplished 1990s woman, comfortable in her identity as a Jew, who has achieved acceptance in the greater society but seems to lack true community. As the century came to a close, one could more clearly see the attraction that the Jewish habitat had for the non-Jew. As Streisand so vividly shows us and as the non-Jewish author Pat Conroy wrote, Tom Wingo — at this point and time — "could have been quite happy." He professes to love Susan. Yet, when asked why he is leaving her to go home to his wife, he answers, "I loved her longer." For Tom, not only had he loved his wife longer, but with her came his children, his family. Susan admits that it is these values that attracted her to him in the first place. "One of the things that I always liked about you is that you're the kind of guy who goes back to his family."

Yet by virtue of her liaison with Tom she has also won back family, her son Bernard. What insight does this film provide? America was changing. The Jew once sought acceptance, then assimilation and societal entrée. By the 1990s, the American Jew was firmly entrenched. The Jew, the new person on the block, had finally established residence, and would not move.

AVALON AND *LIBERTY HEIGHTS*

THE SPIRIT OF FAMILY — REMEMBERING BETTER

AVALON

In *Avalon*, a highly acclaimed film released in 1990, audiences and reviewers alike saw a saga of Jewish immigrants who arrived in America as part of the great wave of European newcomers during the first quarter of the twentieth century. Initially, writer-director Barry Levinson emphatically repudiated that *Avalon* was a film about the immigrant experience. In interviews, Levinson consistently pointed to his picture as a film about "the importance of family and the inevitability of leaving the nest." "It drove me nuts," he said at the time. "Why do they keep going on?"[1] Some twenty years later, he looked back:

> When you do a specific piece of work and you had something in mind and then you're getting "the immigrant experience" and "the coming to America" — yeah, I understand that, but that's not really what my focus was. That's probably what I was responding to at that time . . . what happened and how the world changed is what I was more fascinated by. . . . In the end of the day it's not my film. It's however it's perceived by the individual and their experience in watching it.[2]

Whether intended or not, Barry Levinson does indeed succinctly and dramatically impart a superb portrait of the American Jewish immigrant experience in the early part of the twentieth century, from the arrival of Jews in

America to their adaptation to the American way of life and their struggle to claim a slice of "the American pie." In *Avalon*, one sees a family come together in a new home and the inevitable breakup of that same family as each of five brothers marries and has children. *Avalon* is about the unfolding experience of a new American Jewish society in formation. According to Michael Kassel, "*Avalon* contains an uncanny historical accuracy that allows for historians and students of popular culture to treat the film's family as a 'real' entity that can be evaluated on its own terms." [3] What *Avalon* provides is a moving portrait of Jewish life in America and a wonderful opportunity for the student of American history to better comprehend the dynamics of that period.

Avalon is the third in a series of four personal films situated in Baltimore, Levinson's so-called "Baltimore stories." He both wrote and directed *Diner* in 1982 when he was forty, followed by *Tin Men* in 1987. *Avalon* was drawn "out of remembrances of stories" from Levinson's childhood. [4] *Liberty Heights*, the fourth of the Baltimore films, followed in 1999. Levinson, an accomplished screenwriter, producer, and director, had also directed such films as *The Natural* (1984), with Robert Redford; *Good Morning Vietnam* (1987), with Robin Williams; *Rain Man* (1988), for which he won an Academy Award for best director; *Bugsy* (1991), with Warren Beatty; and *Wag the Dog* (1997), with Dustin Hoffman, Robert De Niro, and Anne Heche. His screenwriting credits include *High Anxiety* (1977) along with *And Justice for All* (1979). He has also produced dozens of films. The story of *Avalon* and the Krichinsky family is drawn from experiences on both sides of Levinson's family:

> I was always intrigued by some of the stories my grandfather told me. . . .
> But for a long time I couldn't make any sense of them in terms of how they
> could be used in a movie. But then I began to think of them in terms of his
> story . . . and my father's life. My father's side of the family was Orthodox,
> kosher: kept two sets of dishes, no cooking on Saturday. My mother's side
> of the family didn't follow the dietary laws at all . . . completely different
> ways of seeing things, in one extended family. [5]

Levinson described how he assembled the film:

> I kind of borrow bits and pieces from one person and another and mix
> them all up and create these composites in order to satisfy the story that

you want to tell and the character arc that you want to tell. So yes, my grandfather actually did have this jazz club. He was a wallpaper hanger. There were five Krichinsky brothers that came to America. They did have family circles. All those things were all true. Within it, it becomes the writer's mind of how you blend and travel through and composite characters that tell your story in the way you want to tell it.[6]

In the film, the five Krichinsky brothers arrive in Baltimore prior to the onset of World War I, the latter four helped by the first, who had arrived before them. We are keenly aware that each brother is there to provide support for the other. They live in the same community, work side by side in the same paperhanging business. Even when one of the brothers tries a new business venture, as Sam does with his nightclub, there is an understanding that, should the venture fail, the family is there to provide a safety net. Levinson calls their inner-city row house community Avalon, a clear reference to the Avalon of King Arthur, which was an earthly paradise.[7] On one hand, Avalon represents the American immigrant ghetto; on the other, it is a state of mind, drawn from the memory of family members and from Levinson himself. Interestingly enough, Levinson was careful never to define Avalon, though in the closing credits of the film, we see an apartment building that appears to be named Avalon. "You don't know if it's the house, or if it's the neighborhood," said Levinson.[8] For Barry Levinson, Avalon was supposed to be "the time when things were good."[9] He described it to me this way:

When they first were all in America—when they had reached the Promised Land—when the five brothers were there, in that one place. . . . That was the moment. It was the new freedom. It was the spirit of family. And then they moved on from there. That was the touchstone in a sense, probably when the family was at its closest and they were now free and in America. . . . I thought there was something magical about the word and that's the meaning that I had in mind, anyway.[10]

Avalon was like an American shtetl, where family members lived near each other and were there for each other. Though there was a cinema house near where Levinson grew up called Avalon, he claims that there is no connection. He was also not cognizant of another Baltimore connection—that George Calvert, the first Lord Baltimore, the person who petitioned King

Director Barry Levinson at the helm. © New Line Cinema. New Line Cinema/Photofest.

Charles I for the land north of Virginia called Maryland, had earlier established and lived in a colony in Newfoundland called Avalon. Levinson was
also unaware of something else:

> This is the strangest — it gave me goosebumps. Where we shot the family
> . . . where they're out in the street and where they have the streetcar that
> goes by and the family meeting — it's in the row houses. We negotiated to
> shoot on that street in this row house and then we started to have prob-
> lems with the person [who owned the house] — they wanted more money.
> We couldn't afford it, etc. We couldn't make it work. But I said: "I love
> that street so much and like the fact that there's a streetcar track and we
> can put our fake streetcar in there." So we went to the end house — the
> one on the corner — four doors down. It was right on the corner. So we
> parked all of our trucks on the side street, which would be the side of
> the building — if you can picture that. Then the A.D. [assistant director]
> came in and he says, "You've got to come take a look at this." So I said
> "What?" "No, no. Just come with me." So we went there, where all the
> trucks are parked, to the side of the building. And there's an old door. Ap-
> parently, it must have been a rooming house at one time because there's

a side entrance. And above it, in wood that's sort of the beam that runs across, you can just faintly see in its carvings—it says "Avalon." And if you ever see the movie—in the closing credits—there's this shot and it says "Avalon."[11]

Sam Krichinsky (Armin Mueller-Stahl), one of the brothers and the grandfather of Michael (who represents Levinson), serves as storyteller. He weaves the family narrative of half a century, from his arrival in Baltimore until his final days in the Levindale Retirement Community. Throughout the film, even in his last days at Levindale, Sam tries to recall for his children, grandchildren, and even great-grandchild what Avalon represented. Sam's story is all about America, and he provides a powerful history of one Jewish family, his own, in Baltimore. We never find out where he, or even his father, who is brought by the family to America a decade later, came from. It is somehow inconsequential, as this is an American story drawn from memory; this experience, as Ben Halpern referred to it, is the "one-generation experience of the immigrant ghetto, known from its very inception to be out of the frame of history and culture."[12] There is no "before they came to America"; we know what happens after, and the "before" is of no consequence. Whereas Yiddish filmmakers in America would often evoke Eastern Europe in their storylines, it has been rare for an American mainstream moviemaker to introduce a foreign starting point in an American Jewish saga. For Sam, his story and his world begin with his arrival in America, and this moment of beginning becomes the underlying oral narrative as it is told and retold over the course of the film. Somehow, during these memorable years, family lived and worked side by side. The family circle decided matters of import and provided for one another. Avalon was "home," a possible oblique reference to the idealized Eastern European Jewish concept of *heym*, yet totally American in character.

Although his intention may not have been to detail the Jewish immigrant experience, Barry Levinson very much does just that. For many Eastern European Jewish immigrants, there was nostalgia for the old country. Countless Yiddish songs and films recounted a return to the shtetl, the market town where life may not have been better, but living certainly seemed simpler and the family was always present. Levinson's shtetl is Avalon, a place and time in America that no longer exists, but the memory of which he is committed to passing along through *his* vehicle for narrative, the motion picture. This is what grandfather Sam and eventually the young Michael, clearly standing in for Levinson, want to convey to the next generation. When part of the Krichinsky family moves to the suburbs, these close associations are strained. The task Levinson lays out for himself is not to document the American Jewish experience as a whole but to record a fragment of it on film, just as his grandfather tried to transmit it orally.[13] Sam tried to keep the family together by telling the story of his arrival in America at every family gathering, but *Avalon* shows how television eventually supplanted Sam as storyteller. For Barry Levinson, there is a personal commitment that cinema might indeed bring the story to the next generation. Cinema, as he sees it, has the power to be the conveyer of history; it puts forward a new form of expression for history.

Just as the telling and retelling of the story of the Exodus from Egypt has become for Jews a central, unifying connection to the Jewish past, Sam Krichinsky's recollection of a Fourth of July moment becomes emblazoned in the family history. For Sam and his descendants this moment represents their identity, their origin in America. There are no links to Pilgrims or voyages on the Mayflower for this family, which is reflected in how Sam and his wife begin their Thanksgiving dinner: "The Pilgrims started it, whoever they were. . . . It's a funny holiday, if you ask me. Makes no sense."[14] There are also no stories of pogroms or of legendary flight from the Czar's army. Said Levinson:

> They so seldom talked about where they came from that I thought it was just interesting not to be specific. My grandmother never mentioned where she came from. You sort of pieced together that she was from somewhere in Poland, but it was close to the Ukraine. . . . It was all sort of blurry, so I figured why mention the specifics since they seldom wanted to talk about it. . . . They did not have this underlying fondness for where they came from, which, as you grow up, you understand why. It was just the Old Country. . . . It was just sloughed off that way. It was like, why would you even care to know?[15]

It all seems to have begun that Fourth of July day, a visual that opens the film and then recurs throughout. This is, as Pierre Sorlin defined it for film, the "starting point" of the family drama, a historical mechanism that elucidates everything to follow.[16] It is the moment when the Jew arrives in

America, ready to start his new journey. In *Avalon*, that instant begins as fireworks light the sky and Sam Krichinsky begins his narration of the event that would leave an indelible mark, his arrival on July 4, 1914, in Baltimore:

> I came to America in 1914 . . . by way of Philadelphia . . . that's where I got off the boat, and then I came to Baltimore. It was the most beautiful place you've ever seen in your life. . . . There were lights everywhere . . . what lights they had. It was a celebration of lights. I thought they were for me. . . . Sam was in America! I didn't know what holiday it was, but there were lights . . . and I walked under them.[17]

These words and images continually punctuate the film, as time and time again Levinson cuts back to them. In subsequent scenes, as we hear Sam's voiceover, we see him, suitcase in hand, walking along trolley tracks. Above him are red, white, and blue banners crested with an American eagle. "This image," said *Avalon*'s director of photography Allen Daviau, "came from photographs taken during an exposition that was held in Baltimore in 1914. . . . It was called Electric Park. . . . It's an extraordinary visual."[18] Along the path and directly behind him are American flags waving in the wind as fireworks above explode, celebrating not only the Fourth of July but also Sam's arrival in America. Sam Krichinsky, the patriarch, has begun a journey. Because Sam and his brothers took that journey, Barry Levinson and his extended family would be born and grow up in America. Their history also began that day.

Avalon is a film history drawn from stories passed down in family recollections. Although it is ostensibly the reminiscences of one family, that of the Krichinskys,[19] it is very much representative of a period in American Jewish life when multitudes of immigrants came to American cities to find and create new lives. The story woven by Levinson is an amalgam of memories drawn from the experiences of both of his grandparents portraying the evolution and growth of a Jewish family. Its time span is broad, from the World War I period, through socioeconomic change in the 1920s and 1930s, to the dream of upward mobility and the eventual move by some family members from the inner city to the suburbs in the 1940s. In *Avalon*, we witness a powerful and proud account of the Jewish success story in the first half of the century. We also observe the turmoil created as the family moves from the protective and nourishing *Avalon*, where the family is close and central, to

The starting point of Avalon *is Baltimore, July 4, 1914. This image recurs throughout the film.* © *Tristar Pictures. Tristar Pictures/Photofest.*

Three generations of Krichinskys. Sam, the patriarch, remonstrates but accepts that his son and nephew have changed their names to Kaye and Kirk, respectively. Adults: Eve Gordon, Joan Plowright, Armin Mueller-Stahl, Elizabeth Perkins, Aidan Quinn, Kevin Pollak. © Tristar Pictures. Tristar Pictures/Photofest.

the suburbs, where traditions are broken and, as older brother Gabriel forcefully proclaims, family takes a back seat. "Get new relatives. . . . Get relatives that live near you and who you'll wait for! You know what it is? That's what happens when you get to be wealthy."[20] According to H. B. Cavalcanti and Debra Schleef, "Levinson implies that the great danger of suburban life is its detachment. Private living spaces help the family turn inward . . . even family life has become rather private."[21] With changes brought about in the post–World War II era and the move to the suburbs, the American Jewish family as it was in *Avalon* becomes only a memory, one that Levinson wants us not to lose.

There was strong criticism of *Avalon* in the Jewish press and in some academic circles on the grounds that it was not sufficiently Jewish.[22] Similar criticism had been leveled at Levinson's two earlier Baltimore films. This lack of outright Jewishness may have been by design, as Levinson focused on a more universal adjustment to America and the ever-present influence that television had on the family. But Levinson also speaks to the fact that this was his reality:

At the Toronto Film Festival, we got criticized for it not being Jewish enough. I think it's a dilemma for Jewish writers, Jewish filmmakers. It's that you can either be too Jewish or you are not Jewish enough. That's sort of the conundrum. And so they said you know you don't really see all the Jewish things, whatever that may be. I didn't try and shy away from anything. When it was supposed to be there, it was there and [when it wasn't], it wasn't. The fact of the matter in terms of *Avalon*, it was as close to the way it was. We did not have all kinds of menorahs just lying around. We didn't have all of those things. They were not part of my life growing up in Baltimore. It did not have all of that connected to it . . . we were Jewish. We didn't hide the fact that we were Jewish. That was the Jewish world we knew.[23]

Levinson also argued that the Baltimore Jewish experience was different, not like New York: "The immigrant experience in terms of the sweatshops and tenements and the teeming masses, that didn't apply to Baltimore in the same way. Of all the stories that I've ever heard, that kind of struggle didn't apply."[24] Though there are no Passover seders in the film, no religious practices, no synagogues, and no Israel, and though one needs to squint to see the one Jewish gravestone in the cemetery, *Avalon* is nonetheless a film about Jews struggling for their place in America. The film's lack of obvious Jewish visual cues does not mask how authentically Jewish it is. It is a motion picture about Jews assimilating into America, about Jews for whom America itself becomes their religion, and about how a new set of rituals, history, and memory is passed down to ensuing generations. This core element was inspired by one phrase that kept recurring in Levinson's head: "If I knew things would no longer be, I would have tried to remember them better."[25] This is one of the last things that the aging patriarch Sam tells his grandson as the film comes to its conclusion. Though Levinson may initially have protested otherwise, this is very much a film about Jews in America.

A Visual Analysis

A clear visual analysis, examining how the filmmaker crafts a powerful statement through use of images, is often overlooked when cinema is used in a historical context. Levinson, who is both writer and director of this film, is a master of the mise-en-scène, a visual representation of ideas and themes, as well as the positioning and editing of those scenes. In cinema, careful attention needs to be given not only to the dialogue but also to the choice of the images. Levinson's visual punctuation of this film is quite powerful and very Jewish. Therefore, a close reading of the actual *film text* provides a unique lens on the American Jewish experience in the era it examines and a better understanding of film as reflective of history. Interestingly enough, some sequences provide powerful insights into a particular moment in American Jewish history. The clearest example is the recurring flashback to Sam's Fourth of July moment. Yet another wonderful example is a powerful sequence set shortly after the conclusion of World War II. The first scene in the sequence has Sam Krichinsky's brother-in-law, Simka, arriving in Baltimore; he is the brother of Sam's wife, Eva (Joan Plowright). Sam and Eva go to the train station to meet Simka, his wife Gittle, and their daughter Elka, arriving by locomotive. All three are survivors of the Holocaust.

The first shots are of the train's arrival and the steamy, ghostlike Baltimore train station. The platform at first seems almost devoid of people and, with Randy Newman's music as backdrop, this eerie station is visually reminiscent of the steamy train-station scenes in films set during the war. Such a scene, with its peculiar music and the train's arrival, indirectly brings to mind Europe and the deportations of Jews to the concentration camps. But this is Baltimore: we are in America, and this train is bringing the family together, not tearing the family apart. After all, this is somehow what America is all about.

> You can't always envision everything when you're writing it. You've got a lot of things in mind. Then, of course when you're there . . . then you begin to say. "Oh look. This has almost a slight European feel to it here. And if we just push this just a little bit." Sometimes you do it and people pick up on it. It's okay if they don't, but it just adds a little texture to the piece.[26]

In the next scene, the elders are sitting with Simka and Gittle in a drawing room, speaking largely Polish but also some Yiddish and Russian. Levinson purposely does not provide subtitles for the dialogue, leaving those of us unable to understand ignorant about what is going on. At one point, we hear a word that resembles "concentration"; the survivors must be sharing their stories. Through this device, we are made to understand that these were stories not immediately passed on by most survivors to the next generation,

Eva Krichinsky at the train station in Baltimore. She hopes to be united with her brother, who survived the Holocaust and whom she has never met. "Where are the people who know where the people are?" Joan Plowright.

An anteroom where the elders hear from brother Simka and his wife Gittle some of the specifics of what they endured in Europe during the war. They speak in Polish, Russian, and Yiddish; the scene is not subtitled. Aidan Quinn, unidentified actor (Gittle), Ronald Guttman, Joan Plowright.

like Ann (Elizabeth Perkins) and Dottie (Eve Gordon) in the kitchen. Ann and Dottie's generation was often left in the dark about what had happened. As the two women prepare the turkey in the next room, they continue trying to grapple with the extent of the horror, all the while preparing the Thanksgiving meal.

> "I'm not sure she was in a camp. Her husband might have died in the war," Ann tells Dottie. "No, I didn't get that," Dottie responds, and they go back and forth. "It must be. The child couldn't have been born in a concentration camp. I got that they met in a refugee camp and her husband had died. But the refugee camp is really recently and the kid is like . . . six. . . . No. We'll have to ask later." [27]

In Levinson's original screenplay, Ann and Dottie place dishes on the holiday table while they are chatting. In the actual film, Levinson transitions from the drawing room to the kitchen, where the women are preparing dinner. We watch through a close-up as the women place the turkey into the oven, all the while talking about the Holocaust and Simka's family. The oven close-up proves to be an incredibly powerful visual directly relating to the crematoria and the death camps. When I asked Levinson about the scene, he commented:

> It occurred to me when I first wrote it—and it's the difference between when you write something and when you are there and you go, "Wow.

This is interesting!" Why don't we do the scene while it's over the oven because it has this subtext that runs through it all without having to say anything. When I wrote it, it did not occur to me. But it occurred to me once I got into the kitchen and saw . . . the mechanics of what would go on and I thought. "Well, that would be interesting."[28]

As the two women prepare the turkey, Levinson brings us back to the drawing room, where the older immigrant generation—joined by these new arrivals to America—are awaiting the beginning of a feast that is particular to Americans, yet has no real meaning for them. As we will see when at the table Sam proclaims, "The Pilgrims started it, whoever they were," the reason for the holiday is of little interest, but what Simka is relating has the whole family on the edge of their seats. In contrast, Ann and Dottie know very well why they are preparing turkey, but have little comprehension of the events that affected Simka and his family. Meanwhile, the turkey, the American feast, has been placed into the oven, while the women grapple for an understanding of the concentration camps, the ovens. In Europe, ovens had been used one way; in America, ovens are just for preparing food.

We then find ourselves in the basement with the next generation, the children. There is a close-up of a toy German fighter plane, a Messerschmitt, complete with swastika. The kids decide to create what they call a "cliffhanger" (a reference to a movie they had seen earlier) and go about setting the plane on fire. All the youngsters scream with great delight, but for Elka, now separated and sitting apart on the steps, the screams are representative of something entirely different, as Levinson shows us a close-up of the

Busy preparing the Thanksgiving feast, Ann and Dottie can't understand how a child could have survived the war. Elizabeth Perkins, Eve Gordon.

As the two women of the middle generation try to comprehend what took place in the concentration camps, they baste the turkey and ready it for the oven. In America, ovens are for preparing feasts. In Europe, they had other uses. Levinson provides a close-up.

The children are about to set fire to a
German airplane and scream with delight.
The Nazi swastika on the tail of the
plane holds a different meaning for
Elka, who arrived from Europe.
Center-front is Elijah Wood.

Thanksgiving dinner at the Krichinskys' in the suburbs; waiting again for Gabriel.
"The pilgrims started it, whoever they were!" Elijah Wood in foreground.
At the far end of the table are Joan Plowright and Armin Mueller-Stahl.
© Tristar Pictures. Tristar Pictures/Photofest.

swastika in flames. It is another interesting visual twist that Levinson uses
to show the spatial separation of Elka from the rest of the children, the distance in history and culture between her and them, and a foreshadowing that
she and her new immigrant parents will never be fully assimilated into the
family.

*"You cut the turkey without me!" Gabriel
cannot believe that the family started
Thanksgiving dinner without him. He
admonishes his brother Sam for not waiting,
as he and his wife came from far away
to be with family. Lou Jacobi, Armin
Mueller-Stahl.*

Levinson then presents us with the Thanksgiving dinner scene. As mentioned before, the meaning of the holiday is somehow lost on the older generation, except that the family members know that this is a time for everyone to gather. In many Jewish families, Thanksgiving and Passover are the two times in the year when extended families meet. Passover has no place in this film, but the Fourth of July and Thanksgiving, American holidays with no religious connections, are very much present. The Fourth of July represents a beginning for this family; Thanksgiving is characterized by recurring family gatherings that erode with change, moves to suburbia, and the passage of time. This particular year, the pressures of the moment somehow keep the family from waiting for older brother Gabriel, as had always been done in years past, and the others proceed to begin eating without him. The seemingly innocuous act of carving the Thanksgiving turkey without waiting for Gabriel has dire consequences and will prove to be the beginning of the demise of this extended family. Gabriel reacts vehemently: "You started without me?!! You cut the turkey without me?!! Come on; we're going. . . . They start without us, we leave. . . . Your own flesh and blood, and you couldn't wait?!! You cut the turkey?!!"[29] In a curious twist, Thanksgiving, which had brought the Krichinskys together in years past and unites them with millions of Americans who celebrate the same feast, is the holiday that marks the beginning of the dissolution of this Jewish family. When I quizzed Levinson on the circumstances of creating this scene, he replied:

I was looking for something that would show there was going to be a break in a tradition—something that needed to be simple enough that [it] didn't need to be explained. I kind of hit on that idea. . . . I hear from people all over the world that somehow connect to it in ways that you can't [understand]. The best thing about it is that some things are just unexplainable.[30]

The turkey, with its connection in the popular mind to a different starting point in early America, plays a vital role. The visual image of the turkey represents America as much as it does Thanksgiving, a time for the coming together of family. When Mr. Plowman, who has never met a Jew before, finally accedes and invites his daughter's Jewish boyfriend to his Vermont home in *The Young Lions*, he invites him for turkey. Yet in *Avalon*, Levinson merges the American visual of the turkey with the close-up of the oven and all that it connotes. He converts a Jewish visual of the smoke-belching train of death into an American one of survival and reunion. Finally, with a close-up on the knife and turkey, we observe as the bird is carved. In the premature slicing of the turkey there is a symbolic connection to tradition and, contrapuntally, to the breaking of tradition. Had Sam and Jules only waited for Gabriel's arrival, as they had done countless times before, the family's tradition of not starting dinner before everyone has arrived would have been sustained. In Judaism, it is with the slicing by blade at a circumcision, the *brit-mila*, that tradition and a covenant dating back to Abraham is maintained. Circumcision represents the induction of a male child into the Jewish family. But on this Thanksgiving, that continuity with the patriarchs is severed by a different slice of a knife. Gabriel's abrupt departure upon seeing that his family has started eating without him marks the beginning of the breakup of the entire family.

In the final scene of the sequence, Gabriel (Lou Jacobi) and his wife Nellie (Shifra Lerer) make their way to the car, and Sam runs after them to try and salvage the situation. Gabriel then lambastes his brother, connecting loss of the family tradition with Sam's movement to suburbia and the physical and economic separation of the family:

You live miles from nowhere! . . . It's too far, for God's sake! Too far for relatives! Get new relatives. . . . Get relatives that live near you and who you'll wait for! When we lived in Avalon, nobody ate! You wait for everyone before you eat, much less cut the turkey without a brother! You move out here to the suburbs, and you think it doesn't matter any more?

We then watch Gabriel and Nellie get into their car, followed by an extended shot of them driving off, never again to return to the neighborhood. As the car recedes into the distance, separating brothers and ending the sequence, we see an image in sharp contrast to the opening scene, in which a train brings family together. In a visual afterthought, the scene is dramatically broken by Elka's scream as she awakens from a nightmare prompted by the "cliff-hanger." In an impressively plausible way, Levinson, in the course of a sequence lasting only eight minutes, has captured an important snapshot of American Jewish life in the post–World War II period.

At the conclusion of the film, Michael, now grown and married, takes his four-year-old child to visit an elderly Sam at the Levindale Retirement Community. Sam, clearly confused, asks Michael whether he is dating. "I told you, Sam, I'm married. . . . Yes, and this is my son. I named him Sam." The elder Sam responds by telling him that he is "not supposed to name him after the living," referring to the Ashkenazic tradition that children are only to be named for the dead. Michael responds to his grandfather that he is well aware, but with that, Sam affirms Michael's choice: "That's good. . . . That's good. . . . Carry on the family name. . . . That's good."[31] At this telling moment, according to Levinson, "it's the death of religion," for "Michael feels a stronger connection to this man than to his heritage."[32] Michael's feelings clearly reflect those of Levinson; in Michael, we see Levinson's own religious struggle and a tension between ritual and memory, between particularism and a more universalist Americanism.[33] For Levinson, what seems important is that the past and memory are carried into the present, in this case through identification with the elder Sam, however inconsistent this may be with Jewish practice.

This final Levindale sequence ends as the older Sam struggles to remember what Avalon truly was. He concludes by saying these important words: "If I knew things would no longer be, I would have tried to have remembered better." He pauses for a moment as Michael and young Sam prepare to leave, and utters, "I came to America in 1914," for the last time. As Michael and his son leave, young Sam questions his father about Sam's accent and place of origin, to which Michael responds, "He came to America in 1914. He said it was the most beautiful place he's ever seen."[34] The scene dissolves to the recurring visual of Sam's arrival on the Fourth of July, and with this the film concludes. Here again, these last images are very much Barry Levinson speaking, for he (as Michael) has taken over as family storyteller, only through a different medium. Like the elder Sam, he is committed to preserving something from the past and conveying it to the next generation.

It is interesting to note that, although Avalon is not posited by Levinson as a finite space, he waits until the closing credits to show us the apartment building with the word "Avalon." He has held this image for the closing roll of titles. It is also curious that when the family gathers for Eva's funeral, it is held in a cemetery surrounded by row homes. We must be back in Avalon. Does one return to Avalon when he or she dies? As in a storybook, this final image reinforces the mythic quality of Levinson's narrative.

LIBERTY HEIGHTS

In the years following the release of *Avalon*, Barry Levinson spoke of wanting to do more films in the tradition of his other Baltimore films, *Diner* and *Tin Men*. Interestingly enough, Levinson writes of having had no intention of making *Liberty Heights* (1999) until he read a review of one of his films that he felt was anti-Semitic.[35] *Entertainment Weekly* reviewer Lisa Schwarzbaum singled out the Dustin Hoffman character in Levinson's 1998 film *Sphere* as Jewish, even though the script never referred to his religion.[36] Levinson was deeply offended, and it set off memories of growing up with the "childhood impression that everyone in the world was Jewish."[37] These memories became the starting point for *Liberty Heights*. Reacting to Schwarzbaum's review, Levinson said:

> It was a peculiar comment. What it did was—it kicked up this thing. Oh yeah, that would come up. "Are you?" As kids, in terms of being Jewish or non-Jewish, and how you define this thing. . . . It kind of shined a light on something that I hadn't thought about. Then I began to go, "Oh, wait a minute." There was this whole thing about who's Jewish and who's not Jewish and all of that. And I realized that there was a certain kind of antisemitism, not necessarily intended to be this malicious antisemitism, but this antisemitism that is in the fabric of things.

As Levinson continued, "Finally, there was a reason to revisit Baltimore again, not to indulge nostalgia, but to examine race, religion and class distinction."[38] Learning that she had something to do with the making of the film, Schwarzbaum included the following in her review of *Liberty Heights*: "If more people followed Barry Levinson's example and made art after taking issue with something I've written, Hollywood and my mailbox would both benefit. . . . In *Liberty Heights*, Barry Levinson calls a Jew a Jew. And with the freedom born of that unveiling, he flushes a whole lot of schmaltz out of his arteries."[39]

In *Liberty Heights*, Levinson places us at a point in history after the elimination of the immigrant ghetto. "The generation that came to America and came there was confronted by one overwhelming task: to get out, or enable the next generation to get out. This task they accomplished," wrote Ben Halpern.[40] It is 1954, and the Jew is now ostensibly an integrated member of American society. That year, 18.6 percent of all Americans changed their place of residence.[41] "For Jews and non-Jews alike, suburbia during these years became the 'symbol of utopia'—a sign of success, prestige, money, power, and security—'the middle class Shangri-La,'" wrote Jonathan D. Sarna.[42] And in the words of Edward S. Shapiro, "The social and economic profile of American Jews was transformed into one that closely approximated the American ideal."[43] The May 1954 U.S. Supreme Court ruling in *Brown v. Board of Education* not only impacted African Americans by signaling the end of segregation, but it also certified the equal status of Jews within a pluralistic America. The underlying theme of the *Brown* decision—as indeed of the times—was that democracy was a cherished American value and that, as a consequence, no one should be excluded from the mainstream.[44] The Court decision moved America away, as Samuel Heilman noted, from "the notion that only white Christians of European ancestry were entitled to full civil and social rights in this country."[45] In *Avalon*, Levinson provided a brilliant study of the immigrant experience. Now, in *Liberty Heights*, he presents an astute look at a changing American Jewish landscape over the course of one full Jewish calendar year. We hear about the Court's decision over the radio in the opening minutes of the film.

In *Avalon*, there was a fluidity that enabled Sam to move in his quest for a better life. Even in the flashbacks to the Fourth of July 1914, we see Sam walking along the trolley tracks—the path is laid out for him—and it seems very clear where he must go. There are no real obstacles in Sam's quest for assimilation and a slice of the American pie. Yet *Liberty Heights*, seemingly beginning where *Avalon* left off, is a film about distinctions and barriers that were very real in the post–World War II era. Jews had begun to move to the suburbs, where there are fences and limits that regulate access.

Liberty Heights is a film about Jews who want to cross the tracks and move in and out of their suburban ghettos. Levinson ties that transition in a powerful way to the newfound equality and "breaking out" by African Americans in the aftermath of the *Brown* Supreme Court decision. But as Blacks reacted carefully to the decision of the Court, so did Jews — a year after the execution of Ethel and Julius Rosenberg, less than a decade after the Holocaust and the seeming indifference of America and the proliferation of fear set off by McCarthyism. Still, for Jews, a crucial development "was their continued ascent en masse into the American middle class." [46] This was a period of struggle for civil rights, the establishment of Judaism as one of three central religions of America, and (as Levinson tries to show) the breaking or blurring of social and economic barriers. [47] It was also a time of greater physical mobility, as "car culture" more easily provided for the crossing of geographic barriers. As Leonard Fein explains:

> Before the 1950s, when we were still largely a community of immigrants and their children, and when American nativism was still a potent force, we were satisfied with the occasional exploratory expedition to the "other side." But generational and cultural change led, during the fifties, to a headlong rush to explore the new territory that had opened to us. For the individual Jew, the experience was often heady. [48]

The Suburban Ghetto

Liberty Heights begins with a semi-autobiographical exposition of Levinson's early insular Jewish experience, setting the stage for his struggle to leave his suburban American Jewish ghetto to confront the outside world, or, as his mother calls it, the "other kind." The film opens with an image of a suburban street, reminiscent of the street where the Krichinsky family lived after they left Avalon; it is as if Levinson wants us to know that this is part two. The Kurtzmans, relatives of the Krichinskys, live here; except for the grandmother, they are native-born and English is their first language. From this very first visual and the sequence that follows, Levinson provides a singular portrait of American Jewry in the 1950s. In this first image, he transitions us from *Avalon* to *Liberty Heights*. Avalon represented an ideal, namely the "home," the protective urban ghetto that gave comfort to the new immigrant family. Liberty Heights suggests the next step in the American journey, the movement up to the suburbs, and the "attainment of America." But just as Avalon represented an urban ghetto as starting point for the Krichinsky family, Liberty Heights was a suburban ghetto for the next generation that then became a stepping-stone for the generation that followed. Suburban Jews achieved "cultural assimilation," while still maintaining "continued social distinctiveness."[49] It is in this enclosed enclave that the Kurtzman parents achieved what they deemed American success. Yet for the Kurtzman sons it was too confining; they wanted to break away in order to experience more of what they believed America had to offer.[50]

This desire to move and change is represented at the outset as we see cars going up and down the block. One of the changes brought about by suburbia and the drop in the price of the car was the new dominance of the automobile; cars began providing people the mobility with which to travel beyond their own neighborhoods. The film's neighborhood, however, is one where it seems only Jews live. As Levinson pointed out, "It was segregated in Baltimore and many other cities, not just in terms of a black-white issue, but you had Germans in one area and Italians in another area and Jews in another area and Irish over here and the blacks were over here."[51] As we watch the visuals onscreen unfold, we hear Ben (Ben Foster), one of the Kurtzman boys, provide voice-over narration: "I grew up in the northwest section of Baltimore. It was all Jewish. In fact, I didn't even think of it in those terms. I just assumed everyone was Jewish." Levinson shows us a second-grade public-school classroom, drawn from Ben's memory, where nearly all the children are Jewish. "I even thought Paine Duhrer was Jewish. The Paine part didn't sound Jewish, but I just assumed it was a nickname. Her brother's name was Huey, and that certainly sounded Jewish!" Levinson remembered, "Our area was predominantly Jewish where we were. There were three African-Americans in the classroom and . . . On a Jewish holiday, there were like six people in the school. It was that extreme."[52] In the next scene, the director/ writer treats us to the first time Ben had lunch at his friend Butch Johnson's home; there, he discovers food that was not what he was accustomed to eating. "I began to sense that there was a world beyond what I knew. . . . I just never had raw bread before. . . . We always cook it, toast it . . ." When told by Ben of his experience, his mother (Bebe Neuwirth) responds that the Johnsons must not be Jewish. "They're the other kind." Ben continues to relate the story as voice-over, as he writes in his journal, "A couple of years later, I

Fenced out. *The Turkey Hills Swim*
Club is restricted. Evan Neumann,
Gerry Rosenthal.

It is 1954 and Jews join African Americans
and dogs as restricted from entry — but not
for long. Within moments, the boys will
hear on the radio that the U.S. Supreme
Court has ruled in Brown v. Board of
Education *and that Baltimore schools*
will be integrated. Ben Foster.

began to realize 'the other kind' was about 99 percent of the world. I went to school thinking everyone was Jewish. Now I know almost no one is Jewish."

In another brief and skillful scene, Barry Levinson is able to portray yet another serious juncture in a changing America. Again, Levinson's lens provides a unique opportunity to explore a chapter in the history of the American Jew. Here, Jews discover that not only is there a world outside their own, but that the gates that enclose them swing freely. Or do they? No sooner do we learn of Ben's food revelation than he goes on to recall one late-summer day at the Turkey Hills Swim Club. "It's some story that I had heard that led me to think about that. . . . It's hard to believe that it existed. The irony is — or our stupidity is — that we looked at it like a curiosity rather than being really angry about it. We got letters from people saying that it could not have been like that," Levinson told me.[53] The filmmaker presents us with a visually powerful scene of Ben and his two friends looking in at the club, with a fence between them and us — they are spectators. On the other side of the fence we see a number of attractive young men and women enjoying the last days of summer. One in particular, a blonde dancing girl with a cigarette pack on the thigh, draws their attention. The camera tracks the three through the chain-link fence as they move closer to the club's entrance. The fence is particularly important here, because this is a film about breaking barriers and crossing what Levinson sees as artificial boundaries. The boys very much want to go in — but they cannot! As they reach the entrance, the camera, in a reverse angle shot, focuses in on Ben reading a sign: No Jews, Dogs, or Coloreds.

All along, intercut throughout the sequence, we see Ben the narrator on his bed recording the events; he stands in for Levinson recalling his own youth. Here, they are words in a diary; later, they will be images on the screen. The sequence draws to a conclusion as the boys, understanding that they are not welcome, return to their car and turn on the radio. We hear the announcer say, "The school year begins in one week and all public schools will implement the new integration law."[54] Using a close-up of the car radio, Levinson makes a strong point that the situation of Jews in the 1950s is linked to that of African Americans, and indeed it was. We see this in the reluctant alliance of the "Jews" and "Coloreds" on the signage, and we hear it loudly and clearly on the radio. In fact, as Arthur Hertzberg suggests, blacks become the principal allies of Jews during this postwar period.[55] All the more interesting is that the setting is Baltimore, a city that Levinson describes as "both Northern and Southern . . . divided by race, religion and class, as are most cities in the United States."[56] Levinson inherently links segregation in the swim club with the new integration in the classroom. He places this black-Jewish connection in the center of an evolving relationship between Ben and his new African American classmate, Sylvia. Their association will be positive, while at the same time creating great discomfort for both sets of parents.[57]

Crossing Borders

At this point, we are introduced to Van (Adrien Brody), Ben's older brother. While Ben pursues a better understanding of Sylvia and African American culture, Van is the one who actually crosses the boundary between the Jewish suburban ghetto and the outside, non-Jewish world. Van and two of his friends decide to go to a Halloween party a few miles away. In order to "crash the party and meet women," they must cross Fells Road into "gentile turf." As they cross the road, Van's friend, Yussel (David Krumholtz), proclaims: "Get ready folks. Jews are a-comin'!" As they walk into the party, we hear the song lyrics, "Take my hand—I'm a stranger in paradise." Indeed they are, for at the party Van (unlike his brother Ben, who was kept away from the blonde in the swim club by a fence) gets to meet Dubbie, the blonde gentile woman of his fantasies. She is dressed as a fairy princess, complete with wand, ready to grant Van his every wish.[58] Yet their encounter is interrupted when Yussel's identity is discovered and he goes off to fight.

Again, we have a wonderful sequence providing an insightful look into

Jewish life at the time. In the aftermath of the war, with Nazism defeated, anti-Semitism was deemed contemptible. "That new fact of life was the protective lotion that would permit us to wander freely into fields we'd not had the courage to explore before," wrote Leonard Fein.[59] Levinson is showing the struggle in postwar society of Jews wanting to cross boundaries. There was also an expectation that gentile America would exercise good neighborliness and not block their entrée and, indeed, the three "strangers" are invited to "paradise." Yet at the same time, most gentiles wanted to know who the newcomers in the neighborhood were. Yussel does admit that he is from Forest Park, the nearby, largely Jewish neighborhood.[60] But it appears that the cause of the fight is not that Yussel is a Jew, but rather that he won't acknowledge that he is Jewish. The dialogue goes like this: "Jewish? What's the point? It's just a question. . . . Hey, are you Jewish? I don't have to answer. Hey, I was just asking if he was Jewish. . . . He won't even say he's Jewish! . . . Are you Jewish? Say it—and it's [the fight's] over!" On one hand, the three men from the Jewish side of town are there only to explore, but Yussel truly represents a desire not only to explore but also to invade. The three seek "white privilege," but the price of admission, at least here, is an acknowledgement of one's Jewishness, a price that Yussel is not prepared to pay.[61] Levinson explained:

> What I tried to do with *Liberty Heights*, was . . . because we've always talked about anti-Semitism and racism and it's always got some kind of very dark side to it. For a lot of us, it existed, but we didn't necessarily see the dark side of it, because we were curiosities to one another. So among the blacks, there was a curiosity, and among the sort of wealthy gentile community, it was a curiosity. And they were curious about Jews. It wasn't like, "There's a Jew. Beat up the Jew!" There's this Jewish person here and the Jewish person doesn't just readily admit to being Jewish. And for the Jewish person, it's, why do I have to admit that I'm Jewish! I'm Jewish. Why do I have to admit to it? I'm not doing some kind of test with you, you know, for you to understand what your religious background is. Why does that lead to that? I play it out throughout the movie that there's a certain kind of curiosity of it, as opposed to it just being malicious at its heart. That's part of what goes on in America.[62]

In contrast to *Avalon*, this is a film steeped in Jewish moments. It spans, as we have noted, the course of one Jewish calendar year, beginning with

Rosh Hashanah and the new year and ending with the next Rosh Hashanah. There is a Shabbat dinner, High Holiday services, and a strong evocation of Jewish identity. While on one level *Liberty Heights* is a study of the liberties that two sons take in breaking down social and racial boundaries, it is also a look at a Jewish family with strong Jewish traditions and values. Early on, we join the Kurtzmans in synagogue, where father Nate (Joe Mantegna) sits with his sons in an area quite near the *amud*, the place where the cantor recites the prayers; these are seats of honor and prestige. In the 1950s, Americanism fostered an implied need to affiliate with a place of worship, and for the Kurtzmans and other children of the immigrant generation this closeness with other Jews was an essential component of American life. Joining a synagogue was the way to be perceived as a respectable American. "It became a good American value, in new neighborhoods, for second- and third-generation Jews to affirm religion through affiliation with a Jewish house of worship." [63] In their move to the suburbs, wrote Daniel Elazar,

> Jews no longer lived in the same proximity to each other. Under such conditions, Jews who once maintained their Jewishness through organic relationships had to seek more formal associational ties simply to keep these relationships alive. The local synagogue offered the easiest means of making the transition, and given the American context, the most acceptable one. [64]

In the suburbs, nearly two out of every three Jews held membership in a synagogue. The suburban synagogue was their "city on the hill," the symbol of achievement and of having entered American society. [65] It is therefore an important reference point — one that bookends the film — that, at a set point in the Rosh Hashanah service, as the cantor completes the Aleynu prayer, Nate and his friend Charlie leave to go to the local Cadillac dealer to see the new models for the coming year. Just as suburban synagogue membership, especially "front row" membership, was a sign of having made it in America, so was Cadillac ownership. With each Jewish New Year and Rosh Hashanah service came a visit to the Cadillac dealership, a reaffirmation, at least for Nate, of American Jewish success. According to Levinson, that "was his tradition . . . his thing." [66] At the beginning of the film, Nate and his friend Charlie leave as the cantor recites Bayom Hahu (On that day, the Lord will be One and His name One). As they leave the building en route to view the new cars, we get to see the synagogue's imposing exterior. As the film comes to a conclusion a full Jewish calendar year later and Nate and Charlie again leave the Rosh Hashanah service, the camera pans from the cantor and the beautiful synagogue interior to the stately rotunda above them. Then, there is a dissolve to a Cadillac on a rotating pedestal in a dealership showroom. The symbolism seems clear — the synagogue facade is the Jewish community's marker for having "arrived"; the Cadillac is the individual trophy, a symbol of having made it.[67]

Liberty Heights provides a unique opportunity to delve into American Jewish life at a time when the walls that inhibited Jewish entrée into American society began to fall. At the same time, once exposed to America's seductions, Jews were placed in a unique position to reassess their Jewishness freely. In *Avalon*, the Krichinsky cousins become Kaye and Kirk, Americanizing their names like so many of their generation in an effort to break with Jewish identification. In *Liberty Heights*, Yussel, very much wanting to fit in again at a party on the other side of Fells Road and truly become "white folk," dyes his hair blond, claims Scandinavian ancestry, and changes his name to Yates. Yet, even as Yussel becomes Yates, both Ben and Van Kurtzman proudly attend synagogue and join their family at holiday meals. A defining "Jewish moment" comes when Ada Kurtzman, the boys' mother, takes great pride in telling the story of how their father spent months as a youngster training so he could return to the scene where he had been attacked for being a Jew; there, he could properly challenge those who had previously humbled him. This clearly resonates for Ben, for, toward the conclusion of the film, he and two of his friends go back to the Turkey Hills Swim Club with pliers in hand and pull down the sign that had restricted their entrance to the club. As the hand-held camera focuses in on the word "No" on the sign, now in the trashcan, we hear Mandy Patinkin's rendition of the Yiddish song "Belz." This time no one screams out, "Get ready folks. Jews are a-comin'!" It is simply a moment of Jewish power and determination, possibly from a time to come, beyond the 1950s. We watch as the boys walk defiantly onto the dock and, after placing themselves at the end of the swimming area for all to see, take off their shirts; each of the boys sports a letter drawn on his chest, together spelling the word "JEW." Most important, as the club population watches in surprise, no one does anything to intervene. Maybe these are indeed segregation barriers set up in a different time, waiting to be pulled down. Whether this is Levinson's historical rendering of the 1950s or

A powerful visual statement by Barry
Levinson that segregation has ended.

The boys "break in" to the restricted club
and proclaim their identity. Ben Foster,
Evan Neumann, Gerry Rosenthal.

a statement of identification for the imminent turn of the century is left up
to us. In any event, it is a powerful lead-in to the final synagogue sequence
that concludes the film.

In recent years, there have been few boundaries in America that have
limited the movement of Jews. *Liberty Heights* represents Barry Levinson's
struggle with difference and distinction. Through the Kurtzman brothers,
we witness obstacles that Jews once faced and that for some in various quarters still remain. Through Ben, Levinson reminisces while poking fun at
his almost totally Jewish environment when he shows how he was raised
to believe that anyone not Jewish was "the other kind." There is also the
playful back and forth between Yussel and his new non-Jewish friend Trey
about why Arthur Miller's Willy Loman in *Death of a Salesman* was not
more clearly Jewish. On one level, these are swipes at particularism; on another level, they are an appreciation of difference within a pluralistic society.
Through Van, Barry Levinson struggles with the barriers faced in the middle
decades of the last century that left Jews and other minorities outside the
periphery of certain schools, professions, and social activities. In America,
almost all of those walls have since fallen for Jews, but not for everyone.
Though *Liberty Heights* is a film clearly about postwar American Jewry, it is
also very much a look at contemporary society: the pull of America and its
values; the continuing question of particularism as opposed to universalism;
exclusion versus inclusion.

In *Avalon*, immigrant Jews struggle with their entry onto the American
stage and how that appearance affects the family. In *Liberty Heights*, the immigrant memory has faded but the struggle continues with the next generations of Jews who are trying to find a comfortable place both within the

Jewish community and in the larger America that may now accept them but may limit access to others. Barry Levinson provides us with a new source for better understanding American Jewish history. In the final moments of *Liberty Heights*, as the camera pans away from the cantor and up to the rotunda ceiling of the synagogue, we hear Ben's voice-over: "A lot of images fade and no matter how hard I tried, I can't get them back. I had a relative who once said that if I knew things would no longer be, I would have tried to have remembered better." Barry Levinson's films are there to help us not only remember better, but to give us much to consider. Whether *Avalon* and *Liberty Heights* are deemed "not Jewish" or "too Jewish," Levinson clearly is a Jew struggling with many of the issues that American Jews once confronted and continue to face.

Both *Avalon* and *Liberty Heights* provide sensitive studies of twentieth-century American Jewish life. For Levinson, cinema holds the possibility of giving the spectator an authentic feel for the time through total immersion in the medium. Each film is drawn not necessarily from what actually was, but from the filmmaker's memory — his family's past as he remembers it or recollections as they were told to him. With Sam's passing, Levinson knew that these stories would no longer be passed down to the next generation, so he chose to concretize that memory as cinema; in the course of doing so, whatever his filmic intention, he has created important historical documents. As such, as Marc Ferro pointed out, they are "permanent, unchanging." [68] There will be no further writing or revision of the Levinson family history on film, except in a new and different work, which Levinson actually did when he followed *Avalon* with *Liberty Heights*. Still, there remains the possibility of more "Baltimore stories" in the future. Though the filmmaker makes no claim to reproduce the past accurately and disavows any historical intent, these two films do provide a road map for better understanding the periods through which their stories are woven. Although these motion pictures are not works of history, they should be seen as important historical texts that carry a great deal of information and warrant careful study and analysis. In one image, as Pierre Sorlin posits, "one cannot hope to see everything, even if we look at it for a long time." [69] Indeed, these films and the images they contain do lend themselves to different readings and interpretation, depending on who the film reader is and what his or her background might be — another reason to encourage greater visual literacy. They serve not simply as a record of visual reality but also as a register for the feelings and attitudes of the time in which each was made. Barry Levinson has given us powerful dramatizations of two moments in American history with which to better understand who we were and who we are. He joins a growing number of filmmakers who are providing new cinematic canvasses from which we can draw greater clarity from the events that shaped and continue to fashion the American Jewish story.

CHAPTER 7

EVERYTHING IS ILLUMINATED

A NEW DIRECTION IN FILM — SEARCHING
FOR A USABLE PAST

In *Everything Is Illuminated*, Liev Schreiber's 2005 narrative film drawn from the novel by Jonathan Safran Foer, a young American Jewish adult travels to Ukraine in search of identity and self-understanding. Both the twenty-five-year-old Foer and Schreiber, a dozen years older, had a grandparent that led each to a journey — a grandparent representing a connection to some kind of Jewish existence that for each growing up was absent in their home. For Foer, it had been Friday night Shabbat with his grandmother; for Schreiber, Passover seders with his grandfather.

Jonathan Safran Foer's first published fiction, the story "A Very Rigid Search," appeared in the June 18, 2001, issue of the *New Yorker*. That short story grew out of the author's search in the Odessa region of Ukraine for Trachimbrod, a village where his grandfather, whom he never knew, was supposedly rescued from the Nazis at the beginning of the war by a woman named Augustine. Foer made the trip after his junior year at Princeton University:

> I did not intend to write *Everything Is Illuminated*. I intended to chronicle, in strictly nonfictional terms, a trip that I made to Ukraine as a twenty-year-old. Armed with a photograph of the woman who, I was told, had saved my grandfather from the Nazis, I embarked on a journey to Trachimbrod, the shtetl of my family's origins. The comedy of errors lasted five days. I found nothing but nothing, and in that nothing — a

landscape of completely realized absence—nothing was to be found. Because I didn't tell my grandmother about the trip—she would never have let me go—I didn't know what questions to ask, or whom to ask, or the necessary names of people, places, and things. The nothing came as much from me as from what I encountered. . . . I wasn't even close to finding her. The trip was so ill conceived, so poorly planned, so without the research that would have been necessary to have had any hope of accomplishing what I thought was my purpose—finding Augustine—that I never had a chance. But in retrospect, I'm not sure that the purpose *was* to find her.[1]

As the author explained, he was a non-observant Jew, skeptical of anything described as Jewish, "with no felt connection to, or great interest in" his past. Yet it was his complete failure to find Augustine that freed his imagination to write and allowed him to write first the short story, and later his novel. He spent his time and energy on activities he didn't think he cared about: "My writing—what little I did then—began to take on a Jewish sensibility, if not content." As his writing proceeded, Foer described "a strange and exhilarating split—between the Jonathan that *thought* (secular), and the Jonathan that *did* (Jewish)."[2] It was allowance for the coexistence of each that enabled Foer to complete the work.

Jonathan Safran Foer's writing was encouraged at Princeton, particularly by the novelist Joyce Carol Oates, who became a mentor. His short story "A Very Rigid Search" eventually became *Everything is Illuminated*, and the publication in 2002 of this first novel drew a great deal of attention; it soared to the top of the bestseller lists. Foer and his wife, Nicole Krauss (the author of *Man Walks Into a Room* and *The History of Love*), are among a group of contemporary young Jewish writers who are enthralling readers with their artistry. Just as impressive are the efforts of a cadre of capable screenwriters and actors like Liev Schreiber who have decided to try their hand at producing and directing Jewish-themed films. Their creative expression appears to be a way of relaying their individual sagas, of dealing with their personal Jewish journeys. Liev Schreiber, a distinguished actor onstage and in film, is one of those talents who has used cinema as a vehicle for his own personal struggle. His story is representative of this new, exciting development.

Schreiber's primary Jewish connection was through his grandfather, a 1908 refugee from Eastern Europe. Liev had no formal Jewish schooling,

*Liev Schreiber was drawn to Jonathan Safran Foer's novel,
adapting it for the screen in his directorial debut. © Warner Independent
Pictures. Photographer: Neil Davidson. Photofest.*

and his upbringing was void of any real Jewish experience, except that each
year his grandfather would reintroduce the Israelite exodus from Egypt at
the Passover seder. In 1993, with his grandfather's death, Schreiber struggled
to find himself as a Jew and began writing a screenplay about what it meant
to return to the land of his grandfather. "I became curious about his history
in the hope that it would inform my own," he said.[3] Schreiber had always
aspired to be a writer, but a teacher had suggested that he would do well to
pursue acting rather than write. The effort of writing was far harder than he
had imagined. A few years later, he read Foer's short story in the *New Yorker*
about a boy who goes back to Ukraine to find his roots. Said Schreiber:

> When I read the short story I was very moved by it and at the same time
> I thought it was the most hilarious thing I had read in years. . . . When I
> read Jonathan's story I felt deeply connected to it. What's more, he had
> done in fifteen pages what I had been trying to do in about one hundred,
> and he had done it with humor.[4]

Schreiber contacted Foer's agent and a meeting was finally arranged in New
York:

At the time I knew nothing about him [Foer]. I imagined some ninety-year-old Jewish man from Nantucket who only communicates through his agent. I walked in and there was this twenty-something-year-old kid with glasses waving and smiling at me. I remember thinking this must be some guy who's seen "Scream" [that I was in] or something but he kept waving at me so I went over to him and it was Jonathan. I was blown away.[5]

The two met and Schreiber found his vehicle and voice, merging his story with that of Foer. On the surface, the film seems like a simple dramatization of Foer's visit to Eastern Europe. It is much more. The film adaptation of the novel provides a brilliant study of American Jewry's fascination with its Eastern Europe past and a warm rendering of what it means today to be a Jew in America. In an interview, Liev Schreiber revealed what brought him to develop *Everything is Illuminated* into a film:

It really began with my grandfather. It began with a death in the family and a kind of identity crisis that I think comes with that sort of thing. Actors generally suffer from identity crisis to some degree or another. But the one place that I didn't was with my grandfather — I had a real sense of who he was. . . . I panicked that in losing my grandfather I was losing an anchor. I was losing something that I hadn't paid enough attention to when I was younger and it was a resource that I was going to lose. . . . I started to piece together a picture of who he was. That brought me to this idea about the immigrant experience, and about what defines American Jewry.[6]

THE OLD COUNTRY

He asked himself: How did he come to be? Who were his ancestors? How might he understand his place as an American Jew juxtaposed to a world that had seemingly vanished? Just what was his connection with that world? For the film's protagonist, Jonathan, "everything is illuminated in the light of the past." For him, as with the majority of America's Jews, the past lies in Eastern Europe. This concept breaks with a norm that had existed in English-language American cinema for seventy years, which had generally avoided connecting America's Jews with a past beyond America's shores.

Beginning in 1934, with changes in production codes and mainstream American moviemaking, there was a paucity of Jewish-themed movies.[7] In contrast, American Yiddish movies flourished in the 1930s, with most story-lines closely linked to Eastern European Jewish life. It was not infrequent for the film's story to be set in the shtetl, as in Edgar G. Ulmer and Jacob Ben-Ami's 1937 reworking of Peretz Hirschbein's *Grine Felder* (*Green Fields*) or Maurice Schwartz's 1939 adaptation of Sholem Aleichem's *Tevye der Milkhiker* (*Tevye the Dairyman*). There were even situations in which an American protagonist found himself back in the old country, as when Sol Reichman (played by Moishe Oysher) returns to his birthplace, the shtetl of Belz, in Sidney Goldin's 1936 *Dem Khazns Zindl* (*The Cantor's Son*), mentioned in chapter 2. There, he joins his parents and seeks out his childhood sweetheart, his *basherta*—the predestined love of his life. At this time, Eastern Europe, and the shtetl in particular, were seen by most Jews as a vibrant Jewish living space. For Hollywood's mainstream filmmakers it was the farthest thing from their reality, as they anxiously sought to disconnect with that Jewish past. Yet for Yiddish moviemakers and the audience for whom they made their films, the shtetl had become established in the Jewish imagination. As David Roskies pointed out, "The place of the shtetl in the self-understanding of millions of American Jews now became fixed for all time. The shtetl was claimed as the place of common origin (even if it wasn't), the source of a collective folk identity rooted in a particular historical past and, most importantly, as the locus of a new, secular covenant."[8] After the war, with the annihilation of European Jewry and the virtual disappearance of Jewish shtetl life, that "place of origin" was refocused to the west, to America. When American films with Jewish subject matter began to emerge over the next decades, rarely would a film's story reach back to Europe for any connection. It is no mistake that when "the Father" arrives from abroad to join the family in Barry Levinson's *Avalon* (1990), he disembarks a ship from "the Old Country," and the immigrant protagonists' beginnings are set at the port of Baltimore, not somewhere in Europe. Like most films with American Jewish themes produced in the U.S. after World War II, Levinson's *Avalon* had America as its point of origin, its starting point.

By the latter part of the twentieth century, the Holocaust had become more fully rooted in Jewish American identity. In 1993, with the release of Steven Spielberg's *Schindler's List* and the opening of the U.S. Holocaust Memorial Museum in the nation's capital, the Shoah also became firmly affixed on the American cultural map as a whole. Holocaust education was

First-time novelist Jonathan Safran Foer trusted his book in the hands of Liev Schreiber.
Here is Foer, off-set with actor Elijah Wood (left), who plays Jonathan. Photofest.

mandated in a growing number of states and there was greater familiarity with the atrocities that had occurred during World War II. There was also a better understanding that all Americans, with the exception of Native Americans, came from somewhere else. For American Jews, as Alan Mintz pointed out, "the indelible images of the Holocaust have filled in that blurred vacancy with a sharply etched picture of the place they came from. If the knowledge of that place and its culture remains vague, at least the sense of loss and sadness elicited by the Holocaust has an address to which to attach itself." [9] With the fall of the Soviet Union and easier access for Americans to that part of the world, it became more common for American Jews, like Foer and Schreiber's Jonathan, to journey east to better understand who they were. Eastern Europe was seen more and more as the supreme Jewish sacred burial ground and pilgrimage site.

Equipped with a snapshot of his grandfather and Augustine taken in the "old country," protagonist Jonathan leaves for Ukraine in search of answers, just as Jonathan Safran Foer had done in real life a few years before. Schreiber and Foer's journeys differed; Schreiber was searching for a beginning, a starting point in his family's history. For Foer, a third-generation American Jew whose grandfather had fled the Nazis, his exploration was more complex and intimately tied to the Shoah. Foer had been impacted by a traumatic event, in this case the Holocaust, and his passion was connected to a more inaccessible past. With the actual witnesses to the atrocities dying off — often without providing oral histories — Foer turned to what the Belgian scholar Philippe Codde called a "postmemorial approach" — creating myths and fairy tales to fill in absent history.[10] "Postmemory," wrote literary scholar Marianne Hirsch, "is a powerful and very particular form of memory precisely because its connection to its object or source is mediated not through recollection but through an imaginative investment and creation."[11] So Foer invents a family history for himself in his novel. When adapting Foer's novel for film, Schreiber, out of cinematic necessity, strips away much of that mythology and history. Though Schreiber's grandfather's past was not connected to the Shoah, memory and history still played a similar role.

NOVEL INTO FILM

Foer's narrative weaves the novel that Jonathan is working on — an imagined century and a half-history of Trachimbrod — with the "reality" of his search for the family's shtetl. As the contemporary section moves back in time, the imagined history moves forward, with "reality" and "fiction" coming together in the final scene. Foer's novel is filled with stories of generations of Trachimbrod inhabitants. Schreiber, needing to create a tight and flowing narrative film, moved away from the collective history of the town, putting aside that aspect of Foer's novel to instead concentrate on Jonathan's personal quest. The impetus for the script was Foer's original short story, and though Schreiber considered incorporating a bit of eighteenth-century Trachimbrod, he realized early on that such a project would be too big and costly. In this way, Schreiber confined himself mostly to Foer's original short story, "A Very Rigid Search," and Foer was perfectly comfortable with this:

> Liev's extremely charismatic and it's very easy to get caught up in what he cares about and I really trusted him straight away. I had no idea what he was going to do with the book but I knew that he cared about it and whatever he did would be a reflection of that caring rather than any other motive one might have for making a movie.[12]

Foer was available to work with Schreiber, and the novelist collaborated when asked: "Along the way Liev would ask my advice and I gave him that but I never wanted to do any more. . . . Liev did it all from start to finish. . . . I really trusted Liev's artistic integrity."[13]

That novel and film differ is not uncommon in cinema. In fact, there is great disparity between Foer's book and Schreiber's motion picture. As the French film theorist Jean Mitry wrote, "the novel is a narrative that organizes itself in the world, while the cinema is a world that organizes itself into a narrative."[14] Schreiber did not deviate a great deal from the guideline set out in the original *New Yorker* short story, but he provided a different flow. A narrator of both the short story and film, Alexander Perchov, played in the film by Eugene Hutz, is a local translator and son of the owner of a tour company that specializes in helping Jewish tourists search for their roots. Alexander has an affinity for malapropisms, and his misuse of language provides the humor that carries us through the early part of the film. Alexander did not have a high opinion of Jews—"I had the opinion that Jewish people were having shit between their brains." Nor could he comprehend how "they paid father very much currency in order to make vacations *from* America to Ukraine."

The first image we encounter, as opening titles come onscreen, is a microscopic view of something quite unclear—what we will later see is a pendant with an inlaid grasshopper, which Jonathan will take from his grandfather Safran's night table shortly after his death. Just what information does this piece of jewelry carry that we scrutinize it so carefully, so many times magnified? The camera then moves to a picture of a young boy wearing a *tallit*—a prayer shawl, possibly Jonathan's grandfather's bar mitzvah picture—and then zooms out. Then comes a panoramic pan across a scrapbook-like wall with sepia-toned pictures of generations of family, ostensibly Jonathan's, pinned over a wall map of Ukraine, with some route outlined in red marker. In the middle of the pan, Alexander begins his narration, and after a close-up of the prose that Alexander is writing, the sequence ends as the camera moves to a snapshot of Jonathan's grandfather with Augustine in a field. Already, with this first montage of photographs, Schreiber is juxtaposing Jonathan's collection of stills with Alexander's rebuke of memory. "I was of the opinion that the past is past and like all that is not now it should remain buried along the side of our memories. But this was before the commencement of our very rigid search, before I encountered the collector—Jonathan Safran Foer," says Alexander. For Alexander the past is past—that is until he meets Jonathan.

After the photo montage, the first "chapter" begins in the cemetery as Jonathan, played by a conspicuously bespectacled Elijah Wood, visits the grave of the man for whom he is named, Safran Foer. As genealogist Arthur Kurzweil reminds us, the cemetery is an excellent place to begin one's search for roots, as the gravestone generally carries a great deal of information.[15] In this scene, the real Jonathan Safran Foer has a cameo role as a man blowing the leaves from in front of the graves, as if to clear away anything that might get in the way of uncovering his history. But Safran's stone only carries his name and the years of his birth and death. Though there is little to be learned here, these images are the start of Jonathan's "very rigid search." The drive from the cemetery across town that begins Jonathan's road trip and quest to learn more about his grandfather is slow and dramatic. As they drive away, the urban American homes serve as a visual contrast to the post-Soviet Ukrainian countryside that we will presently encounter.

The rest of this chapter/sequence has Jonathan, at various stages of his youth, gathering things that are connected with special family moments. In the very next scene, we see him visiting with his seemingly ailing grandmother who appears to be having trouble breathing properly. Opening her eyes in bed, she sees him and with a deep smile turns to her side to reach for a photograph and necklace that sit in a book on her night table. The necklace has a gold Magen David, a Jewish star, on a chain; the photo of a man and a woman in a field reads "Augustine and Me, Trachimbrod 1940" on the back. "Your grandfather wanted you to have this—it is for your collection!" she tells him. Jonathan studies the photograph as he sits across the room against a stark white wall with his shadow deeply embedded on the wall behind him. The walls of grandmother's room have few pictures, and with the exception of a vintage photo over her bed of a couple that we don't recognize, the room seems quite austere. In contrast, in black and white, there are Jonathan and his shadow punctuating these bare surroundings. "Who is Augustine? Grandma!" asks Jonathan. The shadow envelops the room as the curious Jonathan, looking for answers to a past about which he knows little, is transposed against the bare white walls and sheer white curtains that provide no answers. Neither does his grandmother.

But the photo and necklace do possibly carry a clue. Though the story of Jonathan's grandfather that goes back to Eastern Europe was never shared, he does want Jonathan to have the photograph from Trachimbrod. The camera pans up over the white bedsheets and we see an elderly man—it is Safran,

Jonathan's grandmother passes on a necklace with a Magen David—a Jewish star—and the photograph of Augustine together with her husband, Jonathan's grandfather. Jana Hrabetova.

Jonathan in his grandmother's bedroom with swaths of shadows. Jana Hrabetova, Elijah Wood.

with his eyes closed. As our eyes focus on the serene Safran, the sheets are pulled up over his face (alluding to his demise), and the camera moves to the left to focus on the amber pendant seen earlier, now positioned on the night table. A Jonathan from an earlier age takes the pendant, pondering what information he can draw from this artifact in what will eventually become his investigation of his family past. The sequence ends in an entirely different room, in what seems to have become Jonathan's "laboratory," with plastic bags, photographs filling one entire wall, and a picture of Safran Foer all alone on a second wall. The only artifact seen below the picture is the pendant, an object from the past, suspended in time and space, that must have a story. Next, we see all types of artifacts, many rich with Jewish connection: a lock of hair, a photograph, and a child's toy. The investigator is collecting clues for his "very rigid search." Memorabilia connect and identify historical events and real persons in this family. These things form Jonathan's memory and inform his identity. Jonathan calls himself "a collector." He later tells us that he collects "because I'm afraid I'll forget." Collecting objects is his way of gathering and preserving memory. This wall becomes Jonathan's starting point in his journey to try and understand himself and create his own history. That story is all the more remarkable in that it not only connects past and present, but also joins Old World with New. Generations before, Yiddish movies provided a nostalgic connection for immigrant Jews to the old country, but none of that exists here. This is not nostalgia. This young American Jew of the new millennium simply wants to "fill in the void," to understand who he is and from whence he comes.

Jonathan's "laboratory"—his wall of memories. © Warner Independent Pictures. Photographer: Neil Davidson. Photofest.

CHAPTER TWO

Chapter 1 concludes as Jonathan removes the lone ziplock bag that is tacked below Safran Foer's picture on the side wall; inside is the amber pendant with the inlaid grasshopper. Jonathan carefully scrutinizes the ornament under a magnifying glass. He then vigilantly reviews the Trachimbrod picture of Safran and Augustine in the field, only to see that in the photo Augustine is wearing that very pendant. It needs clarity; it requires illumination! What of this pendant? Who is Augustine? Why was her pendant on the night table next to Safran when he died? Why did Jonathan's grandmother later give him the photo, yet decline to tell him more? What was Augustine's relationship to Safran Foer? As we ponder these questions, the scene transitions and we see an inscription describing chapter 2 in Jonathan's journey: "The commencement of a very rigid search." To be sure, in *Everything Is Illuminated*, this search is driven by the mystery, set during the Holocaust, that surrounds Jonathan's grandfather and a woman named Augustine. Schreiber has carefully laid out his protagonist's personality and the mystery and drama that will inspire his journey to Ukraine, his exploration of the past.

Alexander, son of the Ukraine-based Jewish heritage tour operator, is to navigate Jonathan's journey. About the same age as Jonathan, he is fixated on American popular culture and is unclear as to why Americans come *in search* of memory. Joining him is his grandfather, a recent widower, also named Alexander, who feigns blindness and would rather not be bothered. He clearly is not a big enthusiast of Jews, yet here he is. In the course of Jonathan's search for his grandfather's hometown, he bonds with his guide and translator, Alexander, who, over the course of the excursion, goes through his own self-discovery. These three, along with Alexander Sr.'s dog, set out to search for Trachimbrod. Using the trope of journey, a literary device employed by Foer and common in both Yiddish fiction and contemporary cinema, their road trip of self-discovery begins when Jonathan is picked up at the train station and greeted with great fanfare by a group of itinerant musicians hired by Alex. As Jonathan comes off the train, there is already a blending of cultures as the musicians give their interpretation of the American national anthem. As their search moves forward, the reality and actuality of Trachimbrod becomes almost secondary as the two begin their pursuit not only of what was but what might have been.

An important element of the film is the developing relationship of these two contemporaries, who by circumstance of history wind up in America and Ukraine. One is the grandson of a survivor of the Holocaust who fled Europe just in time, the other the grandson of someone who remained, witnessed, and experienced the events of that time. As they get to know each other, there is a growing awareness of what Anna Ronell calls "an unlived possibility," that were it not for certain historic events and calamities, these two children whose grandparents both came from this part of the world might be living side-by-side in the shtetl they are seeking to find.[16] We see this in the novel when Jonathan, asked why he has come, responds to Alex: "I want to see Trachimbrod. . . . To see what it's like, how my grandfather grew up, where I would be now if it weren't for the war."[17] In the film, Jonathan considers where he would now be if his grandfather had not come to America. "You would be Ukrainian like me," responds Alex. Still, Liev Schreiber's own history is not the same as Foer's — there were no Nazis that gave impetus to Schreiber's grandfather's flight from Europe, no real mysteries surrounding that exodus.

Jonathan Safran Foer went to Eastern Europe to seek out his grandfather's story, just as Liev Schreiber tried to learn more about his heritage. Each is Third Generation — they both had a grandfather who fled Eastern

Europe and made his way to America. Both men sought to learn more of their family's past. Whereas for a filmmaker of the previous generation, like Barry Levinson, that exploration might lead to Ellis Island or the Port of Baltimore, both of these men really want to go back farther, to search in Europe. Foer, a grandchild of a survivor of the Shoah, had been shut out, not privy to that experience. Schreiber, whose father came to America long before World War II, was also kept from knowing of his grandfather's life in Europe. This shared experience united the two. Jonathan Safran Foer was denied access to the stories of his family's past, left only with little more than a photograph and a pendant. Schreiber's experience was really not all that different:

> My grandfather didn't want to know from Ukraine or Poland. And you ask the average Jew [in the next generation], they didn't want to talk about Europe. To hell with Europe! My God, go run as fast as you can and don't ever look back! . . . The grandparents don't want to tell it, they don't want to talk about it. They don't want to know from it, and I understand that. . . . That was part of what intrigued me about this story![18]

The Holocaust scholar Gary Weissman observed a phenomenon that some "non-witnesses," particularly American Jews, who have no immediate family connection to the Shoah, nonetheless see themselves as Third Generation.[19] Schreiber's connection to Jewish history was through the Passover seder, when Jews are asked to see themselves as if *they* had left Egypt. So too, many Jews see themselves as having imaginatively survived the Shoah. Novelist and film director are in this way bonded.

Jonathan the character gave Schreiber what he needed, the "post-memory" invention of a narrative. With the artifacts provided as part of that story, Schreiber went forward with his film. Both author and filmmaker saw the possibilities that lay before them with their trip back to this old world. As Ronell noted:

> The scarcity of Jewish material remains in this vanished world only contributes to the imaginative potential of this space. The same cannot be said of the landscape, much of which survived the war and the Soviets unchanged; this is why traveling to Eastern Europe holds such an incomparable grip on the Jewish imagination. Furthermore, exploring the shtetls of Ukraine leaves one with an eerie feeling as one walks along the streets

lined with synagogues that are now philharmonic halls and teachers' colleges, with Jewish houses that are now lodging houses and cafeterias. The Jewish spirit emanates from the place although there are no Jews.[20]

As the heritage tour car carrying Jonathan, Alex, Alex's grandfather, and Sammy Davis Junior, Junior, the "seeing eye bitch," moves across the countryside in its "very rigid search," we see both beauty and decay in an attempt to provide some realism for a vanished Jewish world and a shtetl destination that appears nowhere on a map. The contrast between lushness and devastation is clear, between a world that once flourished and is now eradicated understood. As they close in on their destination, Grandfather remarks, "This was the most fertile land in Eastern Europe. . . . *Before the war*, this was the most beautiful place in the world." We see that the Second World War has clearly had an impact on all of their lives, but the story is yet to unfold.

IN SEARCH OF TRACHIMBROD

The shtetl was largely abandoned as subject or setting for Jewish-themed cinema with the demise of Yiddish movies in 1950. In the few American narrative films where there is a shtetl, it is usually a fictional town, as in Sholem Aleichem's make-believe Anatevka of Norman Jewison's *Fiddler on the Roof* (1971). Trachimbrod also exists as a fiction, something created and imagined by Foer and Schreiber. In the novel, Alex states, "There was nothing. . . . When I utter 'nothing' I do mean there was nothing."[21] In the film, Alex makes his way through a field of sunflowers and arrives at the doorstep of a house where an elderly woman awaits him. He questions her not only about Trachimbrod, but about Jonathan's photograph. Although the woman initially is reluctant to respond to his queries, she finally turns to him and states boldly, "You are here. I am it!" But just where is he? What is this house, surrounded by sunflowers with an entranceway of clean white sheets blowing in the wind outside? Who is this woman and what does she mean by her statement? Have they finally met Augustine, the woman in the photo with grandfather Safran? No, but apparently they have encountered Lista, one of the few survivors of the town and witness to the Trachimbrod annihilation. Schreiber described his decision making in setting the scene thus:

Have they found Trachimbrod? A field of sunflowers with a house in the middle and white laundry hanging outside to dry. Alexander Jr. walks the walk. Eugene Hutz. © Warner Independent Pictures. Photographer: Neil Davidson. Photofest.

The first image that I had was actually an endless field of laundry. That was my first image — that it was a house in the midst of 150 acres of laundry hanging out to dry. But it felt too "on the nose" to me, so I came up with sunflowers and I didn't even know until long after that it was the national flower of Ukraine. . . . There's something about the sunflowers — you know they're six feet tall; they've got big heads and skinny bodies; they look like people; and they follow the trajectory of the sun, so their heads actually move over the course of a day. And the idea of Lista. . . . She seemed to me . . . as a caretaker of sorts — that she was preserving Trachimbrod. And the sunflowers for me were evidence of the souls, the lost souls of Trachimbrod. . . . She was very much alone, but very much surrounded by beings. That house sticks out like a sore thumb in the middle of that field, so you have a real sense of isolation [of] this person who is sort of living in a box with a label on it, but at the same time surrounded by sunflowers — all these protectors of this . . . testament. They are a testament to the existence of that place which has vanished off the map.[22]

The three—Alex Jr., Jonathan, and Alex Sr.—find a collector's trove in Lista's house.
Eugene Hutz, Elijah Wood, Boris Leskin. © Warner Independent Pictures.
Photographer: Neil Davidson. Photofest.

The inside of Lista's house is filled with cardboard boxes of all shapes, each with a different label: dust, menorahs, silver, underwear, figurines—Lista is the keeper of memory. One cannot help calling to mind the walls of Jonathan's room filled with memorabilia. "She too is a collector!" Alex proclaims. When Alex asks Lista if she "has anyone," she responds that she has "all of them." Who are they? "They are Trachimbrod!" Lista then pulls out a box marked "In Case," first taking out a wedding ring and then, when quizzed again about the photo that Jonathan brought with him, a series of pictures from another box. With these photographs, Lista will begin to clarify a history and fill in a void. She shows them a period photo of Safran, Jonathan's grandfather, who looked just like Jonathan, with two women. It turns out that she is one of these women; the other is her sister Augustine. But it is only later that she will provide the answer to how Jonathan's grandfather managed to flee to America and explain the role that Augustine played in his escape. Lista then turns to Alexander Senior and shows him a different picture, of Borukh, one of the townspeople "who adored books." At this critical moment, Grandfather asks to be alone with Lista, and Alex and Jonathan go outside. As Alexander Senior and Lista confront truth inside, Alex ponders who his grandfather really is and what he does not know of *his* grandfather's past. At this point, Jonathan remarks that Alex's undershirt is inside out. As the young men stand outside on the porch and Grandfather and Lista remain inside the house, this inside/outside moment turns into a questioning of what truth might be hidden inside. Jonathan then traps a grasshopper in his glasses case and places it in one of his ziplock bags. This grasshopper that he will collect and bring home provides a connection to the amber pendant that he brings with him from home and that he noticed adorning Augustine's neck in the photo. Alex asks, "Why do you do this?" "I guess sometimes I'm afraid I'll forget," is Jonathan's response. Lawrence Baron sees the grasshopper trapped in amber as symbolizing "how memory freezes a moment in time, in general, and Jonathan's obsession with preserving memory, in particular."[23] Memory, as we see in this work, can be illuminating, enlightening. But that grasshopper, locked forever in the amber pendant, has provided a key to unlocking this family's secrets. Maybe this grasshopper from Trachimbrod, locked into Jonathan's glasses case, will provide another lens for the probe into his origins.

Lista studies Jonathan. He bears a remarkable resemblance to his grandfather.
Laryssa Lauret, Elijah Wood. © Warner Independent Pictures.
Photographer: Neil Davidson. Photofest.

Alex's grandfather is left alone with Lista. We are never quite made aware of what they talk about. It is reminiscent of the scene in *Avalon* where the elders meet with Simka and Elka and speak in foreign languages, not subtitled in English. It seems clear that when Lista showed him the picture of Borukh, he was deeply moved, and the resemblance between Alexander Senior and Borukh is strong. Still, we know little of the grandfather, other than the fact that he seems to hate the Jews from whom, over the years, he has made his livelihood. He appears a virulent anti-Semite, but as the movie progresses he seems to mellow, particularly after he carefully sees and studies Jonathan's photograph of Safran and Augustine during a meal. There is also a moment of great impact for the grandfather, when earlier, stopping on the side of a road, he scrutinizes a pit filled with wreckage from a different time. The camera, in a crane shot, moves over his head in a sweeping view of the terrain below. It is there that we first encounter a flashback, through the grandfather, to a time during the war when Jews were lined up for execution. It is unclear at first who is the executioner and who is the one about to be executed. Only through subsequent flashbacks does Alex's grandfather's relationship to this piece of history become less ambiguous. Was he a Nazi? An accomplice? Someone who got away? No matter what happened to him, it becomes all the more clear that he survived this moment to live another day, carrying that memory with him. Interestingly, Foer and Schreiber chose different paths for Grandfather's story — in the novel, he is a gentile accomplice in the tragedy; in the film, he survives the execution and disassociates himself for the remainder of his life from anything Jewish. In both novel and film, the grandfather chooses to conclude his story in much the same way, though for different reasons. In both cases, that leaves the two, Jonathan and Alexander, with a very special connection: they are both grandchildren of a survivor. They, like their creators Foer and Schreiber, are members of the Third Generation.

Lista wants to bring everyone to the river Brod, where she tells them that they have reached Trachimbrod. They stand by a memorial stone, set in the ground, that commemorates those massacred there. "This is all that is left. They destroyed everything. Only a few were able to get out before they came," says Lista. Jeremy Shere interprets the role of the monument:

The monument's purpose is historical, to "stand in memory" of the former inhabitants of the destroyed shtetl and thereby literally to take their place as the last remnant of a disappeared people. Yet the monument's function is also ironic, of course, since it, like the shtetl depicted in *Illuminated*, is itself a fiction. It is through fiction, finally, that the shtetl most fully comes to life and thus it is the act of imaginative writing [and filmmaking], in place of and even in opposition to history, that makes possible the character's (and the reader's) fullest engagement with the shtetl. The absence of an available shtetl past, in other words, both paves the way for and necessitates a fictional, mythic surrogate.[24]

It is there, at the site, that Lista finally unravels the story of what took place and how Augustine had been murdered. It also becomes clear, through flashback, what had happened to Alexander's grandfather not far from this place. Jonathan leaves the group and walks toward the riverbank where he gathers some earth, as if taking it from a holy place, and places it into two ziplock bags; he presents one of the bags to Grandfather.

Upon returning to the house, Jonathan gives Lista the amber pendant and she in turn presents him with the box marked "In Case," along with the wedding ring, which turns out to be Augustine's. She had hidden it in the ground, in a jar, prior to her murder, "in case someone should come searching one day," Lista says. "It does not exist for you. . . . You exist for it. . . . You have come because it exists!" she continues. As the boys walk away, she turns to Grandfather and asks whether the war is over. "Yes," responds Grandfather and indeed, she has finally been liberated from the memory that she was responsible to keep and that had confined her. Grandfather, on the ride from Trachimbrod, will touch his grandson with great tenderness and affection, seemingly for the first time. For Grandfather, too, has been freed as he finally comes to grips with the past that he had repressed. The survivor is about to surrender his forged life! There may even be guilt for having survived. Alexander Senior's own internal war has come to an end. His feigned blindness gives way to illumination.

Foer and Schreiber sought out the shtetl as a way to solidify their own identity as Jews in America. Historically, Jews have struggled with their special connection to their past in Eastern Europe, a place that for a majority of Jews had been home to their ancestors. This search for the "home" represents a real issue for America's Jews. Sidra Ezrahi questions whether this "invisible" European graveyard has become a new mythical anchor for the Jewish ethos and whether "destruction seems to have territorialized exile as a lost home." She elaborates:

A pattern does begin to suggest itself: what was destroyed becomes over time an authentic original that can be represented but not recaptured; it becomes accessible to the pilgrim/tourist only as an unredeemed ruin, subject to a nonproprietary gaze. Hence the Holocaust may have turned the European exile from a place in which Home is imagined to a "real" home that can only be recalled from somewhere else and reconstructed from its shards.[25]

As the Holocaust has become more and more part of the Jewish psyche, there has evolved a special connection to the memory-sites, even for the American who could not trace loss to this calamity. Combining this with American Jewry's unique relationship with the State of Israel, and a Jew's religious connection with the *land* of Israel, this idea of *home* becomes far more complicated. For most American Jews, however, America is home and Europe and Israel or other points of connection represent part of the Jewish fiber that makes one a proud American.

Schreiber began developing *Everything is Illuminated* in the aftermath of September 11. "I really wanted to make a film to remind everybody else of who we were as Americans. We were *their* grandchildren, and we were *their* refugees. What we're doing was we were just trying to survive and re-build our lives and make this place. And that's what was so wonderful about democracy, and the idea of the Melting Pot, the idealistic idea."[26]

Everything Is Illuminated concludes with a visit by Alex and his family to Trachimbrod, where Grandfather has now been buried. Stones are placed on Grandfather's grave, much as Jonathan had done when visiting his grand-father's grave as the film began. The two gravestones look remarkably simi-lar. Memorial prayers are recited by the yarmulke-adorned males by the graveside, and there seems to be some affirmation that their lives, too, are tied to a common Jewish past previously unknown.

In Alex's final narration in the film, he says, "I have reflected many times upon our rigid search. It has shown me that everything is illuminated—in the light of the past. It is always along the side of us—on the inside looking out. Like you say! Inside out! Jonathan—in this way I will always be along the side of your life and you will always be along the side of mine." Jonathan and Alexander, Third Generation, both grandchildren of Trachimbrod, who live on opposite sides of an ocean, now share a common memory, their story, their Haggadah to be shared with their offspring. This personal Jewish his-tory is reflective of a new kind of American moviemaking, firmly rooted and

Jewishly identified, that does not run away from its historical starting point. As Liev Schreiber has suggested, stressing that this is a point made by the film as distinct from the book, "We don't have to worry about memory if we invest in history . . . and that *that* will now allow those people from our past, and those stories to 'be along the side of us' in our present and our future."[27]

NOTES

PREFACE

1. Arthur M. Schlesinger Jr., foreword to *American History/American Film: Interpreting the Hollywood Image*, ed. John E. O'Conner and Martin A. Jackson (New York: Frederick Ungar, 1979), x.

2. John E. O'Connor, ed., *Image as Artifact: The Historical Analysis of Film and Television* (Malabar, FL: Krieger, 1990), 110.

3. K. R. M. Short, ed., *Feature Films as History* (Knoxville: University of Tennessee Press, 1981), 28.

4. Marc Ferro, *Cinema and History* (Detroit: Wayne State University Press, 1988).

5. Robert Sklar, *Movie-Made America* (New York: Random House, 1975), vi.

6. Michael Paris, "More Than Just Entertainment: The Feature Film and the Historian," in *Using Visual Evidence*, ed. Robert Howells and Robert W. Matson (Berkshire, England: Open University Press, 2009), 126.

7. John Belton, *American Cinema/American Culture* (New York: McGraw-Hill, 1994), xxi.

8. Sklar, *Movie-Made America*, vi.

9. Peter C. Rollins, *Hollywood as Historian* (Lexington: University Press of Kentucky, 1998), 250.

CHAPTER I

1. Neal Gabler, Frank Rich, and Joyce Antler, *Television's Changing Image of American Jews* (New York and Los Angeles: American Jewish Committee and the Norman Lear Center, 2000), 10.

2. Judith E. Doneson, *The Holocaust in American Film* (Philadelphia: Jewish Publication Society, 1987), 16.

3. The U.S. Supreme Court decision in *Brown v. Board of Education* declared that permissive or mandatory segregation in public schools was unconstitutional. *Cooper v. Aaron* (1958) provided the muscle for enforcement.

4. Jonathan D. Sarna, *American Judaism* (New Haven, CT: Yale University Press, 2004), 277.

5. Herbert J. Gans, "Park Forest: Birth of a Jewish Community," in *Commentary on the American Scene: Portraits of Jewish Life in America*, ed. Elliot E. Cohen (New York: Knopf, 1953), 221.

6. It must be pointed out that screenwriter Edward Anhalt's adaptation of the 1948 Shaw novel reflects societal changes between the time Shaw penned the novel (in part during the war) and when the film was released a decade later. Americans related to Germans differently in the two decades. America's relationship with Germany had changed significantly in the fifties, as West Germany had become a close American ally in the Cold War and a friend and benefactor to the State of Israel.

7. Pierre Sorlin, *The Film in History: Restaging the Past* (Totowa, NJ: Barnes and Noble, 1980), 21.

8. J. J. Goldberg, *Jewish Power: Inside the American Jewish Establishment* (Reading, MA: Addison Wesley, 1996), 120.

9. There had been lesser-known films made earlier about Israel. Most notable are *Sword in the Desert* (1949) and *The Juggler* (1953).

10. Leonard J. Fein, *Where We Are? The Inner Life of America's Jews* (New York: Harper & Row, 1988), 79.

11. Howard M. Sachar, *A History of Jews in America* (New York: Alfred A. Knopf, 1992), 730.

12. Omer Bartov, *The "Jew" in Cinema* (Bloomington: Indiana University Press, 2005), 190.

13. Lester D. Friedman, *Hollywood's Image of the Jew* (New York: Frederick Ungar, 1982), 215.

14. Patricia Erens, *The Jew in American Cinema* (Bloomington: Indiana University Press, 1984), 302.

15. For an interesting analysis, see Robert Stam and Ella Shohat, "*Zelig* and Contemporary Theory: Meditations on the Chameleon Text," in Charles L. P. Silet's *The Films of Woody Allen: Critical Essays* (Lanham, MD: Scarecrow Press, 2006), 198–216.

16. Gabler, Rich, and Antler, *Television's Changing Image*, 17.

17. Peter Novick, *The Holocaust in American Life* (Boston: Houghton Mifflin, 1999), 214.

18. Hasia Diner, *The Jews of the United States* (Berkeley: University of California Press, 2004), 321.

19. Sorlin, *The Film in History*, 16.

20. D. W. Griffith, as quoted in Robert Brent Toplin, *Reel History: In Defense of Hollywood* (Lawrence: University Press of Kansas, 2002), 198.

21. Irving Howe, *World of Our Fathers* (New York: Harcourt Brace Jovanovich, 1976), 642.

CHAPTER 2

1. Cass Warner Sperling, *Hollywood Be Thy Name* (Lexington: University Press of Kentucky, 1998), 18.

2. Ibid.

3. Ibid.

4. Ibid., 27.

5. Reminiscences of Samson Raphaelson, June 1959, Columbia Center for Oral History, Columbia University, New York.

6. Samson Raphaelson, "Birth of *The Jazz Singer*," *The American Hebrew*, October 14, 1927, 812.

7. Ibid.

8. Ibid.

9. Arthur Hertzberg, *The Jews in America* (New York: Columbia University Press, 1997), 184.

10. Harry Jolson, *Mistah Jolson*, as told to Alban Emley (Hollywood: House-Warvan Publishers, 1951), 47.

11. For more about Arnstein, see Michael C. Steinlauf, "Mark Arnshteyn and Polish Jewish Theater," in *The Jews of Poland between Two World Wars*, ed. Yisrael Gutman, Ezra Mendelsohn, Jehuda Reinharz, and Chone Shmeruk (Hanover, NH: Brandeis University Press, 1989), 399–411.

12. See Eric A. Goldman, "*The Jazz Singer* and Its Reaction in the Yiddish Cinema," in *When Joseph Met Molly*, ed. Sylvia Paskin (Nottingham, England: Five Leaves, 1999), 39–48.

13. Sholem Asch, *America*, trans. James Fuchs (New York: Alpha Omega Publishing, 1918), 118–119.

14. Ibid., 122–123.

15. Sampson Raphaelson, "The Day of Atonement," *Everybody's Magazine* 46, January 1922, 51. The story is reprinted in Robert L. Carringer, *The Jazz Singer* (Madison: University of Wisconsin Press, 1979), 147–167. A few years later, Raphaelson changed the spelling of his first name to "Samson."

16. Raphaelson, "The Day of Atonement," 52.

17. Ibid.

18. Hertzberg, *Jews in America*, 185.

19. Asch, *America*, 123.

20. Raphaelson, "The Day of Atonement," 52.

21. Ibid., 53.

22. Ibid., 54.

23. Ibid., 55.

24. Samson Raphaelson, *The Jazz Singer* (New York: Brentano's, 1925), 150.

25. This was also the underlying theme of Arnstein's play, *Der Vilner Balabesl* (*The Vilna Petit-Bourgeois*).

26. Audrey Kupferberg, *Take One* 6/2 (January 1978): 29.

27. Sperling, *Hollywood Be Thy Name*, 120–121.

28. George Jessel, *So Help Me* (Cleveland: World Publishing Company, 1943), 64.

29. *Jewish Daily Forward*, September 9, 1925.

30. Hertzberg, *Jews in America*, 203.

31. Sperling, *Hollywood Be Thy Name*, 89.

32. Jolson was actually signed to a contract for the picture on May 27, and the May 28 issue of *Moving Picture World* carried the news.

33. Jack Warner, *My First Hundred Years in Hollywood* (New York: Random House, 1965), 175.

34. George Jessel, *The World I Lived In*, with John Austin, (Chicago: Henry Regnery Company, 1975), 67.

35. Ibid., 88.

36. Ibid., 67.

37. Neal Gabler, *An Empire of Their Own: How the Jews Invented Hollywood* (New York: Anchor Books, 1988), 141.

38. Ruth Perlmutter, "The Melting Pot and the Humoring of America: Hollywood and the Jew," *Film Reader* 5 (1982): 249.

39. Jessel, *The World I Lived In*, 67.

40. Sperling, *Hollywood Be Thy Name*, 123.

41. Asch, *America*, 118.

42. Joyce Antler, *You Never Call! You Never Write! A History of the Jewish Mother* (Cambridge: Oxford University Press, 2007), 25.

43. Irving Howe, *World of Our Fathers* (New York: Harcourt Brace Jovanovich, 1976), 176.

44. Irv Saposnik, "Jolson, the Jazz Singer and the Jewish Mother: Or How My Yiddishe Momme Became My Mammy," *Judaism* 43, no. 4 (Fall 1994): 436.

45. Howe, *World of Our Fathers*, 176.

46. For more on *The Jazz Singer*, see J. Hoberman, "Is 'The Jazz Singer' Good for the Jews?" *Village Voice*, January 7–13, 1981, 32–33; Steve Whitfield, "Jazz Singers: A Hollywood Bomb — But Inadvertently, an Accurate Portrayal of the American Jewish Condition," *Moment*, March/April 1981, 19–25; J. Hoberman and Jeffrey Shandler, eds., *Entertaining America: Jews, Movies and Broadcasting* (Princeton, NJ: Princeton University Press, 2003), 77–80; Joel Rosenberg, "What You Ain't Heard Yet: The Languages of The Jazz Singer," *Prooftexts* 22, no. 1/2 (Winter/Spring 2002): 11–54.

47. Performers of the time often mimicked African American minstrel singers by applying a black tar to their faces.

48. Michael Rogin, *Blackface, White Noise: Jewish Immigrants in the Hollywood Melting Pot* (Berkeley: University of California Press, 1998), 79. See also Perlmutter, "Melting Pot," 248–249, and Rosenberg, ("What You Ain't Heard Yet," see note 46), who does an extensive analysis on this subject.

49. Howe, *World of Our Fathers*, 183.

50. Mark Slobin, "Putting Blackface in Its Place," in Hoberman and Shandler, *Entertaining America*, 97.

51. We had previously seen this Yom Kippur image, the cantor in white, at the beginning of the film when he sings the Kol Nidre, and also as an overlay when Jack goes to the theater to hear Yossele Rosenblatt.

52. Cantor Rosenblatt was invited to Hollywood specifically to be a part of this film. Apparently it was a special request of Ben Warner to his sons. Rosenblatt, who was a fan of the cinema, was excited by the opportunity, even arranging a meeting with Charlie

Chaplin. See Samuel Rosenblatt, *Yossele Rosenblatt: The Story of His Life, As Told by His Son* (New York: Farrar, Straus and Young, 1954). Rosenblatt, who was extremely pious, agreed to appear on film only on the condition that he would not sing any actual liturgy, but only "songs." Rosenblatt's appearance on camera is static and rigid; some scholars have looked at this as having purpose. In reality, in other film recordings — onstage — of the great cantor, he shows the same demeanor. The exception to this is his performance in the 1933 film travelogue *Dream of My People*, where throughout, particularly in a rowboat in the middle of the Jordan River, he is highly animated.

53. Saposnik, "Jolson, the Jazz Singer," 436.

54. Joseph Green, interview with the author, April 14, 1977, New York.

55. Ted Merwin, in *In Their Own Image: New York Jews in Jazz Age Popular Culture* (New Brunswick, NJ: Rutgers University Press, 2006), offers various opinions about the film's closing scenes.

56. Fein, *Where Are We*, 4.

57. Quoted in Fein, *Where Are We*, 9.

58. David Weinberg, "The 'Socially Acceptable' Immigrant Minority Group: The Image of the Jew in American Popular Films," *North Dakota Quarterly* 40, no. 4 (Autumn 1972): 64.

59. Scott Eyman, *The Speed of Sound: Hollywood and the Talkie Revolution* (New York: Simon and Schuster, 1997), 142.

60. See Laura Mulver, "Now You Has Jazz," *Sight & Sound* 9, no. 5 (May 1999): 18.

61. Sperling, *Hollywood Be Thy Name*, 134–135.

62. Sklar, *Movie-Made America*, 152.

63. Presentation made at first Academy Award ceremony, May 16, 1929, in the Blossom Room of the Hollywood Roosevelt Hotel in Los Angeles.

64. Eyman, *Speed of Sound*, 68.

65. In 1956, Moishe Oysher reprised his role as a cantor's son in the English-language *Singing in the Dark*, the story of a Holocaust survivor who has amnesia only to gain back the memory of his terrible past. The film enjoyed limited success and wound up being Oysher's last motion picture.

66. Alistair Cooke, "Al Jolson Dies on Crest of a Wave," *The Guardian*, October 25, 1950.

67. "The Jazz Singer," *Cue*, January 24, 1953.

68. Shawn Levy, *King of Comedy* (New York: St. Martin's Press, 1996), 4.

69. Richard Natale, "Neil Diamond Cuts Up," *Los Angeles Times*, February 10, 2001.

70. John Leland, *New York Times Magazine*, July 22, 2001, 18.

CHAPTER 3

1. See K. R. M. Short, "Hollywood Fights Anti-Semitism," in *Film and Radio Propaganda in World War II*, ed. K. R. M. Short (Knoxville: University of Tennessee Press, 1983): 146–172.

2. One such novel, Arthur Miller's *Focus* (1945), received little attention. The novel was adapted for the cinema in 1947. It was finally made into a movie in 2001.

3. Arnold Forster (associate director of the Anti-Defamation League of B'nai B'rith), as quoted in J. J. Goldberg, *Jewish Power: Inside the American Jewish Establishment* (New York: Addison-Wesley, 1996), 119.

4. Marianne R. Sanua, *Let Us Prove Strong: The American Jewish Committee, 1945–2006* (Waltham, MA: Brandeis University Press, 2007), 44.

5. Howard M. Sachar, *A History of the Jews in America* (New York: Alfred A. Knopf, 1992), 621.

6. Sklar, *Movie-Made America*, 269.

7. Michel Ciment, *Kazan on Kazan* (New York: Viking Press, 1974), 57. Steven Alan Carr makes the argument that the films offered "a postwar response to the Holocaust." See Steven Alan Carr, "Jew and Not-Jew: Anti-Semitism and the Postwar Hollywood Social Problem Film," in *The Modern Jewish Experience in World Cinema*, ed. Lawrence Baron (Waltham, MA: Brandeis University Press, 2011), 266–272.

8. It simply would have been near-impossible in 1947, with existing production codes enforced through the Breen Production Code Office, which was the arm of the film industry that reviewed and regulated content of films, to make a film about homosexuality. This was the first novel of future screenwriter and director Richard Brooks, born Ruben Sax.

9. Betty Lasky, RKO—*The Biggest Little Major of Them All* (Englewood Cliffs, NJ: Prentice-Hall, 1984), 195–196.

10. Adrian Scott, "Censorship and Stereotypes," *Saturday Review*, April 30, 1949, 9.

11. Edward Dmytryk, interview with Lester Friedman, circa 1982, Syracuse, New York. George Eastman House Motion Picture Department Collection, Rochester, New York.

12. Scott, "Censorship and Stereotypes."

13. Taking an option meant making a payment to tie up the story for a finite period of time. At the conclusion of that period, one could choose to exercise the option by making additional payments or let the option run out. According to Dmytryk (Friedman interview), the cost for the option was $1,000.

14. Laura Z. Hobson, *Laura Z.: The Early Years and Years of Fulfillment* (New York: Donald I. Fine, Inc., 1986), 434.

15. Scott, "Censorship and Stereotypes."

16. Dore Schary, interview with the author, April 23, 1975, New York.

17. The head drama coach was Moss Hart.

18. Keith Kelly and Clay Steinman, "*Crossfire*: A Dialectical Attack," *Film Reader* 3 (February 1978): 110.

19. Bernard Rosenberg and Harry Silverstein, eds., *The Real Tinsel* (New York: Macmillan, 1970), 141.

20. Edward Dmytryk, *It's a Hell of a Life But Not a Bad Living* (New York: Times Books, 1978), 89.

21. Dore Schary, 1961, Oral History Research Project, Columbia University, New York.

22. Interoffice correspondence, N. Peter Rathvon to Dore Schary, February 12, 1947. Dore Schary Collection, Wisconsin Historical Society Archives, Madison.

23. Schary, Oral History Project.

24. Schary, interview with the author.

25. The new title was proposed in March by Ben Saeta at RKO, who received fifty dollars from the studio.

26. Schary, interview with the author.

27. *Time*, February 14, 1944, as quoted in Hobson, *Early Years*, 30.

28. Hobson, *Laura Z.*, 30.

29. Ibid.

30. Ibid., 401.

31. Stephen J. Whitfield, "The Paradoxes of American Jewish Culture," in *American Jewish Identity Politics*, ed. Deborah Dash Moore (Ann Arbor: University of Michigan Press, 2009), 257.

32. Hobson, *Laura Z.*, 404.

33. Zanuck was a Protestant from Wahoo, Nebraska. His Dutch Jewish–sounding last name often led to his being mistaken for a Jew. His studio was often referred to as the "Goy Studio."

34. In fact, recently uncovered files show that the FBI had a file on Zanuck and was carefully following his activities.

35. Leonard Mosley, *Zanuck: The Rise and Fall of Hollywood's Last Tycoon* (New York: McGraw Hill, 1985), 140.

36. George F. Custen, "Over 50 Years, a Landmark Loses Some of Its Luster," *New York Times*, November 16, 1997, http://www.nytimes.com.

37. Hobson, *Laura Z.*, 434.

38. Ibid.

39. Ibid.

40. J. J. Goldberg points out that when newly elected Wisconsin Senator Joseph McCarthy joined the anti-Communist fray, he placed a Jew, New York lawyer Roy Cohn, at his right hand, "both for effect and to keep anti-Semitism out of his hearings" (Goldberg, *Jewish Power*, 118).

41. Mosley, *Zanuck*, 227.

42. Elia Kazan, *A Life* (New York: Alfred A. Knopf, 1988), 331.

43. Ibid.

44. Leon Gutterman, "A Movie About Anti-Semitism: An Interview with Moss Hart," no date. Anti-Defamation League of B'nai B'rith Microfilm Files, New York. Gutterman wrote extensively for the Jewish Telegraphic Agency.

45. By this time, Hart had already authored *Lady in the Dark*, and with George S. Kaufman had written such hits as *Once in A Lifetime* and *The Man Who Came to Dinner*.

46. Steven Bach, *Dazzler: The Life and Times of Moss Hart* (New York: Alfred A. Knopf, 2001), 277.

47. Kitty Carlisle Hart, interview with the author, May 23, 2005, New York.

48. Bach, *Dazzler*, 277.

49. Ibid., 237.

50. Gutterman, "Movie About Anti-Semitism."

51. Hobson, *Laura Z.*, 436.

52. Kazan, *A Life*, 332.

53. Ibid., 332–333.

54. Elia Kazan, interview with the author, February 6, 1975, New York. See Eric A. Goldman, "The Fight to Bring the Subject of Antisemitism to the Screen," *Davka* 5, no. 3 (Fall 1975): 24.

55. Gutterman, "Movie About Anti-Semitism."

56. Laura Z. Hobson, *Gentleman's Agreement* (New York: Simon and Schuster, 1947), 178.

57. Ibid.

58. *Gentleman's Agreement*, special features (Beverly Hills: Twentieth Century-Fox, 2003), DVD.

59. Hobson related that Hart told Zanuck of her participation and that Zanuck offered to pay her, but she refused (*Laura Z.*, 432). Zanuck subsequently sent her gold jewelry as a thank-you. As to how much Hart was paid for writing the screenplay, Kitty Carlisle related in her biography that "the studio underpaid Moss so badly that to assuage their consciences, when we left Los Angeles they gave him a whopping big wooden-bodied Chrysler station wagon as a bonus." Kitty Carlisle Hart, *Kitty: An Autobiography* (New York: Doubleday, 1988), 141. Hobson also wrote that the Hollywood press reported that "Zanuck had to come up with $150,000 to induce Moss to do this" (*Laura Z.*, 432).

60. Kazan, interview with the author.

61. Kazan, *A Life*, 331.

62. Mel Gussow, *Darryl F. Zanuck: Don't Say Yes Until I'm Finished Talking* (New York: Da Capo Press, 1971), 150.

63. Kazan, interview with the author.

64. Kazan, *A Life*, 334.

65. Ibid.

66. The sales department at RKO had done a study to determine whether *Crossfire* would make money and concluded that it could not.

67. Bach, *Dazzler*, 276.

68. Neal Gabler, *An Empire of Their Own: How the Jews Invented Hollywood* (New York: Anchor Books, 1988), 355.

69. Congressional Record, 91, pt. 6 (July 18, 1945), 7735, as quoted in Gabler, *Empire of Their Own*, 357–358.

70. Thomas Doherty, *Cold War, Cool Medium* (New York: Columbia University Press, 2003), 21.

71. Gabler, *Empire of Their Own*, 361–362.

72. Both Adrian Scott and Edward Dmytryk were called before the HUAC on October 23 and deemed "unfriendly witnesses." Both wound up being found in contempt of Congress, given prison terms, and fired by RKO. Dmytryk chose to testify before the Committee in 1951. Elia Kazan was only subpoenaed by the HUAC in 1952.

73. "Pix with Anti-Semitism Themes May Narrow Down to Only 20th's and RKO," *Variety*, June 11, 1947, 3, 21.

74. Thomas F. Brady, "Hollywood Tackles the Facts of Life," *New York Times*, March 16, 1947, x5. *Focus* was finally made into a film by Neal Slavin in 2001.

75. Dore Schary, *Heyday: An Autobiography* (Boston: Little Brown and Company, 1979), 156.

76. Actual cost of production was reportedly $543,000. According to Dmytryk, the combined salaries for the three leads was $375,000, leaving very little for the production (Friedman interview). See also Darryl Fox, "*Crossfire* and HUAC: Surviving the Slings and Arrows of the Committee," *Film History* 3, (1989): 29–37.

77. Adrian Scott, "Some of My Worst Friends," *Screen Writer* (October 1947): 3.

78. Dmytryk, interview with Friedman.

79. Eileen Bowser, program notes for *Crossfire*, Museum of Modern Art Department of Film, May/June 1979.

80. Dmytryk, interview with Friedman.

81. Kelly and Steinman, "*Crossfire*," 115.

82. Dmytryk, *Hell of a Life*, 90.

83. Kelly and Steinman, "*Crossfire*," 115.

84. Leonard J. Leff and Jerold L. Simmons, "Film into Story: The Narrative Scheme of *Crossfire*," *Literature/Film Quarterly* 12, no. 3 (1984): 171.

85. Dmytryk, interview with Friedman.

86. Schary, in Rosenberg and Silverstein, *The Real Tinsel*, 141. Schary wrote that he never knew Scott and Dmytryk to be "brethren," i.e., be involved in the Communist party, and that when he asked them about their activities prior to their testimony before HUAC, they denied party affiliation.

87. Much of Schary's extensive correspondence with Hart can be found at the Wisconsin Historical Society Archives in Madison.

88. Adrian Scott, "You Can't Do That!" *Screen Writer* (August 1947): 4.

89. Schary, *Heyday*, 157.

90. Correspondence files, Dore Schary Collection, Wisconsin Historical Society Archives.

91. Ibid.

92. Dore Schary to Darryl F. Zanuck, July 31, 1947. Dore Schary Collection.

93. Schary, *Heyday*, 157.

94. Schary, interview with the author.

95. Arthur Hertzberg, *The Jews in America* (New York: Columbia University Press, 1997), 291.

96. Gabler, *Empire of Their Own*, 349.

97. Kazan, interview with the author.

98. Ibid.

99. Goldberg, *Jewish Power*, 116.

100. Jack Wertheimer, "Antisemitism in the United States: A Historical Perspective," in *Antisemitism in America Today*, ed. Jerome Chanes (New York: Birch Lane Press, 1995), 49–50.

101. Charles H. Stember, ed., *Jews in the Mind of America* (New York: Basic Books, 1966), 78–82.

102. Ibid., 82–83.

103. Kazan, interview with the author.

104. Smith was well connected, a close associate of Senator Huey Long of Louisiana and Theodore G. Bilbo, former governor of Mississippi.

105. Elliot E. Cohen, "Mr. Zanuck's 'Gentleman's Agreement,'" *Commentary* 5, January 1948, 51.

106. John Slawson to Walter S. Hilborn, May 5, 1947. American Jewish Committee Archives, New York.

107. Schary, interview with the author.

108. Ibid.

109. Letter from Slawson to Hillborn. In it, the AJC executive noted that he believed the filmmakers to be good-intentioned but misguided.

110. Diary entry from unsigned source (possibly attorney Walter S. Hilborn of Loeb & Loeb), April 4, 1947. American Jewish Committee Archives.

111. Thomas Doherty, *Hollywood's Censor: Joseph I. Breen and the Production Code Office* (New York: Columbia University Press, 2007), 220.

112. Joseph M. Proskauer to Ralstone R. Levine, April 4, 1947. Wisconsin Historical Society Archives.

113. N. Peter Rathvon to Ralstone R. Levine, April 22, 1947. Wisconsin Historical Society Archives.

114. Letter from Slawson to Hillborn.

115. Schary, interview with the author.

116. Telegram from Ned Depinet to Schary, July 17, 1947. Dore Schary Collection.

117. Schary, interview with the author.

118. New York–based Executive Vice President Ned E. Depinet to Dore Schary, August 7, 1947. Dore Schary Collection.

119. Dore Schary to F. Hugh Herbert, June 16, 1947. Dore Schary Collection.

120. David Robinson to Dore Schary, April 22, 1947. Dore Schary Collection.

121. Schary, interview with the author.

122. John Slawson to Frank Trager, May 13, 1947. Anti-Defamation League of B'nai B'rith Microfilm Files, New York.

123. The list of impressive attendees included Albert Furth of *Fortune Magazine*, film theorist Siegfried Kracauer, and anthropologist Margaret Mead. Interestingly, also present were John Slawson and Dick Rothschild.

124. David M. Levy, "*Crossfire*: The Case of Propaganda in a Mystery Film," no date. Anti-Defamation League of B'nai B'rith Microfilm Files.

125. Ibid.

126. Study by ADL, conducted by Louis Raths of New York University and Frank Trager of ADL. ADL Archives, New York.

127. Darryl Fox, "*Crossfire* and HUAC," 34.

128. Schary, *Heyday*, 157.

129. Ad in *Los Angeles Times*, October 8, 1947.

130. Bosley Crowther, "*Crossfire* Puts the Fact of Bigotry on the Screen," *New York Times*, July 27, 1947.

131. "The Boy with the Fair Hair," *Time*, October 20, 1947, 92.

132. Elliot E. Cohen, "Letter to the Movie-Makers," *Commentary* 3 (August 1947): 111–112.

133. Edward S. Shapiro, *A Time for Healing: American Jewry Since World War II* (Baltimore: Johns Hopkins University Press, 1992), 26.

134. Hertzberg, *Jews in America*, 298.

135. Cohen, "Letter to the Movie-Makers."

136. S. Andhil Fineberg, "Danger Seen in Movies That Fight Antisemitism," *Intermountain Jewish News* (Denver), October 30, 1947.

137. Elliot E. Cohen to Dore Schary, September 23, 1947. Dore Schary Collection.

138. Schary, interview with the author.

139. Dore Schary, "A Letter to Elliot Cohen from a Moviemaker, *Commentary* 4, October 1947, 344.

140. Ibid.

141. J. Harold Sachs, memorandum, July 15, 1947. Anti-Defamation League of B'nai B'rith Archive.

142. Richard E. Gutstadt to Dore Schary, September 23, 1947. Dore Schary Collection.

143. Dore Schary to Richard E. Gutstadt, September 29, 1947.Dore Schary Collection.

144. S. Andhil Fineberg, memorandum on *Crossfire*, October 22, 1947. ADL Microfilm Archives.

145. Dorothy M. Nathan, memorandum, October 1, 1947. American Jewish Committee Archive.

146. Eileen Creelman, "'Gentleman's Agreement,' Well Directed Discussion of Social Antisemitism," *New York Sun*, November 12, 1947.

147. Bosley Crowther, "Antisemitism Assaulted Boldly on the Screen," *New York Times*, November 16, 1947.

148. Kazan, *A Life*, 333.

149. Jeff Young, *Kazan: The Master Director Discusses His Film* (New York: Newmarket Press, 1999), 48.

150. Ibid., 50–51.

151. George F. Custen, *Twentieth Century's Fox: Darryl F. Zanuck and the Culture of Hollywood* (New York: Basic Books, 1997), 297.

152. Elliot E. Cohen, "Mr. Zanuck's 'Gentleman's Agreement.'"

153. Schary, *Heyday*, 157.

154. Irwin C. Rosen, "The Effects of the Motion Picture 'Gentleman's Agreement' on Attitudes toward Jews," *Journal of Psychology* 26 (October 1948): 525–536.

155. Russell Middletown, "Ethnic Prejudice and Susceptibility to Persuasion," *American Sociological Review* (October 1960): 686.

156. Ibid.

157. Dore Schary, "Censorship and Stereotypes," *Saturday Review of Literature* 32, no. 18, April 30, 1949, 8.

158. Schary, interview with the author.

159. Ibid.

160. Both men were blacklisted and sentenced to a year in prison. In 1951, after a stint in England, Dmytryk testified before the HUAC and was removed from the blacklist.

161. K. R. M. Short, "Hollywood Fights Antisemitism, 1945–1947," in *Feature Films as History*, ed. K. R. M. Short (Knoxville: University of Tennessee Press, 1981), 180.

162. Such public Jewish debate over motion pictures would continue over the years, with one of the more glaring examples being Mel Gibson's 2003 release of *The Passion of the Christ*.

CHAPTER 4

1. Irwin Shaw, interview with Miriam Varon, October 12, 1977. William E. Wiener Oral History Library of the American Jewish Committee, New York Public Library. When the family made their name change, Irwin and his younger brother David were furious; the two even considered changing their name back when they were in their twenties.

2. Ibid.

3. George Plimpton, ed., *The* Paris Review *Interviews: Writers at Work, Fifth Series* (New York: Penguin, 1981), 145.

4. Paul V. Beckley, *New York Herald Tribune*, April 3, 1958, 15.

5. Edward Dmytryk, *It's a Hell of a Life But Not a Bad Living* (New York: Times Books, 1978), 225.

6. Robert LaGuardia, *Monty: A Biography of Montgomery Clift* (New York: Avon, 1978), 170.

7. Patricia Bosworth, *Montgomery Clift* (New York: Harcourt Brace Jovanovich, 1978), 316–317.

8. Ibid., 315.

9. Irwin Shaw, *The Young Lions* (Chicago: University of Chicago Press, 2000), 42.

10. "Vital Statistics," prepared by Twentieth Century-Fox, proudly lists Jacob Ben-Ami in the credits and provides a short bio, but the scene is gone. It apparently was cut at the last moment. The press notes call Ben-Ami "America's most distinguished actor," making his screen debut as Jacob Ackerman, Noah's father. He agreed to "cross the continent to play the one-day but key role at the urging of Montgomery Clift, an old friend and fan." Dated January 16, 1958. Production notes dated February 26 omit Ben-Ami. According to Dmytryk, Spyros Skouras, who was president of the studio, went to a screening of the completed film (*Hell of a Life*, 231). After applauding, he then demanded that half an hour be taken out. Producer Al Lichtman was ill and died on February 20, so he could not fight for the film.

11. Shaw, *Young Lions*, 201.

12. Edward S. Shapiro, *A Time for Healing: American Jewry since World War II* (Baltimore: Johns Hopkins University Press, 1992), 7.

13. Ibid., 2.

14. Shaw, interview with Varon.

15. Charles H. Stember, "The Recent History of Public Attitudes," in *Jews in the Mind of America*, ed. Charles H. Stember (New York: Basic Books, 1966), 95–99.

16. Martin Franzmann wrote "Thy Strong Word" while he was chair of the Exegetical Department at Concordia Seminary in St. Louis.

17. Pierre Sorlin, *The Film in History: Restaging the Past* (Totowa, NJ: Barnes and Noble, 1980), 21.

18. Dmytryk, interview with Friedman (see chap. 3, n. 11).

19. Shaw, interview with Varon.

20. Dmytryk, interview with Friedman.

21. Miller's *Focus* was adapted for film by Kendrew Lascelles and directed by Neal Slavin. It was completed in 2001.

22. Arthur Miller, *Focus* (New York: Penguin, 2001), v.

23. Sidra DeKoven Ezrahi, *By Words Alone: The Holocaust in Literature* (Chicago: University of Chicago Press, 1980), 185.

24. Ibid.

25. Shaw, interview with Varon.

26. Robert Mandel's 1992 film *School Ties*, written by Dick Wolf, tackles anti-Semitism in the 1950s. In one telling scene, David Greene (played by Brendan Fraser), finding a Nazi swastika drawn over his bed in his dorm room, tacks up a notice on the dorm's bulletin board seeking redress from the person or persons who did the act. The scene is an homage to a similar scene in *The Young Lions*, in which Noah Ackerman tacks his note up in the barracks. In *The Young Lions*, Noah meets his detractors; in *School Ties* nobody is ready to fight David. A striking difference is that Noah is frail and David is physically overpowering, a statement of the times in which each film was made.

27. Shaw, interview with Varon.

28. Deborah Dash Moore, "How World War II Changed a Generation and Remade America," in Moore, *American Jewish Identity Politics*, 35.

29. Shaw, interview with Varon.

30. Shaw, *Young Lions*, 16–17.

31. Shaw, interview with Varon.

32. Michael Shnayerson, *Irwin Shaw: A Biography* (New York: G. P. Putnam's Sons, 1989), 227.

33. Ibid., 251.

34. Dmytryk, *Hell of a Life*, 220.

35. Edward Anhalt, together with his wife Edna, had won an Academy Award for *Panic in the Streets* (1950). The two had worked together professionally, but after their divorce, Anhalt tackled writing projects alone and worked solo on *The Young Lions*. He won a second Oscar for *Becket* in 1964.

36. Dmytryk, *Hell of a Life*, 221.

37. Shnayerson, *Irwin Shaw*, 252.

38. Ibid.

39. Shaw, interview with Varon.

40. Brando and Clift shot only one scene together, and in it Brando lies dead. According to Dmytryk, the two did not hit it off when, as principal photography commenced, they met each other for the first time in Paris over dinner (*Hell of a Life*, 224). Coincidentally, they were both born in Omaha, Nebraska, three and a half years apart in age.

41. LaGuardia, *Monty*, 171.

42. *Look* magazine, April 15, 1958, 55.

43. Patricia Bosworth, *Marlon Brando* (New York: Viking, 2001), 133.

44. Ibid., 134. Elia Kazan had directed Brando in *A Streetcar Named Desire* (1951), *Viva Zapata* (1952), and *On the Waterfront* (1954), which garnered Brando an Academy Award.

45. Dmytryk, *Hell of a Life*, 228. See also Judith Crist, "Echoes of War, Nazism in *The Young Lions*," *New York Herald Tribune*, March 30, 1958.

46. Lawrence Grobel, *Conversations with Brando* (New York: Hyperion, 1991), 121.

47. Shnayerson, *Irwin Shaw*, 252–253.

48. *Look* magazine, April 15, 1958, 55.

49. Grobel, *Conversations*, 119.

50. Ben Hecht, *A Flag Is Born* (New York: American League for a Free Palestine, 1946), 47–48.

51. Ibid., 2–4.

52. Shaw, interview with Varon.

53. Plimpton, *Paris Review Interviews*, 145.

54. Ilan Avisar, *Screening the Holocaust: Cinema's Images of the Unimaginable* (Bloomington: Indiana University Press, 1988), 114–115.

55. James R. Giles, *Irwin Shaw* (Boston: Twayne Publishers, 1983), 82.

56. Lawrence Baron, "The First Wave of American 'Holocaust' Films, 1945–1959," *American Historical Review*, 115/1 (February 2010): 106.

57. Sidney Bernstein, chief of the Psychological Warfare Division of the Supreme Headquarters Allied Expeditionary Force Film Section, as quoted on a PBS *Frontline* website (http://www.pbs.org/wgbh/pages/frontline/camp/faqs.html). The Public Broadcasting Service's broadcast of *Memory of the Camps*, a *Frontline* special, was the first public showing of the film in the United States.

58. Orson Welles, Peter Bogdanovich, and Jonathan Rosenbaum, *This Is Orson Welles* (New York: HarperCollins, 1992), 189.

59. Peter Novick, *The Holocaust in American Life* (New York: Houghton Mifflin, 1999), 103.

60. Leon Jick, "The Holocaust: Its Uses and Abuses in the American Public," *Yad Vashem Studies* 14 (1981): 308–309.

61. Shapiro, *Time for Healing*, 4.

62. Hasia R. Diner, *We Remember with Reverence and Love: American Jews and the*

Myth of Silence after the Holocaust, 1945–1962 (New York: New York University Press, 2009).

63. Ezrahi, *By Words Alone*, 185.

64. Shaw, *Young Lions*, 635.

65. Ibid., 638.

66. Giles, *Irwin Shaw*, 89.

67. Ezrahi, *By Words Alone*, 186.

68. Shaw, *Young Lions*, 646–647.

69. See David Rousset, *The Other Kingdom* (New York: Fertag, 1982).

70. The Struthof-Natzweiler Nazi concentration camp was located thirty-one miles southwest of Strasbourg. According to the Struthof website (http://www.struthof.fr), twenty-two thousand people died there from May 1941 to March 1945. Although there were many "camps" on French soil, Struthof was the only camp that contained a gas chamber and was used for extermination. Drancy and Rivesaltes were transit camps, from which people were sent to extermination camps, and Gars was a detention camp.

71. This was disputed land, claimed by Germany but taken by France after World War I.

72. Dmytryk, *Hell of a Life*, 227.

73. "Vital Statistics," prepared by Twentieth Century-Fox.

74. Giles, *Irwin Shaw*, 99.

75. Ibid., 102.

76. LaGuardia, *Monty*, 176–177.

77. See Will Herberg, *Protestant, Catholic, Jew; An Essay in American Religious Sociology* (Garden City, NY: Doubleday, 1955).

CHAPTER 5

1. Christopher Andersen, *Barbra: The Way She Is* (New York: William Morrow, 2006), 43.

2. Barbara W. Grossman, http://www.jewish-theatre.com/visitor/article_display .aspx?articleid=1514, Jewish Women's Archive, 2005.

3. As quoted in *Where Are We? The Inner Life of America's Jews*, by Leonard Fein (New York: Harper & Row, 1988), 224.

4. Sydney Pollack, commentary, *The Way We Were*, DVD.

5. Arthur Laurents, *Original Story By: A Memoir of Broadway and Hollywood* (New York: Alfred A. Knopf, 2000), 254.

6. Ibid., 257.

7. Barbra Streisand, in The Way We Were: *Looking Back*, documentary film included with the DVD release of *The Way We Were*, Michael Arick, director, 1999.

8. Laurents, *Original Story By*, 258.

9. Paul Cowan, in *The Golden Land on the Silver Screen* (Teaneck, NJ: Ergo Media Inc., 1985), DVD.

10. Anzia Yezierska, *The Open Cage: An Anzia Yezierska Collection* (New York: Persea Books, 1979), 15–16.

11. Marshall Sklare, *The Jew in American Society* (New York: Behrman House, 1974), 94.

12. Samuel Heilman, *Portrait of American Jews: The Last Half of the Twentieth Century* (Seattle: University of Washington Press, 1995), 16.

13. Milton R. Konvitz, "The Quest for Equality and the Jewish Experience," in *Jewish Life in America: Historical Perspectives*, ed. Gladys Rosen (New York: The Institute of Human Relations Press of the American Jewish Committee and Ktav, 1978), 33–34.

14. Sklare, *Jew in American Society*, 94.

15. Ibid., 95.

16. Sidney Goldstein, "American Jewry, 1970: A Demographic Profile," in Sklare, *Jew in American Society*, 148.

17. Hasia Diner, Shira Kohn, and Rachel Kranson, eds., *A Jewish Feminine Mystique? Jewish Women in Postwar America* (New Brunswick, NJ: Rutgers University Press, 2010), 4.

18. Sylvia Barack Fishman, *Double or Nothing: Jewish Families and Mixed Marriage* (Waltham, MA: Brandeis University Press, 2004), 4.

19. Although Robert Redford was considered the perfect actor for the role, he initially refused the part because he did not want to come across as a "sex object." After several failed attempts by coproducer Julia Phillips and others to sign him, Sydney Pollack—who had been hired to direct and was a friend of Redford's—approached him. After numerous refusals and modifications of the script, Redford finally signed.

20. "Barbra Streisand Interview," *Agenda* 14 (Agenda Feminist Media, 1992): 44.

21. Some of Streisand's biographers claim that the treatment was fifty pages, but Laurents remembers sending her 125 pages.

22. Streisand, in *Looking Back*, documentary.

23. Tom Santopietro, *The Importance of Being Barbra* (New York: Thomas Dunne Books, 2006), 76.

24. Robert Redford, interview by Oprah Winfrey, *The Oprah Winfrey Show*, November 10, 2010.

25. Laurents, *Original Story By*, 258.

26. Steven M. Cohen, *American Modernity and Jewish Identity* (New York: Tavistock Publications, 1983), 82.

27. Egon Mayer, "A Demographic Revolution in American Jewry," in Moore, *American Jewish Identity Politics*, 271.

28. *The National Jewish Population Survey 2000–2001* (New York: United Jewish Communities, 2003), 16.

29. For example, Hubbell pleads with the director of the film he is writing to allow him to stay on, agreeing to write it the way the director wishes. Interestingly, this scene was added to the original screenplay, possibly by Alvin Sargent or David Rayfiel, to expand Hubbell's character.

30. Rosh Hashonoh (Rosh Hashanah) is the Jewish New Year, and the Festival of

Shavuos (Shavuot) is the feast of weeks that follows Passover by seven weeks and is traditionally considered the time of the giving of the Torah at Sinai.

31. Barbra Streisand, written responses to questions posed by the author, November 29, 2011.

32. Patricia Erens, *The Jew in American Cinema* (Bloomington: Indiana University Press, 1984), 323.

33. Beekman Place is an opulent area on New York's East Side in midtown.

34. Barry Gross, "No Victim, She: Barbra Streisand and the Movie Jew," *Journal of Ethnic Studies* 3/1 (Spring 1975): 37.

35. The original screenplay had a campus YCL fellow traveler (played by James Wood), who was subpoenaed by the House Committee on Un-American Activities, inform on Katie, naming her as a "subversive."

36. Streisand, in *Looking Back*, documentary.

37. Pollack, in *Looking Back*, documentary.

38. There were various discussions of making a sequel, but Robert Redford would never agree to be part of any such project.

39. James Spada, *Streisand: Her Life* (New York: Crown, 1995), 457.

40. Streisand, written responses to questions posed by the author, November 29, 2011.

41. It should be noted that Redford was also not interested initially in working with Streisand in *The Way We Were*, as he found the part of Hubbell quite limited in the original treatment.

42. Andersen, *Barbra*, 316.

43. *New York Daily News*, October 25, 1975, 1.

44. The 1990 National Jewish Population Survey's 52 percent intermarriage figure was found to be flawed. The number was closer to 38 percent, a figure that still caused great concern. See "Highlights of CJF National Jewish Population Survey," at www.jewishdatabank.org.

45. J. J. Goldberg, "New Study Debunks 52 Percent Intermarriage Rate," jweekly.com, January 14, 2000. Sociologist Bruce Phillips, in a November 15, 2011, post to JewishJournal.com, concurred that the approach used was highly problematic.

46. Hertzberg, *Jews in America*, xii.

47. Henry Feingold, introduction to Shapiro, *Time for Healing*, xii.

CHAPTER 6

1. Barry Levinson interview, Encore Movie Channel, multiple broadcasts, March 2001.

2. Barry Levinson, interview with the author, October 23, 2011, Baltimore, MD.

3. Michael B. Kassel, "The American Jewish Immigrant Family in Film and History: The Historical Accuracy of Barry Levinson's *Avalon*," *Film & History* 26, nos. 1–4, 52. See also Paul Haspel, "Avalon Lost: Suburbanization and Its Discontents in

Barry Levinson's *Avalon*," *The Journal of American Culture* 31, no. 4 (December 2008): 383–392.

4. Barry Levinson, interview in *Avalon* production notes, Baltimore Pictures, 1990.

5. Mervyn Rothstein, "Barry Levinson Reaches Out to a Lost America," *New York Times*, September 30, 1990, II, 13.

6. Levinson, interview with the author.

7. In reality, there was no such neighborhood in Baltimore, only a movie theater by that name.

8. David Thompson, "Barry Levinson," in *Levinson on Levinson*, ed. David Thompson (Winchester, MA: Faber and Faber, 1992), 108.

9. Rothstein, "Levinson Reaches Out."

10. Levinson, interview with the author.

11. Ibid.

12. Ben Halpern, "America Is Different," in *The Jew in American Society*, ed. Marshall Sklare (New York: Behrman House, 1974), 86.

13. See Steven J. Whitfield, "Making Fragmentation Familiar: Barry Levinson's *Avalon*," *Studies in Contemporary Jewry* 14 (1998): 49–64.

14. Barry Levinson, *Avalon, Tin Men & Diner: Three Screenplays* (New York: Atlantic Monthly Press, 1990), 319.

15. Levinson, interview with the author.

16. Pierre Sorlin, *The Film in History: Restaging the Past* (Totowa, NJ: Barnes and Noble, 1980), 42.

17. Levinson, *Three Screenplays*, 243.

18. George Turner, "*Avalon*, Cinematic Time Machine," *American Cinematographer* (October 1990): 47.

19. Krichinsky is Levinson's mother's family name.

20. Levinson, *Three Screenplays*, 321–22.

21. H. B. Cavalcanti and Debra Schleef, "Cultural Loss and the American Dream: The Immigrant Experience in Barry Levinson's *Avalon*," *Journal of American and Comparative Cultures* 24, issue 3–4 (Fall/Winter 2001): 19.

22. Barry Levinson, "Baltimore, My Baltimore," *New York Times*, November 14, 1999, IIa, 30. See also Jack Fischel's review in *Midstream* (February/March, 1991): 46–47.

23. Levinson, interview with the author.

24. Thompson, *Levinson on Levinson*, 108.

25. Ibid., 100.

26. Levinson, interview with the author.

27. Levinson, *Three Screenplays*, 316–17.

28. Levinson, interview with the author.

29. Levinson, *Three Screenplays*, 321.

30. Levinson, interview with the author.

31. Levinson, *Three Screenplays*, 371.

32. Jesse Kornbluth, introduction to Levinson, *Three Screenplays*, xxi.

33. Like Michael, Levinson named one of his children Sam.

34. Levinson, *Three Screenplays*, 372.

35. Levinson, "Baltimore, My Baltimore."

36. Schwarzbaum's review (February 20, 1998) described the Dustin Hoffman character, Norman Johnson, as "an emphatic Jewish psychologist . . . not officially Jewish; he's only Hoffman . . . noodgey and menschlike." The reviewer goes on to write, "You do the math," because the character wants to call home.

37. Levinson, "Baltimore, My Baltimore."

38. Ibid.

39. Lisa Schwarzbaum, review of *Liberty Heights*, *Entertainment Weekly*, EW.com, November 19, 1999.

40. Halpern, "America Is Different," 85–86.

41. Albert I. Gordon, *Jews in Suburbia* (Boston: Beacon Press, 1959), 1.

42. Sarna, *American Judaism*, 282.

43. Shapiro, *Time for Healing*, 125.

44. Heilman, *American Jews*, 15.

45. Ibid.

46. Shapiro, *Time for Healing*, 125.

47. Hertzberg, *Jews in America*, 304–321. Hertzberg cites several sources on the question of "arriving."

48. Fein, *Where Are We*, 186–187.

49. Gans, "Park Forest: Birth of a Jewish Community," in Cohen, *Commentary on the American Scene*, 221. Though Gans is specifically writing about Park Forest, a Chicago suburb, his analysis is applicable here.

50. We see one example of the clash of cultural assimilation with Jewish particularism when Ben, one of the Kurtzman sons, unabashedly dresses as Adolf Hitler for Halloween, to the horror of his mother and grandmother.

51. Barry Levinson, in press production notes prepared by Baltimore Pictures for *Liberty Heights*, 1999, 10.

52. Levinson, interview with the author.

53. Ibid.

54. The result of the Supreme Court decision in *Brown v. Board of Education* (1954).

55. Hertzberg, *Jews in America*, 322.

56. Levinson, "Baltimore, My Baltimore."

57. There is unease as well in the forced business relationship that evolves between Nate, Ben's father, and Little Melvin, a local black petty criminal.

58. In fact, later in the film, Van is granted his wish, a chance to sleep with Dubbie. His inability to consummate the act can take us into a lengthy discourse on Jewish men and non-Jewish women in American cinema.

59. Fein, *Where Are We*, 187.

60. Levinson grew up in Forest Park.

61. See Karen Brodkin, *How Jews Became White Folks and What That Says About*

Race in America (New Brunswick, NJ: Rutgers University Press, 1995); and Warren Rosenberg, "Coming Out of the Ethnic Closet: Jewishness in the Films of Barry Levinson," *Shofar* 22, no. 1 (Fall 2003): 29–43.

62. Levinson, interview with the author.

63. Jeffrey S. Gurock, "Twentieth-Century American Orthodoxy's Era of Non-Observance, 1900–1960," *Torah u-Madda Journal* 9 (2000): 97.

64. Daniel J. Elazar, *Community and Polity* (Philadelphia: Jewish Publication Society, 1976), 177.

65. Hertzberg, *Jews in America*, 311–312.

66. Levinson, interview with the author.

67. Leonard Fein, in a totally different context (*Where Are We*, 182), writes of the Aleynu prayer as illustrating the tension in Judaism between particularism and universalism. In *Liberty Heights*, a rendition from the Aleynu of Bayom Hahu has multiple meanings. Not only is it a reference to that day — the specialness of the Jewish New Year and the day Nate and Charlie go to see the new Cadillacs — but it serves as a contrast between the particular character of the synagogue and the universal American nature of the Cadillac.

68. Marc Ferro, *Cinema and History* (Detroit: Wayne State University Press, 1988), 159.

69. Sorlin, *Film in History*, x.

CHAPTER 7

1. A conversation with Jonathan Safran Foer, *Everything Is Illuminated* reader's guide, www.hmhbooks.com/readers_guides/foer.

2. Previous quotations, ibid.

3. Liev Schreiber, interview in *Everything Is Illuminated* production notes, Warner Independent Pictures, 2005.

4. Ibid.

5. Ibid.

6. Liev Schreiber, interview with the author, April 11, 2007, New York.

7. See Chapter 1.

8. David G. Roskies, *The Jewish Search for a Usable Past* (Bloomington: Indiana University Press, 1999), 57.

9. Alan Mintz, *Popular Culture and the Shaping of Holocaust Memory in America* (Seattle: University of Washington Press, 2001), 163.

10. Philippe Codde, "Transmitted Holocaust Trauma: A Matter of Myth and Fairy Tales?" *European Judaism* 42, no. 1 (Spring 2009): 64.

11. Marianne Hirsch, *Family Frames: Photography, Narrative, and Postmemory* (Cambridge, MA: Harvard University Press, 1997), 22.

12. Jonathan Safran Foer, interview in *Everything Is Illuminated* production notes, Warner Independent Pictures, 2005.

13. Ibid.

14. Jean Mitry, "Remarks on the Problem of Cinematic Adaptation," *The Bulletin of the Midwest Modern Language Association* (Spring 1971): 8.

15. Arthur Kurzweil, *How to Trace Your Jewish Roots* (Teaneck: Ergo Media, 1997), DVD.

16. Anna P. Ronell, "Three American Jewish Writers Imagine Eastern Europe," *Polin* 19 (2007): 387.

17. Jonathan Safran Foer, *Everything is Illuminated* (New York: Harper Perennial, 2003), 59.

18. Schreiber, interview with the author.

19. Gary Weissman, *Fantasies of Witnessing: Postwar Efforts to Experience the Holocaust* (Ithaca, NY: Cornell University Press, 2004), 19.

20. Ronell, "Three Writers," 375.

21. Foer, *Illuminated*, 184.

22. Schreiber, interview with the author.

23. Lawrence Baron, "Imagining the Shoah in American Third Generation Cinema," *The Jewish Role in American Life, An Annual Review* 6 (2008): 111. Baron, in addition to writing an interesting analysis, makes a number of important statements about the power of cinema.

24. Jeremy Shere, "Imagined Diaspora: The *Shtetl* in Allen Hoffman's 'Small Worlds' and Jonathan Safran Foer's 'Everything is Illuminated,'" *Polin* 22 (2010): 459.

25. Sidra DeKoven Ezrahi, *Booking Passage: Exile and Homecoming in the Modern Jewish Imagination* (Berkeley: University of California Press, 2000), 17.

26. Schreiber, interview with the author.

27. Ibid.

Abrams, Nathan. *The New Jew in Film: Exploring Jewishness and Judaism in Contemporary Cinema*. New Brunswick, NJ: Rutgers University Press, 2012.

Andersen, Christopher. *Barbra: The Way She Is*. New York: William Morrow, 2006.

Antler, Joyce. *You Never Call! You Never Write! A History of the Jewish Mother*. Cambridge: Oxford University Press, 2007.

Asch, Sholem. *America*. Translated by James Fuchs. New York: Alpha Omega Publishing, 1918.

Avisar, Ilan. *Screening the Holocaust: Cinema's Images of the Unimaginable*. Bloomington: Indiana University Press, 1988.

Bach, Steven. *Dazzler: The Life and Times of Moss Hart*. New York: Alfred A. Knopf, 2001.

Baron, Lawrence. *Projecting the Holocaust into the Present: The Changing Focus of Contemporary Holocaust Cinema*. Lanham, MD: Rowman & Littlefield, 2005.

————, ed. *The Modern Jewish Experience in World Cinema*. Waltham, MA: Brandeis University Press, 2011.

Bartov, Omer. *The "Jew" in Cinema: From the Golem to Don't Touch My Holocaust*. Bloomington: Indiana University Press, 2005.

Belton, John. *American Cinema/American Culture*. New York: McGraw-Hill, 1994.

Bernheimer, Kathryn. *The 50 Greatest Jewish Movies: A Critic's Ranking of the Very Best*. Secaucus, NJ: Birch Lane, 1998.

Bosworth, Patricia. *Marlon Brando*. New York: Viking, 2001.

————. *Montgomery Clift: A Biography*. New York: Harcourt Brace Jovanovich, 1978.

Brady, John. *The Craft of the Screenwriter*. New York: Simon and Schuster, 1981.

Brodkin, Karen. *How Jews Became White Folks and What That Says About Race in America*. New Brunswick, NJ: Rutgers University Press, 1995.

Brooks, Richard. *The Brick Foxhole*. New York: Harper & Brothers, 1945.

Buhle, Paul. *From the Lower East Side to Hollywood: Jewish American Popular Culture*. New York: Verso, 2004.

Burstein, Janet. *Telling the Little Secrets: American Jewish Writing since the 1980s*. Madison: University of Wisconsin Press, 2006.

Carr, Steven Alan. *Hollywood & Anti-Semitism: A Cultural History up to World War II*. Cambridge, UK: Cambridge University Press, 2001.

Carringer, Robert L. *The Jazz Singer*. Madison: University of Wisconsin Press, 1979.

Chanes, Jerome A., ed. *Antisemitism in America Today: Outspoken Experts Explode the Myth*. New York: Birch Lane Press, 1995.

Ciment, Michel. *Kazan on Kazan*. New York: Viking Press, 1974.

Cohen, Elliot E., ed. *Commentary on the American Scene: Portraits of Jewish Life in America*. New York: Knopf, 1953.

Cohen, Sarah Blacher, ed. *From Hester Street to Hollywood: The Jewish-American Stage and Screen*. Bloomington: Indiana University Press, 1983.

Cohen, Steven M. *American Modernity and Jewish Identity*. New York: Tavistock Publications, 1983.

Conroy, Pat. *The Prince of Tides*. Boston: Houghton Mifflin, 1986.

Custen, George F. *Twentieth Century's Fox: Darryl F. Zanuck and the Culture of Hollywood*. New York: Basic Books, 1997.

Desser, David, and Lester D. Friedman. *American-Jewish Filmmakers: Traditions and Trends*. Urbana: University of Illinois Press, 2004.

Diner, Hasia R. *The Jews of the United States*. Berkeley: University of California Press, 2004.

——————. *We Remember with Reverence and Love: American Jews and the Myth of Silence after the Holocaust, 1945–1962*. New York: New York University Press, 2009.

——————, and Beryl Lieff Benderly. *Her Works Praise Her: A History of Jewish Women in America from Colonial Times to the Present*. New York: Basic Books, 2002.

——————, Shira Kohn, and Rachel Kranson, eds. *A Jewish Feminine Mystique? Jewish Women in Postwar America*. New Brunswick, NJ: Rutgers University Press, 2010.

Dinnerstein, Leonard. *Anti-Semitism in America*. New York: Oxford University Press, 1994.

Dmytryk, Edward. *It's a Hell of a Life But Not a Bad Living*. New York: Times Books, 1978.

Doherty, Thomas. *Cold War, Cool Medium: Television, McCarthyism and American Culture*. New York: Columbia University Press, 2003.

——————. *Hollywood's Censor: Joseph I. Breen and the Production Code Office*. New York: Columbia University Press, 2007.

Doneson, Judith E. *The Holocaust in American Film*. Philadelphia: Jewish Publication Society, 1987.

Elazar, Daniel J. *Community and Polity*. Philadelphia: Jewish Publication Society, 1976.

Erens, Patricia. *The Jew in American Cinema*. Bloomington: Indiana University Press, 1984.

Eyman, Scott. *The Speed of Sound: Hollywood and the Talkie Revolution, 1926–1930*. New York: Simon and Schuster, 1997.

Ezrahi, Sidra DeKoven. *Booking Passage: Exile and Homecoming in the Modern Jewish Imagination*. Berkeley: University of California Press, 2000.

——————. *By Words Alone: The Holocaust in Literature*. Chicago: University of Chicago Press, 1980.

Fein, Leonard J. *Where We Are? The Inner Life of America's Jews*. New York: Harper & Row, 1988.

Feingold, Henry. *A Time for Searching: Entering the Mainstream, 1920–1945*. Baltimore: Johns Hopkins Press, 1992.

Ferro, Marc. *Cinema and History*. Detroit: Wayne State University Press, 1988.

Fishman, Sylvia Barack. *Double or Nothing: Jewish Families and Mixed Marriage*. Waltham, MA: Brandeis University Press, 2004.

Foer, Jonathan Safran. *Everything Is Illuminated*. New York: Harper Perennial, 2003.

Freedland, Michael. *Jolson*. New York: Stein and Day, 1972.

Friedman, Lester D. *Hollywood's Image of the Jew*. New York: Frederick Ungar, 1982.

———, and David Desser. *American-Jewish Filmmakers: Traditions and Trends*. Urbana: University of Illinois Press, 2004.

Fuchs, Lawrence H. *The Political Behavior of American Jews*. Glencoe, IL: Free Press, 1956.

Gabler, Neal. *An Empire of Their Own: How the Jews Invented Hollywood*. New York: Anchor Books, 1988.

———, Frank Rich, and Joyce Antler, *Television's Changing Image of American Jews*. New York and Los Angeles: American Jewish Committee and the Norman Lear Center, 2000.

Gertel, Elliot B. *Over the Top Judaism: Precedents and Trends in the Depiction of Jewish Beliefs and Observances in Film and Television*. Lanham, MD: University Press of America, 2003.

Giles, James R. *Irwin Shaw*. Boston: Twayne Publishers, 1983.

Gittler, Joseph B., ed. *Jewish Life in the United States: Perspectives from the Social Sciences*. New York: New York University Press, 1981.

Goldberg, J. J. *Jewish Power: Inside the American Jewish Establishment*. Reading, MA: Addison Wesley, 1996.

Goldberg, Judith. *Laughter through Tears: The Yiddish Cinema*. East Brunswick, NJ: Fairleigh Dickinson University Press, 1983.

Goldman, Eric A. *Visions, Images and Dreams: Yiddish Film Past and Present*. Revised edition. Teaneck, NJ: Holmes and Meier, 2011.

Goldscheider, Calvin. *The American Jewish Community: Social Science Research and Policy Implications*. Atlanta: Scholars Press, 1986.

Goldstein, Sidney, and Calvin Goldscheider. *Jewish Americans: Three Generations in a Jewish Community*. Lanham, MD: University Press of America, 1985.

Goldstein, Sidney, and Alice Goldstein. *Jews on the Move: Implications for Jewish Identity*. Albany: State University of New York Press, 1996.

Gordon, Albert I. *Jews in Suburbia*. Boston: Beacon Press, 1959.

Greenspoon, Leonard J., and Ronald A. Simkins, eds. *Studies in Jewish Civilization 17*. Omaha, NE: Creighton University Press, 2006.

Grobel, Lawrence. *Conversations with Brando*. New York: Hyperion, 1991.

Gussow, Mel. *Darryl F. Zanuck: Don't Say Yes Until I Finish Talking*. New York: Da Capo Press, 1971.

Hart, Kitty Carlisle. *Kitty: An Autobiography*. New York: Doubleday, 1988.

Hecht, Ben. *A Flag Is Born*. New York: American League for a Free Palestine, 1946.

Heilman, Samuel. *Portrait of American Jews: The Last Half of the 20th Century*. Seattle: University of Washington Press, 1995.

Heinze, Andrew R. *Adapting to Abundance: Jewish Immigrants, Mass Consumption and the Search for Jewish Identity*. New York: Columbia University Press, 1990.

Herberg, Will. *Protestant, Catholic, Jew; An Essay in American Religious Sociology*. Garden City, NY: Doubleday, 1955.

Hertzberg, Arthur. *The Jews in America: Four Centuries of an Uneasy Encounter — A History*. New York: Columbia University Press, 1997.

Higham, Charles. *Warner Brothers*. New York: Scribner, 1975.

Hirsch, Marianne. *Family Frames: Photography, Narrative, and Postmemory*. Cambridge, MA: Harvard University Press, 1997.

————, and Irene Kacandes, eds. *Teaching the Representation of the Holocaust*. New York: Modern Library Association of America, 2004.

Hoberman, J. *Bridge of Light: Yiddish Film between Two Worlds*. Revised edition. Hanover, NH: University Press of New England, 2010.

————, and Jeffrey Shandler, eds. *Entertaining America: Jews, Movies and Broadcasting*. Princeton, NJ: Princeton University Press, 2003.

Hobson, Laura Z. *Gentleman's Agreement*. New York: Simon & Schuster, 1947.

————. *Laura Z.: The Early Years and Years of Fulfillment*. New York: Donald I. Fine, Inc., 1986.

Howe, Irving. *World of Our Fathers*. With the assistance of Kenneth Libo. New York: Harcourt Brace Jovanovich, 1976.

Howells, Richard, and Robert W. Matson. *Using Visual Evidence*. Berkshire, England: Open University Press, 2009.

Insdorf, Annette. *Indelible Shadows: Film and the Holocaust*. Revised edition. Cambridge, UK: Cambridge University Press, 2003.

Jessel, George. *So Help Me: The Autobiography of George Jessel*. Cleveland: World Publishing Company, 1943.

————. *The World I Lived In*. With John Austin. Chicago: Henry Regnery Company, 1975.

Jolson, Harry. *Mistah Jolson*. As told to Alban Emley. Hollywood, CA: House-Warvan Publishers, 1951.

Kazan, Elia. *A Life*. New York: Alfred A. Knopf, 1988.

Kugelmass, Jack, ed. *Key Texts in American Jewish Culture*. New Brunswick, NJ: Rutgers University Press, 2003.

LaGuardia, Robert. *Monty: A Biography of Montgomery Clift*. New York: Avon, 1978.

Langdon, Jennifer E. *Caught in the Crossfire: Adrian Scott and the Politics of Americanism in 1940s Hollywood*. New York: Columbia University Press, 2010.

Lasky, Betty. *RKO — The Biggest Little Major of Them All*. Englewood Cliffs, NJ: Prentice-Hall, 1984.

Laurents, Arthur. *Original Story By: A Memoir of Broadway and Hollywood*. New York: Alfred A. Knopf, 2000.

————. *The Way We Were*. New York: Harper & Row, 1972.

Levinson, Barry. *Avalon, Tin Men & Diner: Three Screenplays*. New York: Atlantic Monthly Press, 1990.

Levy, Shawn. *King of Comedy: The Life and Art of Jerry Lewis*. New York: St. Martin's Press, 1996.

Merwin, Ted. *In Their Own Image: New York Jews in Jazz Age Popular Culture*. New Brunswick, NJ: Rutgers University Press, 2006.

Miller, Arthur. *Focus*. New York: Penguin, 2001.

Miller, Randall M., ed. *Ethnic Images in American Film and Television*. Philadelphia: The Balch Institute, 1978.

Mintz, Alan. *Popular Culture and the Shaping of Holocaust Memory in America*. Seattle: University of Washington Press, 2001.

Moore, Deborah Dash, ed. *American Jewish Identity Politics*. Ann Arbor: University of Michigan Press, 2009.

————, and Paula Hyman. *Jewish Women in America*. New York: Routledge, 1997.

Mosley, Leonard. *Zanuck: The Rise and Fall of Hollywood's Last Tycoon*. New York: McGraw Hill, 1985.

Novick, Peter. *The Holocaust in American Life*. Boston: Houghton Mifflin, 1999.

Oberfirst, Robert. *Al Jolson: You Ain't Heard Nothing Yet*. San Diego: A. S. Barnes, 1982.

O'Connor, John E., ed. *Image as Artifact: The Historical Analysis of Film and Television*. Malabar, FL: Krieger, 1990.

————, and Martin A. Jackson. *American History/American Film: Interpreting the Hollywood Image*. New York: Frederick Ungar, 1979.

Paskin, Sylvia, ed. *When Joseph Met Molly: A Reader on Yiddish Film*. Nottingham, UK: Five Leaves, 1999.

Quart, Leonard, and Albert Auster. *American Film and Society Since 1945*. Westport, CT: Praeger, 1991.

Raphaelson, Samson. *The Jazz Singer*. New York: Brentano's, 1925.

Roffman, Peter, and Jim Purdy. *The Hollywood Social Problem Film: Madness, Despair, and Politics from the Depression to the Fifties*. Bloomington: Indiana University Press, 1981.

Rogin, Michael. *Blackface, White Noise: Jewish Immigrants in the Hollywood Melting Pot*. Berkeley: University of California Press, 1998.

Rollins, Peter C. *Hollywood as Historian: American Film in a Cultural Context*. Lexington: University Press of Kentucky, 1998.

Rose, Peter, ed. *The Ghetto & Beyond: Essays on Jewish Life in America*. New York: Random House, 1969.

Rosen, Gladys, ed. *Jewish Life in America: Historical Perspectives*. New York: The Institute of Human Relations Press of the American Jewish Committee and Ktav, 1978.

Rosenberg, Bernard, and Harry Silverstein, eds. *The Real Tinsel*. New York: Macmillan, 1970.

Rosenberg, Joel. "Jewish Experience on Film—An American Overview." *American Jewish Yearbook* 96 (1996): 3–50.

————, and Stephen J. Whitfield, eds. "The Cinema of Jewish Experience." *Prooftexts* 22, no. 1/2 (Winter/Spring 2002).

Rosenblatt, Samuel. *Yossele Rosenblatt: The Story of His Life, As Told by His Son*. New York: Farrar, Straus and Young, 1954.

Roskies, David G. *The Jewish Search for a Usable Past*. Bloomington: Indiana University Press, 1999.

Rousset, David. *The Other Kingdom*. New York: Fertag, 1982.

Sachar, Howard M. *A History of the Jews in America*. New York: Alfred A. Knopf, 1992.

Samberg, Joel. *Reel Jewish*. Middle Village, NY: Jonathan David, 2000.

Santopietro, Tom. *The Importance of Being Barbra*. New York: Thomas Dunne Books, 2006.

Sanua, Marianne R. *Let Us Prove Strong: The American Jewish Committee, 1945–2006*. Waltham, MA: Brandeis University Press, 2007.

Sarna, Jonathan D. *American Judaism*. New Haven, CT: Yale University Press, 2004.

Schary, Dore. *Heyday: An Autobiography*. Boston: Little Brown, 1979.

Schickel, Richard. *Elia Kazan: A Biography*. New York: HarperCollins, 2005.

Shandler, Jeffrey. *While America Watches: Televising the Holocaust*. New York: Oxford University Press, 1999.

Shapiro, Edward S. *A Time for Healing: American Jewry since World War II*. Baltimore: Johns Hopkins University Press, 1992.

—————, ed. *Yiddish in America: Essays on Yiddish Culture in the Golden Land*. Scranton, PA: University of Scranton Press, 2008.

Shaw, Irwin. *The Young Lions*. Chicago: University of Chicago Press, 2000.

Shnayerson, Michael. *Irwin Shaw: A Biography*. New York: G. P. Putnam's Sons, 1989.

Short, K. R. M., ed. *Feature Films as History*. Knoxville: University of Tennessee Press, 1981.

—————, ed. *Film and Propaganda in World War II*. Knoxville: University of Tennessee Press, 1983.

Silverman, Charles. *A Certain People: American Jews and Their Lives Today*. New York: Summit Books, 1985.

Sklar, Robert. *Movie-Made America: A Social History of American Movies*. New York: Random House, 1975.

Sklare, Marshall, ed. *The Jew in American Society*. New York: Behrman House, 1974.

—————. *The Jews: Social Patterns of an American Group*. Glencoe, IL: Free Press, 1959.

Slobin, Mark. *Tenement Songs: The Popular Music of the Jewish Immigrants*. Urbana: University of Illinois Press, 1982.

Smith, Judith E. *Visions of Belonging: Family Stories, Popular Culture and Postwar Democracy, 1940–1960*. New York: Columbia University Press, 2004.

Sorlin, Pierre. *The Film in History: Restaging the Past*. Totowa, NJ: Barnes and Noble, 1980.

Spada, James. *Streisand: Her Life*. New York: Crown, 1995.

Sperling, Cass Warner. *Hollywood Be Thy Name: The Warner Brothers Story*. Lexington: University Press of Kentucky, 1998.

Stember, Charles H., ed. *Jews in the Mind of America*. New York: Basic Books, 1966.

Taub, Michael. *Films about Jewish Life and Culture*. Lewiston, NY: Edwin Mellon Press, 2005.

Thompson, David, ed., *Levinson on Levinson*. Winchester, MA: Faber and Faber, 1992.

Toplin, Robert Brent. *Reel History: In Defense of Hollywood*. Lawrence: University Press of Kansas, 2002.

Vorspan, Max, and Lloyd P. Gartner. *History of the Jews of Los Angeles*. Philadelphia: Jewish Publication Society of America, 1970.

Warner, Jack L. *My First Hundred Years in Hollywood*. With Dean Jennings. New York: Random House, 1965.

Weber, Donald. *Haunted in the New World: Jewish American Culture from Cahan to the Goldbergs*. Bloomington: Indiana University Press, 2005.

Weissman, Gary. *Fantasies of Witnessing: Postwar Efforts to Experience the Holocaust*. Ithaca, NY: Cornell University Press, 2004.

Welles, Orson, Peter Bogdanovich, and Jonathan Rosenbaum. *This Is Orson Welles*. New York: HarperCollins, 1992.

Whitfield, Stephen J. *The Culture of the Cold War*. Baltimore: The Johns Hopkins Press, 1996.

——. *In Search of American Jewish Culture*. Hanover, NH: Brandeis University Press, 1999.

——. *Voices of Jacob, Hands of Esau: Jews in American Life and Thought*. Hamden, CT: Archon Books, 1984.

Yezierska, Anzia. *The Open Cage: An Anzia Yezierska Collection*. New York: Persea Books, 1979.

Young, Jeff. *Kazan: The Master Director Discusses His Film*. New York: Newmarket Press, 1999.

Zuckerman, Bruce, ed. "The Impact of the Holocaust in America." *The Jewish Role in American Life, An Annual Review 6*. West Lafayette, IN: Purdue University Press, 2008.

INTERVIEWS

Dmytryk, Edward. Interview with Lester Friedman. Circa 1982, Syracuse, New York. George Eastman House Motion Picture Department Collection, Rochester, New York.

Green, Joseph. Interview with the author. April 14, 1977, New York.

Hart, Kitty Carlisle. Interview with the author. May 23, 2005, New York.

Kazan, Elia. Interview with the author. February 6, 1975, New York.

Levinson, Barry. Interview with the author. October 23, 2011, Baltimore, MD.

Raphaelson, Samson. June 1959, Columbia Center for Oral History, Columbia University, New York.

Schary, Dore. Interview with the author. April 23, 1975, New York.

Schary, Dore. Oral History Research Project, Columbia University, 1961.

Schreiber, Liev. Interview with the author. April 11, 2007, New York.

Shaw, Irwin. Interview with Miriam Varon. October 12, 1977. William E. Wiener Oral History Library of the American Jewish Committee, Dorot Division, New York Public Library.

Streisand, Barbra. Written responses to questions posed. November 29, 2011, Los Angeles.

Avalon. Written and directed by Barry Levinson. Baltimore/Spring Creek Pictures, 1999. Culver City, CA: Columbia TriStar Home Video, 2000.

Crossfire. Directed by Edward Dmytryk. RKO Studio Pictures, 1947. Burbank, CA: Warner Home Video, 2005.

Everything Is Illuminated. Written and directed by Liev Schreiber. Warner Independent Pictures, 2005. Burbank, CA: Warner Home Video, 2006.

Gentleman's Agreement. Directed by Elia Kazan. Twentieth Century-Fox, 1947. Beverly Hills, CA: 20th Century Fox Home Entertainment, 2002.

The Golden Land on the Silver Screen. Directed by Eric A. Goldman. Teaneck, NJ: Ergo Media Inc., 1985.

How to Trace Your Jewish Roots: A Journey with Arthur Kurzweil. Directed by Eric A. Goldman. Teaneck, NJ: Ergo Media Inc., 1987.

The Jazz Singer. Directed by Alan Crosland. Warner Brothers, 1927. Burbank, CA: Warner Home Video, 2007.

The Jazz Singer. Directed by Michael Curtiz. Warner Brothers, 1952. Burbank, CA: Warner Home Video, 2002.

The Jazz Singer. Directed by Ralph Nelson. NBC Lincoln-Mercury Startime TV, 1959. Santa Monica, CA: Inception Media Group, 2012.

The Jazz Singer. Directed by Richard Fleischer. EMI Films, 1980. Troy, MI: Anchor Bay, 2002.

Liberty Heights. Written and directed by Barry Levinson. TriStar Pictures/Baltimore Pictures, 1999. Burbank, CA: Warner Home Video, 2000.

"Like Father, Like Clown." Directed by Brad Bird and Jeffrey Lynch. *The Simpsons: The Complete Third Season*. Twentieth Century-Fox Film Corporation, 1991. Beverly Hills, CA: 20th Century Fox Home Entertainment, 2003.

The Prince of Tides. Directed by Barbra Streisand. Columbia Pictures, 1991. Culver City, CA: Columbia TriStar Home Entertainment, 2001.

The Way We Were. Directed by Sidney Pollack. Columbia Pictures, 1973. Culver City, CA: Columbia TriStar Home Video, 1999.

The Way We Were: *Looking Back*. Documentary film included with the DVD release of *The Way We Were*. Directed by Michael Arick. Culver City, CA: Columbia TriStar Home Video, 1999.

The Young Lions. Directed by Edward Dmytryk. Twentieth Century-Fox, 1958. Beverly Hills, CA: 20th Century Fox Home Entertainment, 2001.

Page numbers in italics refer to illustrations.